POOR LEO'S 2002 COMPUTER ALMANAC

Leo Laporte

CONTENTS AT A GLANCE

201 West 103rd Street
Indianapolis, Indiana 46290

POOR LEO'S 2002 COMPUTER ALMANAC

Copyright © 2002 by Que ® Corporation

International Standard Book Number: 0-7897-2691-2

Library of Congress Catalog Card Number: 2001096821

Printed in the United States of America

First Printing: December 2001

04   03   02   4

Trademarks

Warning and Disclaimer

ASSOCIATE PUBLISHER
Dean Miller

ACQUISITIONS EDITOR
Angelina Ward

DEVELOPMENT EDITOR
Maureen McDaniel

MANAGING EDITOR
Thomas F. Hayes

PROJECT EDITOR
Tonya Simpson

TECHTV BUSINESS DEVELOPMENT
Dee-Dee Atta

TECHTV EXECUTIVE EDITOR
Regina Lynn Preciado

INDEXER
Kelly Castell

PROOFREADER
Mary Ann Abramson

TEAM COORDINATOR
Cindy Teeters

INTERIOR DESIGNERS
Karen Ruggles
Anne Jones

COVER DESIGNER
Planet 10

PAGE LAYOUT
Mark Walchle

FOREWORD

This book is not For Dummies. It's for the normally intelligent human being who occasionally feels befuddled by technology. That means you. And me. And pretty much anyone who ever encounters a computer. The truth is we all feel like dummies from time to time. But I'm here to tell you it's not your fault. It's the computer's fault. Honest.

I'm all for taking responsibility for your life, but when it comes to computer hardware and software, you shouldn't take the blame. These things really are hard to use. And even though we often feel like it must be our fault if we can't get them to do what we want, it's really the fault of the bozos who design this stuff.

Computer hardware and software designers just can't seem to figure out how to make their products easy to use. And that's a design flaw. When something is well designed, it makes sense. It's easy to use because it's intuitive. You don't have to consult a 500-page manual to figure out how to turn it on. You can say that about your toaster, your TV, even your car, but not about computers.

I'll share a little secret with you. Computers don't make sense a lot of the time, even to experts. And when the so-called experts try to explain how to use computers, they often make things worse. That's because they live and breathe this stuff. They don't remember a time when they didn't know how to use a computer. It's in their bones. In other words, computer experts don't speak our language. They might as well be from another planet.

This book was written by humans, for humans. Inside you'll find tips, explanations, and advice in plain English. And because we Earthlings like to laugh, there are some funny things, too. After all, what's the point if you're not having fun?

I've organized the material as an almanac because I didn't want you to confuse it with a computer manual. After all, who reads computer manuals? It's not a reference book, either. There are other books that do a much better job of that.

Think of *Poor Leo's Computer Almanac* as a companion. I hope you'll keep this book by your side all year long. Turn to it for amusement, encouragement, or just to learn a little about your PC. By the end of the year I bet you'll be able to call yourself an expert—even if you do hail from planet Earth.

ABOUT THE AUTHOR

Leo Laporte has made it his mission to help people master technology since 1984. He has worked in radio and television and is currently host of *The Screen Savers* on TechTV. His writing has appeared in numerous books and magazines and on the Web at `www.leoville.com`. Leo lives in Northern California with his wife, two children, two goats, two cats, and a guinea pig named Lucy Grifter.

DEDICATION

For Jennifer, my beloved and my friend.

ACKNOWLEDGMENTS

A lot of the material in this book comes from my television show, *The Screen Savers* on TechTV. Every night we help real users solve real problems in plain English. We like to think of it as saving the world one computer at a time. And our show's motto is "It's not your fault!"

My name is on the cover, but the words in this book were written by many people who have worked hard to make *The Screen Savers* and TechTV the best place anywhere to learn about technology. Special credit goes to the people who make our Web site, www.thescreensavers.com, a fun and interesting place to visit. Our Web executives over the years have included John Gilles, Regina Lynn Preciado, and Tom Merritt. Writers for the Web site include Marina Chotzinoff, Josh Lawrence, Greg Melton, Megan Morrone, Michelle Von Wald, Mike Street, and Karen Whitehead.

Contributors from the television side include Phil Allingham, Roger Chang, Martin Sargent, Robert Herron, Chris Kraus, and David Prager.

It takes 41 people to put *The Screen Savers* on the air every night. I know. I've counted. And each of them put a piece of him- or herself into this book. I want to send special props to my onscreen peeps, Martin Sargent, Scott Herriott, Megan Morrone, and Jessica Corbin, and especially to my co-hosts on *The Screen Savers*, Kate Botello and Patrick Norton. I couldn't do the show without you, and there's no way this book would exist without your contributions.

Regina Lynn Preciado and her researcher, Patricia Moore, helped compile three years of writing from many different sources into the book you see before you. If I'm the Almanac's father, Regina's definitely its mother; and it didn't take her any nine months, either. Thank you, Regina.

Most of all, I'd like to acknowledge you. It's never easy to tackle something new and unfamiliar. Sometimes technology even appears actively hostile to the novice. By buying this book you're sending a signal to your computer that you're the boss. It might not be your fault, but from now on, you're definitely in charge.

TELL US WHAT YOU THINK!

As the reader of this book, *you* are our most important critic and commentator. We value your opinion and want to know what we're doing right, what we could do better, what areas you'd like to see us publish in, and any other words of wisdom you're willing to pass our way.

As an associate publisher for Que, I welcome your comments. You can fax, e-mail, or write me directly to let me know what you did or didn't like about this book—as well as what we can do to make our books stronger.

Please note that I cannot help you with technical problems related to the topic of this book, and that due to the high volume of mail I receive, I might not be able to reply to every message.

When you write, please be sure to include this book's title and author as well as your name and phone or fax number. I will carefully review your comments and share them with the author and editors who worked on the book.

Fax: 317-581-4666

E-mail: feedback@quepublishing.com

Mail: Dean Miller
Que Corporation
201 West 103rd Street
Indianapolis, IN 46290 USA

COMPUTER RESOLUTIONS

It's a brand new year: A good time to make some promises to your PC. Try these on for size:

- I promise I'll stop slapping you upside the monitor every time you slow down to a crawl.

- I promise to keep the kids from spilling Jell-O on your keyboard.

- Next time, I promise I'll back up my data before the hard drive crashes.

- I promise to take security seriously and take the steps necessary to keep you safe.

- I'll keep your screen clean and your cables wrapped.

- I won't swear if you lose my digital baby pictures.

- I won't tear out your cables when I can't get the printer to work.

- I promise not to stuff you in the closet as soon as a speedier system comes along.

Fortunately, thanks to the little book you hold in your hand, you might be able to keep some of those important resolutions. Just pick it up every day and follow our instructions. Back up regularly. Keep your antivirus up to date. And never, ever, open e-mail attachments.

Your computer might be an inanimate object, but that doesn't mean it doesn't need a little TLC. For the next 12 months, treat it like a friend, and maybe it will stop treating you like the enemy.

TUESDAY, JANUARY 1

MAC TIP

A $9 piece of shareware, Appearance Hopper (www.whpress.com/mac/), lets you assign any installed font as the large or small system font, the small heading font, or the Finder views font.

JANUARY'S QUIZ

What is VoIP?

- a. Internet telephony
- b. Unix software
- c. Node generator
- d. Volleyball company

See January 31 for the answer.

GEEK SPEAK

RAM (*Random Access Memory*; pronounced "ram") is a type of computer memory that can be accessed randomly; that is, any byte of memory can be accessed without touching the preceding bytes. RAM is the most common type of memory found in computers and other devices, such as printers.

WEDNESDAY, JANUARY 2

WEB TIP

Top-level domain suffixes tell you right away what kind of site you're visiting.

These are the most common domain name suffixes on the Internet, including the seven new suffixes approved in 2000:

- **aero**—Air transport (new)
- **biz**—Business (new)
- **com**—Commercial business
- **coop**—Cooperatives (new)
- **edu**—Educational institution
- **gov**—Government agency
- **info**—All uses (new)
- **mil**—Military
- **museum**—Museums (new)

- **name**–Individuals (new)
- **net**–Miscellaneous
- **org**–Nonprofit organization
- **pro**–Professionals (new)

The following list shows the code suffixes of countries with heavy Internet traffic:

- **au**–Austria
- **br**–Brazil
- **ca**–Canada
- **fr**–France
- **hk**–Hong Kong
- **il**–Israel
- **in**–India
- **it**–Italy
- **mx**–Mexico
- **tw**–Taiwan
- **uk**–United Kingdom

THURSDAY, JANUARY 3

WINDOWS TIP

If you're suffering from an unreliable computer, or you seem to be losing data, it could be due to damaged sectors on your hard drive. One way to check to see whether this is the case is to test your hard drive sector by sector. Before you do anything else, back up your computer and all your data; then, follow these steps:

1. From the Start menu, choose Programs.
2. Select Accessories.
3. Select System Tools.
4. Choose ScanDisk.
5. Under Type of Test, choose Thorough.

This enables your computer to scan for bad sectors.

If this doesn't work, go to your DOS prompt (go to the Start menu, select Run, and type `command`). In the DOS window, type `scan disk`. This launches an interface that does the same thing, but without the Windows overhead. When prompted, choose to perform a surface scan.

FRIDAY, JANUARY 4

LAPORTE SUPPORT

Q: Can you use a camcorder as a netcam?

A: Not only is it possible to use a video camera in lieu of a netcam, but the video camera produces a better picture than most netcams.

Netcams, which are small video cameras that plug into your computer, are inexpensive for a reason. They have a fixed focal length, no special features, and they serve one purpose: to get your image across the Internet. Camcorders—those big video cameras that record to VHS—cost hundreds of dollars, have lots of features, and provide a better-quality picture. Whether you can use your camcorder with your equipment depends on how you want to use your computer video.

Many video-capture cards on the market enable you to hook the video camera directly into your computer. The video-capture card turns the analog data from your video camera into bits that the computer can process.

After you have installed the card and drivers, turning your camcorder into a netcam is merely a matter of connecting the video camera, which just means plugging it into the Video In slot on your computer. Your software should recognize the video camera.

SATURDAY, JANUARY 5

FOR GEEKS ONLY

Two heads might be better than one, but are two computer processors better than one?

The answer depends on what you plan to do, and how many things you do at once. Using multiple processors to share the work is called *symmetric multi-processing*, or *SMP*. My main workhorse system sports dual Pentium III processors and Windows XP Professional. The operating system automatically shares tasks across the two processors, which means I seldom have to wait while the computer works. I can open my e-mail, burn a CD, and write these words all at the same time. Even better, when I use programs that also support multiple processors, like Adobe Photoshop, I'll get an even bigger performance boost.

If you go with a dual-processor system, you'll need to use an operating system that recognizes both CPUs. That's Windows NT, 2000, XP Professional, Linux, or Mac OS X. The Home edition of Windows XP, Windows 95, 98, and Me do not support multi-processing. They won't see the second processor at all.

A new mobo, two processors, and a new install of Windows XP Professional does cost a fair amount of cash. For most people, a single fast processor is plenty, even if you do more than one thing at a time. That's especially true if you're a gamer. Very few games can take advantage of multi-processing. You'd be better off putting the money into a fast processor, lots of memory, and a really good video card.

SUNDAY, JANUARY 6

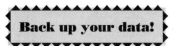

Back up your data!

PROTECT YOURSELF

Trojan horses are malicious programs that run in the background and can give a hacker access to your system over the Internet. To detect a Trojan horse virus on your computer, download the latest definitions from your antivirus software manufacturer, and then run a virus scan.

If your antivirus software doesn't detect anything, but you still suspect infection, visit the Symantec Anti-Virus Research Center at `www.sarc.com`. SARC offers free removal tools for all the major Trojan horse viruses.

MONDAY, JANUARY 7

LAPORTE SUPPORT

Q: *Like many PC users, I am not an idiot, and I resent getting cautionary screens every time I examine my Windows folder. Is there any way to reveal ALL files, get around Access Denied, and abolish the annoying warning in Windows Explorer?*

A: Considering the damage people can do by rooting around in the Windows folder, I can understand Microsoft's warnings, but you intrepid explorer types can turn them off fairly easily.

First, reveal the invisible system files. Open your Windows folder and select Folder Options from the View menu. Click the View tab and select the Show All Files button. You also might want to uncheck Hide File Extensions for Known File Types. Click OK.

Now re-enter the Windows folder. To turn off the warning forever, delete a file called `folder.htt` from inside the Windows folder. Every Windows folder contains this file; it stores folder customizations, including the warning message.

TUESDAY, JANUARY 8

MAC TIP

You can decide from which drive to boot in one of two ways. The first is the tried and true Startup Disk control panel. The second is very handy if you reboot and realize you forgot to change the startup disk.

As you turn on your computer, hold down the Option key. A blue window eventually will appear, listing all the drives with bootable operating systems on them. Click the drive you want. The round arrow on the left rescans for drives. After you've selected your drive, click the straight arrow on the right to continue booting.

GEEK SPEAK

Bit is short for binary digit, the smallest unit of information on a machine. A single bit can hold only one of two values: 0 or 1. More meaningful information is obtained by combining consecutive bits into larger units. For example, a byte is composed of 8 consecutive bits.

WEDNESDAY, JANUARY 9

 ## WEB TIP

AOL is a great way to get online for the first time, but as you become more sophisticated, you might find yourself disappointed by its limitations. Chief among these is its miserable e-mail function. Wouldn't it be nice to use a more complete e-mail program with AOL? You can, but it will cost you.

EnetBot is a program that will make any standard e-mail program work with AOL mail. Download a copy from `www.enetbot.com`. You can try it for free for 30 days, but after that you'll have to pay $19.95 to buy the program.

You also can get your AOL mail with any browser through the AOL Web site (`aolmail.aol.com`). It's no more sophisticated than the built-in AOL e-mail, but it does greet you with that cheery "You've Got Mail!"

Incidentally, did you know that the guy who says "You've got mail" is named Elwood Edwards? He even has his own Web page at (where else) AOL: `members.aol.com/voicepro/`.

THURSDAY, JANUARY 10

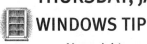 ## WINDOWS TIP

You might never have noticed it, but your computer comes with a Pause key. It's to the right of the function keys at the top of your keyboard. Pause doesn't work in most Windows applications, but it's great for stopping the text that scrolls by during boot up, such as when you want to read the list of virus updates. When you're finished reading, press any key to continue.

FRIDAY, JANUARY 11

 ## LAPORTE SUPPORT

Q: I read in a magazine that if you install a second 56k modem, you can download information faster. Is this true?

A: It's true, but you need two modems, two phone lines, and the cooperation of your Internet service provider to get higher speeds.

Windows provides support for this technique called *multilink PPP*. The settings are buried away in the Dial-up Networking entry for your ISP. Open the Dial-up Networking or Network Connections folder, right-click on the dial-up connection you want to change and select Properties from the pop-up menu, and then click the Multilink tab. When you have a second modem installed, you can add it to the Multilink window.

Multilink users report download speeds of 80–100Kbps–twice the speed of normal 56k modems. Upload speeds don't change much.

ISPs often charge extra for doing this–after all, you're using double the resources. The typical charge is an extra $4–$10 per month, but it can be more.

SATURDAY, JANUARY 12
FOR GEEKS ONLY

It's a magic milestone like the three-minute mile, the Dow crossing 10,000, and Elizabeth Taylor's 12th husband. Both Intel and AMD shipped processors last year that broke the one gigahertz mark. That's more than one billion cycles per second–250 times faster than the first IBM PCs at about half the price.

But does anybody need all that power? No way, unless you're calculating rocket trajectories or rendering *Toy Story 3*. So, why do Intel and AMD spend so much money designing chips no one needs? Bragging rights. Each wants to be able to say it has the fastest chip on the planet.

For the rest of us, 500 megahertz do just fine. You're better off putting the extra money into more memory, a faster hard drive, or a bigger screen.

Meanwhile, the chip giants face another challenge. They need to dream up applications that demand enough power to require these multi-gigahertz processors.

Hey, if they can come up with a CPU that can clean the house, feed the kids, and walk the dog, sign me up.

SUNDAY, JANUARY 13

Back up your data!

PROTECT YOURSELF

The software that comes with Wi-Fi (a.k.a. 802.11b) products often has built-in features for security and network selection.

If you're running a wireless network, be sure to use these security settings, unless you want anyone who's in the neighborhood to be able to get on your network. (Incidentally, they call this *wilding*—Wireless Internet LAN Discovery—and it's a growing sport that can have some serious consequences for the victim.) Always require a password for access to your wireless network. And turn on WEP, the wireless encryption protocol. WEP is not 100% foolproof, but it does provide some security.

The Wireless Ethernet Compatibility Alliance (www.wirelessethernet.org) publishes good information on Wi-Fi. According to a WECA report on Wi-Fi security and privacy, "the likelihood of [a security] attack being mounted is very small, given the difficulty and cost of the attack versus the typical value of the stolen data." The report is available on the WECA site, but you need Adobe Acrobat (which you can download at www.adobe.com) to read it.

MONDAY, JANUARY 14

LAPORTE SUPPORT

Q: *What's the difference between a bad cluster and a bad sector?*

A: Functionally, there's no difference. Hard drives are divided into sectors, like a pie. A cluster is a piece within a sector.

You might see `bad cluster` or `bad sector` warnings appear onscreen while running ScanDisk. ScanDisk looks for errors and tries to repair them. It's normal for a hard drive to have a few bad sectors, but if you see a continual increase in bad sectors, it means your hard drive is failing. Back up your data and get a new hard drive.

TUESDAY, JANUARY 15

MAC TIP

The Macintosh can automatically set its time using the Date & Time System Preference in Mac OS X. Open Date & Time and click the Network Time tab. Enter `time.apple.com` into the NTP server field, and then click Start. Click the Stop button, and then click Start again just to be sure it knows to set itself.

GEEK SPEAK

The *hard drive* is the place on a computer where data is stored and retrieved. All of a computer's programs are also stored on the hard drive.

TODAY IN COMPUTER HISTORY

On January 15, 1998, Apple executives announced that Apple was once again profitable. This announcement followed two years of losses. Credit for turning around the company goes to interim CEO, Steve Jobs, who earns only $1 a year for his efforts.

Later, the board of directors gave Jobs a Gulfstream V private jet worth $90 million by way of thanks.

WEDNESDAY, JANUARY 16

WEB TIP

If you get a `Certificate Authority Is Expired` message when trying to reach a secured Web site, it's time to upgrade your browser.

Those certificates verify the identity of Web sites you visit. This is especially important on e-commerce sites. When you give someone your credit card information, you want to be darn sure they are who they say they are.

But all certificates expire. The certificates that came with older versions of Netscape Navigator and the Mac version of Microsoft's Internet Explorer expired at the end of 1999. You still can use your old browser to buy things on the Web, but it's a good idea to upgrade to the new version as soon as you can. That way, you get all the latest features, security enhancements, *and* updated certificates.

THURSDAY, JANUARY 17

WINDOWS TIP

To change a file association, follow these steps:

1. Double-click My Computer.
2. Choose View, Folder Options.
3. Click the File Types tab.
4. A list of applications shows up onscreen. Select the application you want to change and choose Edit.
5. You now can choose the type of file, the default extension, and what you want the application to do with the file.

Also, you can single-click a file (`.mp3`, `.doc`), hold down the Shift key, right-click the highlighted icon, choose the Open With command, and then choose Always Open With This Program.

FRIDAY, JANUARY 18

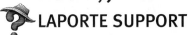

LAPORTE SUPPORT

Q: *How do I clear out unwanted addresses on my Web browser's Address bar? I'm stuck with mistyped URLs.*

A: Covering your tracks is easy, but the technique varies from browser to browser:

- In Internet Explorer 5, go to the Tools menu, select Internet Options, and click Clear History.
- In Netscape 4.7, go to the Edit menu, choose Preferences, click the Navigator listing in the left pane, and then click the Clear Location Bar button.
- AOL 5.0 uses Internet Explorer as its browser, so repeat the steps for IE5 as shown previously. To clear AOL's history and keyword bar, go to the My AOL menu, select Preferences, and click the Toolbar button. Press the Clear History Now button to clear the entries.

SATURDAY, JANUARY 19

FOR GEEKS ONLY

Want a computer but have only a couple of 20s and a 10 spot? No problem. You can start your Linux or programming career today for less than $50.

You can find cheap 486 and 386 computers for $10 to $30 online. Monitors are a dime a dozen if you don't worry much about size and resolution. Be sure you get a computer with a CD-ROM drive, though. Find deals at eBay, in local newspaper classified ads, and in thrift stores.

Buy smart. Read all the fine print before you hand over your money.

Now that you have the hardware, install Linux. For help, visit TechTV's Linux Superguide (www.techtv.com/superguides/linux). Linux works great, even on older machines, and it can run on hard drives as small as 500MB.

Boom. You're done. Now you have to buy some books on Linux, but you've got a PC for less than $50. You can learn the intricacies of Linux, and you'll be able to get a job as a Linux administrator. Or, you can teach yourself how to program in one of several different programming languages that come free with the operating system.

SUNDAY, JANUARY 20

AOL TIP

Are you tired of having an e-mail box full of unsolicited e-mail? Are you worried that your kids might be sent an e-mail with a link to an X-rated Web site? Are you going to scream if you get another "make a million bucks instantly" e-mail?

One of the biggest complaints I hear from AOL users regards the amount of spam they get. Well, you can take steps to protect yourself against unwanted e-mail:

1. Click the Mail Center icon in your toolbar.
2. Choose Mail Controls.
3. Click Set Up Mail Controls.
4. Select the Screen Name account you want to modify. Here, you can choose the setting that best suits your needs. I recommend you choose Block Email From the Listed AOL Members, Internet Domains, and Addresses. This is where you can add e-mail addresses of people who have sent you spam. This way you won't receive any more unwanted e-mails from that address. You also can add Web sites you don't want your kids to access.

MONDAY, JANUARY 21

LAPORTE SUPPORT

Q: Being new to Windows PCs, I'm not sure: What is the right mouse button used for?

A: You can use Windows perfectly well without ever clicking the right mouse button. On the other hand (or finger, as it were), using the right button— known as *right-clicking*—is one of the best ways to get things done in Windows.

Right-clicking pops up a "context-sensitive" menu containing commands that make sense in the current situation. For example, right-clicking an icon produces a list of commands to open it, delete it, rename it, and so on.

Try right-clicking everywhere in Windows. You never know what handy commands you might discover.

TUESDAY, JANUARY 22

SHORTCUT: MAC OS X

- **Command+H** hides the top window in any application.
- **Command+Option+D** hides or shows the dock.
- **Command+M** minimizes a window.

TODAY IN COMPUTER HISTORY

On January 22, 1984, Macintosh's "1984" commercial aired during the Super Bowl. In this controversial advertisement, a "big brother"-type scene was interrupted by a woman wearing a Mac logo on her shirt. The ad stated that in a few days, Macintosh would show the world why 1984 would not be like *1984*. The commercial aired only once, but you can see it for yourself at www.uriah.com/apple-qt/1984.html. At least until Apple reads this.

WEDNESDAY, JANUARY 23

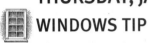

WEB TIP

The U.S. Postal Service sells stamps on the Web at www.stampsonline.com. But why use stamps at all when you can print postage directly onto envelopes with your computer?

You pay a little more than you would at the post office, but it's a lot more convenient because you can download postage directly from the Internet.

The USPS allows a number of companies to sell computer postage, including Stamps.com (www.stamps.com), Pitney Bowes's ClickStamp Online (www.pitneyworks.com), and Simply Postage (www.simplypostage.com). For an up-to-date list, visit www.usps.com/ibip.

THURSDAY, JANUARY 24

WINDOWS TIP

If right-clicking the desktop to create a new folder is too slow for you, try these three keystrokes whenever you have a folder open:

- Alt+F
- W
- Enter

A new, untitled folder will appear within the currently open folder. (The keystrokes might differ in various versions of Windows. If these don't work, experiment!)

FRIDAY, JANUARY 25

LAPORTE SUPPORT

Q: *Will any keyboard work on any computer?*

A: You should be able to use any keyboard with any computer as long as you have the right connectors.

The original IBM PCs and compatibles used a big, AT-style connector. Almost all PCs sold in the last few years use USB or a smaller connector called PS/2. You can get an older AT-style keyboard working on a PS/2 system with a $5 adapter available at any computer store. There are also USB to PS/2 adapters.

Macs have evolved, too. The original Macintosh keyboards used the ADB port. Newer Macs use USB, but if you really hate to give up your old Mac keyboard, Dr. Bott (www.drbott.com) sells a USB-to-ADB adapter for about $50.

SATURDAY, JANUARY 26
FOR GEEKS ONLY

You've certainly been asked to "insert the Windows CD" when making system configuration changes. Here's my question to you: Do you know where your Windows installation CD is located? I sure don't. I never use it for system changes because I keep all the files Windows needs on my hard drive. (This tip works only with Windows 95/98/Me. Windows XP users will have to keep a copy of their install disk where they can find it.)

The best way to do this is to install Windows from the hard drive in the first place. The install files have the .CAB extension. Before you install Windows, copy the contents of the Windows install folder from the CD to a folder on your drive, something like C\WINDOWS\ INSTALL\. Then, pop out the CD, and run the Setup program from the install directory on your hard drive. Not only will the install go faster, but Windows will forevermore look there for the files it needs. Many manufacturers do this, storing the files in the C:\WINDOWS\OPTIONS\CABS\ directory. Check there right now—you already might have all the files you need on your drive. The install files take up about 125MB, a negligible amount on today's big drives.

But what if you already have Windows installed? No sweat. You still can trick Windows into looking for its files on the hard disk first. Copy the installation files from the CD as before. Make a note of where you've put them. For this example we'll use C:\WINDOWS\ OPTIONS\CABS\.

Now we need to modify Windows's Registry file. Windows stores many key settings in this file, so be careful with it. If you inadvertently damage your registry, boot from a rescue disk and use the command SCANREG /RESTORE to restore a previous, undamaged version.

To modify the Registry, follow these steps:

1. Go to the Start menu, select Run, and type regedit. This launches the Registry Editor.
2. In the left pane, open HKEY_LOCAL_MACHINE\Software\Microsoft\Windows\CurrentVersion\SETUP.
3. In the right pane, scroll down until you see SourcePath. Double-click it.

4. Change the path (for example, `E:\win98cd\win98`) to your own setup directory (for example, `C:\WINDOWS\OPTIONS\CABS\`). Note: You *must* include the backslash at the end of your path.

5. Close regedit.

After we showed this tip on the air, our favorite tame programmer, Mark Thompson, came up with an easier way. He wrote a program that enables you to change the path of CAB files and also saves the previous path so you can restore it in case of a problem. Search for "BanishCD" at `www.analogx.com` to download it for yourself. It's free and works great.

SUNDAY, JANUARY 27

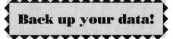
Back up your data!

 ## PROTECT YOURSELF

It's a good idea to run a personal firewall if you have an always-on connection to the Internet, as with a DSL or cable modem. Even if you don't, your banking and online shopping should be safe. Just be sure you see a little gold lock at the bottom of your browser window whenever you're sending private information.

That little gold lock icon tells you your browser is talking to a secure site, and transactions between your browser and the secure Web site are encrypted.

MONDAY, JANUARY 28

 ## LAPORTE SUPPORT

Q: I send a lot of e-mail in HTML format, but not everyone can read it, so I have to send plain text. Why can't they read my HTML formatted e-mails?

A: HTML is a language for Web page design, but lately it's been used to dress up e-mails. Even though programs such as Outlook, Netscape Mail, and Eudora can use HTML to format e-mail, there are many other e-mail programs that don't understand the formatting.

AOL handles HTML e-mail by stripping the formatting out, leaving just the text. Other programs don't do so well. They leave in the computer instructions, making the message look like gibberish.

Unless you know the person you're e-mailing uses an HTML-compatible mail reader, stick with plain old text.

TUESDAY, JANUARY 29

MAC TIP

When you set up Mac OS X, you were given the option to turn off the login password. You can change this setting by opening the Login item in System Preferences:

1. Open System Preferences.
2. Click the Login Window tab.
3. Check the Automatic Login box to turn off the password request at login.
4. Enter the default name and password.

You can always log in as a different user by selecting Log Out from the Apple menu.

To turn the login password feature back on, simply follow steps 1 and 2 and select the turn on the password request at login.

GEEK SPEAK

A *modem* is a device that allows a computer to transmit data over telephone lines. It is still the most common way that people connect to the Internet. Modem is short for modulate-demodulate. That's what a modem does. It modulates the data from your computer into sound that can be transmitted over plain old telephone lines. The modem on the other end demodulates the sound back into data your computer can use.

WEDNESDAY, JANUARY 30

WEB TIP

If you are just looking for text or information, you can speed up a Web search by turning off all the pictures, music, dings, and whistles that Web sites add for dramatic effect.

Go to Internet Options in Internet Explorer. It's located in different places depending on which version you use; check the Tools menu first. After you're inside Internet Options, click the Advanced tab. Uncheck everything under the Multimedia category.

When you go to a site, pictures are represented by empty outlines. If you want to see a picture, view it by right-clicking the empty outline and selecting the menu option Show Picture.

Now you download only what you want to see, without having to download every little logo and ad.

THURSDAY, JANUARY 31

WINDOWS TIP

One of our viewers called and asked how to get a hidden file back. The file is not missing, it's just hiding. To hide a file, right-click it, select Properties, and check Hidden. To view all files, even the hidden ones, follow these steps:

1. Choose Start, Settings, Folder Options.
2. Click the View tab in the Folder Options dialog box.
3. Click Show All Files.
4. Click OK.

JANUARY'S QUIZ: ANSWER

What is VoIP?

Internet telephony, also known as *Voice over Internet Protocol*, or *VoIP*, enables you to make voice contact over the Internet.

This Month's Feature

HOW TO REINSTALL WINDOWS

By Leo Laporte

It often is possible to fix computer problems with a little tweaking here and a little banging there. But if things just won't get better, or if your system seems to be bogged down with old bloated software, it might be time to (insert dramatic organ riff here) reinstall Windows. Don't fret. Like death and root canals, it's something we all have to face sooner or later. Reinstalling Windows can take as little as an hour or as long as a long weekend, depending on how far you want (or need) to go. Here is your complete guide from an expert. I've reinstalled Windows hundreds of times. How do you think I got all these gray hairs?

You can choose from three kinds of reinstalls. In order of difficulty, they are *install in place*, the *slightly clean install*, and the *format and install*. Before you do any of these, it's prudent to take some precautions up front.

Preparation

First, back up your data onto removable media (you should do that regularly anyway). The install in place and clean install shouldn't affect your data, but why take any chances?

While backing up, copy and store your Internet settings. These settings can get clobbered, so it's important to save a copy.

You also should print a system summary so you have information about all your hardware and settings in case you need to revive them. You can do that by opening the System Control Panel, clicking the Device Manager tab, and clicking the Print button. Select the All Devices and System Summary button and prepare to print volumes—as many as 20 pages. Everyone should have an up-to-date copy of this document, though. I recommend making a new one every time you install new hardware.

Emergency Recovery

Now that you know what hardware you've installed, download the latest software drivers for each. You can find these files at manufacturers' Web sites, or search for them at `windrivers.com`. Reinstalling Reinstalling Windows replaces your existing drivers with the Windows default drivers, but because these can be out of date, it's a good idea to have the most recent drivers. Put them on a floppy for easy access.

You also might want to run a program called ERU (Emergency Recovery Utility). It's on your Windows installation disk, or you can download a program that does the same thing. Try Theodore Fattaleh's Emergency Recovery System 98 (search `www.hotfiles.com` for a download). These programs send backup copies of critical system files to a floppy—which is a nice thing to have in a pinch.

Finally, make a working boot disk that can not only start up your machine, but also can provide access to your CD-ROM drive. The Windows 95 boot disk does not do this. Search `techtv.com` for "creating a boot disk" if you need help. And be sure to test your disk before doing anything more.

You probably won't need these recovery tools, but it's nice to know they're there. Frankly, it's something you should do whether you're planning a reinstall or not. Now let's get to the actual reinstallations.

Install in Place

This is the simplest reinstallation, and it often does the trick. Insert your Windows installation disk into your CD-ROM drive and run the setup program. Windows installs on top of your existing installation, preserving all your settings and data. This restores missing and damaged files, and it often fixes an otherwise unreliable machine.

The *install in place* has few side effects, but occasionally some settings disappear, and software that used to work stops working. You might need to reinstall some programs, but that's rare. Before you do the install in place, be sure you have master disks for all programs. If you are using a boot manager to run multiple operating systems, note that reinstalling Windows usually overwrites the master boot record, which can disable your boot manager. Either make a copy of your modified boot record for restoration later, or plan to reinstall your boot manager.

If you don't know what a boot manager is, don't worry. (But if you *must* know, it's a piece of code that enables your machine to boot into different OSes, such as Windows and Linux.)

Slightly Clean Install

Use the slightly clean install when install in place doesn't work. The *slightly clean install* is identical to install in place with one exception: You delete the Windows directory and all its subdirectories first. This is most often required when you have upgraded from Windows 3.1 or Windows 95 to Windows 98. Old files from previous versions of the system often remain in the Windows directory, confusing software and causing crashes. Deleting the Windows directory clears these old incompatible files. Unfortunately, it also deletes the registry and all your settings. Your data should remain intact, but you have to reinstall most applications.

Before you do a slightly clean install, be doubly sure to have all the master disks for your programs available. Allow a day or two to get everything back in working order.

The slightly clean install requires nearly as much work as the format and install, but it saves you the trouble of backing up and restoring your data.

Format and Install (or Clean Install)

If all else fails, there's the slash-and-burn approach: starting over with the *format and install*. But first, understand something: This isn't easy. The format and install requires considerable time, forethought, and patience. Don't do it if you're unsure about what you're doing. Although I've done this many times, and it has always worked eventually, I am not responsible for what might happen if you go ahead with this.

The format and install (which many call a *clean install*) is useful if your system is bogged down with too many programs, crashes inexplicably, or is just plain out of control. I do one of these at least once a year, but some might say I'm a masochist. I recommend that you try the simpler install in place before attempting the all-out format and install. In most cases, simply reinstalling Windows on top of your existing system fixes an unreliable system. The format and install is only for someone who really needs to begin with a clean slate and is willing to make the needed effort. People who take the trouble to do this usually report system operation that's quicker and more reliable than it was since the machine arrived from the factory. That is, after they spend several days reinstalling software, reconfiguring hardware, and pulling their hair out over the little quirks that inevitably show up.

So, now that you know what you're getting into, let's begin.

Prepare for the Format and Install

Double-check that you've taken all the steps laid out in the preceding section. You are going to delete everything, so you must have copies of all data—including everything you can't reproduce. That includes things such as Internet bookmarks, saved games, and program preferences. Don't blame me if you delete your great American novel. And be sure the backup is good. If in doubt, print it out.

You also must have a working boot disk. Otherwise, you won't be able to reinstall Windows. And you need to copy a couple of extra programs to that boot disk, FDISK and FORMAT.

Open a DOS window and type the following commands:

```
COPY C:\WINDOWS\COMMAND\FDISK.EXE A:
```

```
COPY C:\WINDOWS\COMMAND\FORMAT.COM A:
```

Get your Windows installation disk (and the certificate of authenticity with the serial number on it), and the installation disks for all the programs you want to put back on your hard drive. (Be conservative about reinstalling them. Remember that jamming all that junk on the hard drive is what got you here in the first place.) Finally, be sure you have up-to-date drivers for all your hardware.

Got everything? OK. Take a deep breath.

Perform the Format and Install

Boot from the boot floppy you just made, and then restart your machine. After a bunch of grinding and whirring (this is what computing was like in the days before hard drives) you'll see the A: prompt.

Insert your Windows installation disk in the CD drive and type the following commands:

```
D:
DIR
```

If you can see the contents of the CD-ROM drive, you're in business. (If you have more than one hard disk on your computer, your CD might not be D:—use whatever drive letter works.) If not, go back to techtv.com, search for "creating a boot disk," and try again.

We've reached the point of no return. You're going to partition your hard drive. After you do, you are no longer able to recover your data. Reassure yourself that you do indeed have good backups and that you've copied everything you need off the drive, because you're about to kiss it goodbye. Type FDISK.

Now we're going to delete your DOS partitions and create three new partitions. (This is my personal favorite partitioning scheme, but feel free to replace it with one that works for you.) Type 3 to delete partition and then select your Windows partition—that's almost always the Primary DOS Partition. After you've done so, you're committed. Now create three new DOS partitions. The first is for your swap file. Make it about 150MB. Next, create your main Windows partition. Make it as big as you want, but leave 500MB or so free for your final data partition.

Putting the swap file and your data in a separate partition is good for organization, and it also helps make your system a bit more robust. The swap file works faster if it doesn't get fragmented—and it can't get fragmented if it's on a partition by itself. Putting it on the first partition ensures that it's on the fastest part of the hard drive. Separating your data directories onto a partition of your own also helps keep fragmentation down, and it simplifies clean installs in the future. Be sure to give your data partition sufficient space for growth. After you've created your partitions, exit FDISK and reboot from your floppy.

Now you can format each partition, starting with the Windows directory:

```
FORMAT C: /S /V
```

The /S parameter makes the C: drive bootable. /V verifies the format. Format D: (your data directory) and E: (your swap partition) as well using the /V (but not the /S) parameter. Take a break; this might take a while.

After you've formatted your C: drive, copy the Windows installation files to the hard drive. This speeds up the installation and ensures that you have copies of the Windows install files available in the future. No more fumbling for the Windows CD when you install new hardware. All you need is the files in the WIN98 directory; although, if you have a large enough hard drive, you can copy the entire CD to it.

I suggest creating a folder called WIN98 on your hard drive and sticking the files there. After the files are copied, pop out the floppy and restart your machine. It should start up, and you should see the C: prompt grinning at you. Time to begin the installation of Windows. Change to the install directory you just created (CD WIN98, for example) and type SETUP. The setup should begin, and you're in business.

Rebuild the Hard Drive

All done? Good. Everything went okay, I hope. Some of your hardware devices might cause a little trouble, but if they were working before clean install, they'll work again. You just have to coax them with a little TLC and the right drivers and settings.

Now it's time to begin the laborious process of rebuilding your hard drive. First, move the swap file to its new home. Open the System Control Panel, click the Performance tab, and click the Virtual Memory button. Select the Let Me Specify my Own Virtual Memory Settings button. Select the drive you created for a swap file; most likely it is drive E:. Make the minimum and maximum file sizes the same; this forces Windows to create a permanent swap file. That's the fastest kind because Windows doesn't spend any time resizing it. I suggest a file size just one or two megabytes smaller than the partition size, say 149MB. After you click OK a couple of times, you have to restart your computer to let the new settings take effect.

If you created a separate partition for your data files, you also should change the location of the My Documents folder from the default C: drive to your new data drive (on most machines, this is D:). Start by creating folders called My Documents, Downloads, and any other data-oriented folders you'd like to include in your new data partition.

Type the following:

```
D:
CD
MKDIR "My Documents"
MKDIR "Downloads"
```

You then need to use a control panel called TweakUI to change the default location of the My Documents folder. You can get the most recent copy of TweakUI from Microsoft's Web site. Last time I checked it was squirreled away at www.microsoft.com/ntworkstation/ downloads/PowerToys/Networking/NTTweakUI.asp.

TweakUI is an extremely useful control panel that lets you change many user interface settings. Unzip the file you've downloaded, and then right-click the TweakUI.inf file and select Install to install it.

After you've installed TweakUI, open it from the Control Panel, click the My Computer tab, select My Documents in the Special Folders area, and then press the Change Location button. Change the location to D: My Documents. Close TweakUI and delete the My Documents folder from your C: drive. As you install applications, you also might want to change each program's preferences to point to the D: drive for new documents.

Now, restore your data to the D: directory and begin reinstalling your applications. I hope you didn't have any plans for the weekend.

Congratulations, you have completed the full format and install process, the rebuild of your hard drive and, I suspect, improved the speed and reliability of your system in the process. I hope it all went smoothly, but if you had problems along the way, just remember: What doesn't kill you makes you geekier. A successful slash and burn install qualifies you for the title of true Supergeek. Way to go!

INFORMATION WANTS TO BE FREE...EVEN IF IT COSTS MONEY

The tech sector had a big party in 2000. And we spent most of 2001 cleaning up after it. Between free music downloads from Napster and below-cost merchandise from nearly every e-commerce site, we were living in the golden age of free stuff. Then reality set in and the dot-boom went dot-bust. There are two lessons to be learned here.

First, no business can survive long while losing money. And second, people really like the convenience of digital information. The first point is obvious. The second point might take a little more explanation. Here's what I mean.

After an object is turned into bits on a computer—a song, a picture, a book—it's easy to move those bits around, to modify them, to share them. And that's the secret to the success of services like Napster. We want our data to flow freely, to go anywhere. We want to make copies of it, modify it, and share it. That's what the early computer hackers meant when they said that information wants to be free. Free from constraints, but not necessarily free of charge. Given the lessons of the dot-com boom, that's an important distinction.

If we, as consumers, want information to flow freely, we can't demand that it always be free of cost, as well. We tried the no-cost thing and it was a giant bust. Hundreds of companies went out of business. Hundreds of thousands of us were laid off. And we intensified resistance to the idea of information flowing freely.

If you want to have books to read, music to listen to, and movies to enjoy, you're going to have to pay for them. The people who create these things for us deserve to be paid. That's only fair. But when you pay for them, you should be able to do anything you want with them, including turn them into bits on a computer, move them from device to device, copy them, and even share them. That's fair, too.

Information can be free, as long as we're all willing to pay a little bit for the right to use it.

FRIDAY, FEBRUARY 1

EXPERT OPINION

"I have traveled the length and breadth of this country and talked with the best people, and I can assure you that data processing is a fad that won't last out the year."

—The editor in charge of business books for Prentice Hall, 1957

LAPORTE SUPPORT

Q: How do I listen to MP3s while I play a game?

A: You need a card that can handle multiple sound streams simultaneously. If yours can't, it's time to upgrade. I recommend sound cards from Creative, `www.soundblaster.com`. These Sound Blaster cards, either the Live! or the new Audigy, are the industry standard, so they're compatible with everything, and they can play back multiple streams at the same time. They're particularly good for gaming.

SATURDAY, FEBRUARY 2 (GROUNDHOG DAY)

FOR GEEKS ONLY

Older gaming consoles, such as the Sony Playstation, Nintendo 64, and Sega Dreamcast, come equipped with video output designed for your television only. However, you can use them with a computer monitor for super-crisp game action. To do this, you must convert the NTSC signal coming out of the console into a VGA output your computer monitor can handle. Products such as the AverTVBox from AverMedia, `www.avermedia.com`, cost around $150—nearly as much as the game console itself—but they also can be used to watch television on your monitor.

SUNDAY, FEBRUARY 3

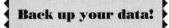

Back up your data!

PROTECT YOURSELF

If you want to keep folks out of your PC, the best way is to turn on the hardware password. When you start your machine, you usually see a message that reads something like `Press DEL to enter SETUP`. On some computers, the key to press might be Esc or F1 or F10. Check your system documentation for details.

After you enter the Setup program, look for an entry for "system password." After you enable the password, your computer won't start without it.

If your system doesn't have a startup password, try Access Denied from www.nt.unets.ru/john/. It's free to try, $19.95 to buy.

Neither of these methods is foolproof, but they deter all but the most determined data thief.

MONDAY, FEBRUARY 4

LAPORTE SUPPORT

Q: *Is there some reasonably reputable site that can set up a full-duplex, troubleshooting link to my PC and tell me what is wrong with it?*

A: You can, indeed, give control of your computer to a remote expert who fixes things as you watch. The best known source for this kind of help is Expertcity.com.

Here's how it works. When you need help, log in to www.expertcity.com and pose your question. Online experts will bid on the job; the cost usually works out to $5 to $20 per question. Expertcity.com handles the billing through your credit card. Use the ratings system to pick an expert in your price range. You then can chat with him or her, and, if necessary, the expert can use Expertcity.com's software to virtually peer into your machine and even take control of it to fix the problem.

The experts don't actually work for Expertcity.com, but the company does check their credentials and offers a money-back guarantee if the fix doesn't take.

TUESDAY, FEBRUARY 5

MAC TIP

The quickest and easiest way to transfer files between a Mac and PC is to use an Ethernet connection. You need an Ethernet crossover cable, which you can buy in an electronics store for less than $20.

If you're using Mac OS X and Windows XP or 2000, turn on file sharing in Windows. The drive should be visible on the Mac without any additional software.

Mac OS 9 and Windows 95/98/Me users will have to buy some additional software to translate between the Windows and Macintosh network file systems. I recommend either Thursby Software's MacSoho (about $50 from www.thursby.com) or Miramar System's PC MACLAN (about $200; from www.miramar.com).

GEEK SPEAK

The *monitor* is the display screen for a computer. It looks much like a small television set, except with better clarity.

A *mouse* is a handheld device that moves the onscreen pointer. A mouse enables a computer user to perform many tasks without using the keyboard.

A *printer* is a device that prints text or pictures directly onto paper.

WEDNESDAY, FEBRUARY 6

WEB TIP

Give your PC a free checkup at PCPitstop.com, which runs your machine through several diagnostic tests and offers tips for improving its performance. Pitstop works with computers running Windows and Internet Explorer 4 or higher.

THURSDAY, FEBRUARY 7

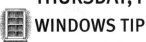

WINDOWS TIP

Every Windows 95/98/Me user should have a rescue disk: a floppy disk with which you can start your system in case of hard drive failure. Use the Add/Remove Programs control panel to create a startup disk. Then, follow these steps to verify that your disk works:

1. Boot from the floppy.
2. When you get the Startup menu, select the CD support option.
3. Put the Windows CD into the CD-ROM drive.
4. At the A:\ prompt, type the letter of your CD-ROM drive. It's usually D:\ or E:\.
5. Type dir to get the directory. Inspect the directory to be sure you can see the contents of the CD-ROM.

If you can boot from the startup floppy and see the contents of the CD ROM, you're in great shape. You have a disk you can use to boot up and reinstall Windows if the need ever arises.

Windows NT, 2000, and XP users can use the installation CD as a startup disk.

FRIDAY, FEBRUARY 8

LAPORTE SUPPORT

Q: *What's the fastest way to launch my screensaver?*

A: A screensaver is an executable file, just like Microsoft Word or any other application. You can create shortcuts that launch your screensaver on command. As an added bonus, you can link to several different screensavers on your desktop. If you're in a pipes kind of mood, you can launch Pipes. If you're in a flower box mood, Flower Box is at your fingertips:

1. Go to the Start menu and choose Find (or Search) and look for files containing .scr.
2. The screensaver executable files are represented with little computers.

3. Right-click the screensaver executable.

4. Choose Create Shortcut.

5. When asked whether to create a shortcut to the screensaver on your desktop, click Yes.

6. When you click the new icon on your desktop, you launch your screensaver.

SATURDAY, FEBRUARY 9

FOR GEEKS ONLY

I'm all for recycling, but that doesn't mean I have to be stuck with the name Recycling Bin on my Windows trash can. The Recycling Bin is not a normal icon; you can't rename it just by clicking on it and pressing F2. Renaming the Recycle Bin requires modifying your Windows Registry. (The usual warnings here: Messing with the Registry can wreak havoc with your PC if you make a mistake, so if you're new to computers, enlist a more experienced friend to help you. If you have problems after applying this hack, boot up with your rescue disk and run SCANREG /RESTORE to restore a working copy of your Registry.)

1. Go to the Start menu, select Run, and type REGEDIT.

2. Select HKEY_CLASSES_ROOT in the left pane.

3. Scroll down to CLSID and click once to expand it.

4. Select {645FF040-5081-101B-9F08-00AA002F954E}.

5. Double-click (Default) in the right pane.

6. The current name of your Recycle Bin is displayed. Change it to whatever you want, and close the Registry Editor.

7. Click the Desktop and press F5 to refresh your shortcuts.

SUNDAY, FEBRUARY 10

Back up your data!

PROTECT YOURSELF

You don't have to be paranoid about viruses, just prudent. The following list shows a couple of things you can do to avoid viruses:

- Inoculate your computer: Install an antivirus program. You can buy a commercial product from Norton, McAfee, and other companies. HouseCall

(housecall.antivirus.com) is an online antivirus that's free for Windows users, as is AVG Anti-Virus System (www.grisoft.com). Use the software to scan everything you download from the Internet or receive via e-mail. And scan your entire hard drive weekly.

- Don't open e-mail attachments, especially those that end in .vbs or .exe. That's the number one way to spread viruses.
- You also can spread viruses if you're e-mailing attachments. Find alternative ways of delivering files, such as embedding images within the e-mail, or use an online storage service to transfer large files.
- Limit physical access to your computer. The fewer people using the computer, the fewer things you have to track.

MONDAY, FEBRUARY 11

LAPORTE SUPPORT

Q: What is virtual memory?

A: Your computer reserves a certain amount of space on your hard drive to use when it runs low on RAM. This "virtual" RAM is much slower than the real thing, but it's better than the alternative: running out of memory and crashing.

Unless you're a real expert, it's best to let your operating system manage the size and location of virtual memory for itself. Always keep a few hundred megabytes free on your hard drive for the virtual memory file.

TUESDAY, FEBRUARY 12

MAC TIP

No Macintosh library is complete without StuffIt Expander (www.aladdinsys.com), the ultimate compression software.

Free from Aladdin, this utility can decompress lots of files, including the following:

- Applelink package
- Arc
- Arj
- BinHex
- Compact Pro
- gzip
- Lha
- MacBinary
- StuffIt
- Tar
- Unix Compress
- UUCode
- Zip

StuffIt Expander also has a Watch Folder feature, which automatically decompresses any new item you add to the folder and puts it where you specify.

Keep the StuffIt Expander icon on your desktop and drag a compressed file onto the StuffIt Expander icon. The file automatically decompresses. The decoded or decompressed file appears in a new folder on your desktop, ready to use.

And yes, Windows users can use StuffIt Expander as well.

GEEK SPEAK

Software means the programs you run on your computer, such as your games, word processor, checkbook program, and your operating system. *Hardware* means the physical parts of the computer and its components. *Firmware* means software that is stored in hardware, usually on memory chips called ROMs or PROMs.

WEDNESDAY, FEBRUARY 13

 WEB TIP

If you save all your downloads to your desktop, you probably have an unruly mess of icons and random executable files. Clear up your desktop and organize your downloads into one folder:

1. Right-click a blank area of your desktop.
2. Select New, Folder.
3. Name the folder My Downloads (or whatever name you fancy) and press Enter.

The next time you download a program, save it in your Downloads folder. Your browser will remember that location and store files there from now on.

THURSDAY, FEBRUARY 14 (VALENTINE'S DAY)

Send online flowers, candy, and promises you don't intend to keep.

Flowers: www.americasflorist.com

Candy: www.sees.com

Promises: greetings.yahoo.com/browse/Holidays/Valentine_s_Day/

 WINDOWS TIP

It's good practice to know what's installed in your computer. To print a complete system inventory in Windows 95/98/Me follow these steps:

1. Right-click My Computer and select Properties.
2. Click the Device Manager tab.
3. Click Print.

4. Select System Summary for a quick view or All Devices and System Summary for a longer detailed report.

In Windows 2000/XP:

1. Right-click My Computer and select Properties.
2. Click the Hardware tab.
3. Click the Device Manager button.
4. Select Print from the View menu.
5. Under Report Type, select System Summary for a quick view or All Devices and System Summary for a longer, detailed report.

Macintosh users can do the same thing using the Apple System Profiler. It's under the Apple Menu on Mac OS 9 and in the Applications/Utilies folder on Mac OS X.

Windows users also can use the Belarc Advisor free from www.belarc.com/Download.html.

FRIDAY, FEBRUARY 15

LAPORTE SUPPORT

Q: How do I control my computer remotely?

A: You can buy commercial remote access software such as LapLink (www.laplink.com) or Symantec's PC Anywhere (www.pcanywhere.com). Microsoft's NetMeeting includes PC remote control now, too. Or try a free program from Bell Labs UK called VNC (www.uk.research.att.com/vnc/download.html), which works slower than the other two but can be used from your Palm. (Mac users, try www.chromatix.uklinux.net/vnc/.)

To speed up VNC, go to www.tightvnc.com to download VNC Tight Encoder. Drop the files into your VNC folder. The next time you start VNC Viewer, click Options and choose Tight Compression. As long as the server to which you're connecting runs a TightVNC server, you get a compressed, fast connection.

For even more speed (with or without TightVNC), choose Restrict Pixels to 8-Bit under Options before you connect. It's much faster when you don't have to transfer 16/24-bit color information.

SATURDAY, FEBRUARY 16

FOR GEEKS ONLY

There's a bewildering range of home networking choices out there. I'll narrow them down to the two I like best.

If each of the computers is within reach of a phone jack, I recommend telephone-line –based networking kits from companies such as D-Link, NetGear, Diamond, and 3COM. These kits use your existing telephone jacks to connect the PCs in your house without interfering with normal telephone service.

The latest version of phone line networking, dubbed PNA 2.0 by the acronym-happy computer industry, is easy to set up and very fast: about 10 million bits per second. It's also relatively inexpensive. You can buy everything you need to network two computers for around $100.

If you want to go wireless, the only system that's anywhere near as fast as PNA 2.0 is the even more bizarrely named IEEE 802.11b or Wi-Fi. Apple's AirPort is the best known example, but you can buy Wi-Fi access points and network cards for PCs, too. Expect to spend $300 for a transmitter and $100 per computer.

SUNDAY, FEBRUARY 17
PRIVACY TIP

People often worry that programs like America Online or Prodigy are sending information from your computer back to the home office. These applications do indeed communicate with the servers back home, but the information exchanged usually is innocuous. You don't have to worry about them fetching your checkbook data or downloading your credit card numbers. Doing so would be completely illegal, and no major company would risk its reputation in that way.

On the other hand, many companies do collect information about your surfing and online buying habits for marketing purposes. You should always check your online service's privacy policy to be sure you can live with the information they collect. Do the same thing with any Web site to which you give personal information.

Many free programs also include something called *spyware*. These programs are ostensibly used to freshen the ad banners built into the programs, but it's also possible that they're exchanging information about your online habits with the advertisers. To find out what spyware is running on your computer, download Ad-aware, free from www.lavasoft.com. The Web site also lists spyware-free alternatives to many popular downloads.

MONDAY, FEBRUARY 18

LAPORTE SUPPORT

Q: I want to delete programs I no longer use so I have more room for other things. I've heard that you can't just drag an application to the Recycle Bin, so how do I get rid of these unwanted programs?

A: To uninstall an application or program you no longer use, follow these steps:

1. Choose Start.
2. Click Control Panel.
3. Click Add/Remove Programs.
4. Select any listed programs you no longer use.
5. Click the Add/Remove Button.

If a program's uninstaller leaves traces of the program lying about, and most do, you can sweep up the crumbs with an uninstaller such as Norton CleanSweep, part of the Norton Utilites, $50 from www.symantec.com/sabu/ncs.

It's a lot easier to delete unwanted programs from a Macintosh. In most cases, trashing the program's folder is sufficient. You also might want to look in the System/Preferences folder for the program's preferences and delete them, as well.

TUESDAY, FEBRUARY 19

MAC TIP

Mac OS 9 users can use the Multiple Users control panel to set different permissions for different users. For example, you can create an account for your grandkids using Panels access to keep them from prying into places they shouldn't:

1. Go to the Apple menu.
2. Select Control Panels.
3. Select Multiple Users.
4. Click New User.
5. Enter a username and password.
6. Click Panels.
7. Expand Show Setup Details (click the arrow).
8. Check the box next to any application you want to allow this user to open.
9. Close the window to save.

Be sure to enable Multiple Users before rebooting.

TODAY IN COMPUTER HISTORY

On February 19, 1985, President Reagan awarded Steve Jobs and Steve Wozniak (the founders of Apple) the National Medal of Technology. This honor, awarded the year following Apple's release of the Macintosh, was to recognize their development of the first personal computer.

WEDNESDAY, FEBRUARY 20

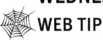

WEB TIP

You can use Internet Explorer to send your friend a URL without cutting and pasting it from your location bar.

Say you're on The Screen Savers Web site in Internet Explorer and you want to tell your friend about a cool article you just read. Instead of cutting and pasting the article or URL into your e-mail client, you can have your browser open your default e-mail client with the text of the message (a clickable URL) already pasted in the text window. All you have to do is type your friend's e-mail address and hit Send!

Just go to your Internet Explorer file menu and click Send. Then, choose Link by E-mail. This opens your default mail client with a clickable link to whichever page was in your browser window. You also can click the link on any story at TechTV.com that says *email this story to a friend* and do just that.

THURSDAY, FEBRUARY 21

WINDOWS TIP

To customize your taskbar (that's the bar with the Start button in it), right-click on any unoccupied area and select Toolbars. From the Toolbars pop-up menu, select Address to add a URL field to your taskbar. Type in a Web address; Windows launches Internet Explorer and takes you there.

If you select Links, Windows adds Internet Explorer's links bar to your taskbar. Choose Desktop to add icons for your Desktop items or choose New Toolbar to add shortcuts to commonly used folders and files.

FRIDAY, FEBRUARY 22

SHORTCUT: WINDOWS

If you have a Windows keyboard—that's a keyboard with a Windows key on the bottom row—you can do all sorts of interesting things with it. For example, press the Windows key and E at the same time to open Windows Explorer.

LAPORTE SUPPORT

Q: Can I assign different functions to my Windows key?

A: If you want to change your Windows key only, try the free WinKey (www.agents-tech. com/winkey/). To control all kinds of keystrokes, try Quickeys (www.cesoft.com). It costs $50, but you can download a 30-day trial version of Quickeys, and it works with many versions of Windows and MacOS.

SATURDAY, FEBRUARY 23

FOR GEEKS ONLY

3D game design is a very advanced subject, among the most advanced in programming. To write your own 3D game, I suggest starting with *The Black Art of 3D Programming* by Andre Lamothe, a book that gives you the basics of writing a 3D engine in C++. It's pretty much a college course in itself, although at $50 or so it costs less than a class. It's the best book I've found for game programmers.

Next, look at someone else's source code. That's the original form of a program, just as the programmer wrote it, before it's turned into machine language. Several open-source 3D gaming projects, such as Crystal Space (`crystal.linuxgames.com`) and Genesis 3d (`www.genesis3d.com`), offer real-world coding examples. If you get really good, you might even want to contribute to the effort.

If you want to learn from the master, John Carmack has released the source code for Quake I at `www.idsoftware.com/archives/sourcearc.html`. Read it and be afraid.

SUNDAY, FEBRUARY 24

Back up your data!

PROTECT YOURSELF

All computer users should be aware of hacking. However, keep things in perspective by doing the following:

- Remember, the chances of your getting hacked are pretty slim—just like your chances of getting burglarized. But it's still a good idea to lock your doors at night.
- Cable modem and DSL users should install a firewall such as ZoneAlarm (`www.zonealarm.com`) or Tiny Firewall (`www.tinysoftware.com`) for protection against outside intruders. They're both free and very effective. Mac OS 9 users can buy a great firewall called NetBarrier for $60 from `www.intego.com`. Mac OS X users already have firewall protection, but they'll need to turn it on. I recommend a script called Brickhouse from `personalpages.tds.net/~brian_hill/brickhouse.html`.
- Don't open e-mail attachments. Never. Ever.
- Buy a good antivirus program and keep it up-to-date.

MONDAY, FEBRUARY 25

LAPORTE SUPPORT

Q: What's VBR, and should I use it?

A: VBR stands for *variable bit-rate recording*. It's used when converting CD audio into MP3 music files.

MP3s can be encoded at a variety of bit rates, from 8,000 to 320,000 bits per second. The higher the bit rate, the bigger the file size and the better the musical quality. Most MP3s are recorded at 128,000 bits per second (or 128Kbps). That gives you a file size of about a megabyte per minute of music and near CD-quality sound. When you choose a single bit rate for your recordings we say you're using CBR, or constant bit-rate recording.

Another way to encode MP3s is to let the recorder choose an appropriate bit rate, depending on the source material. That's variable bit-rate encoding. More complex music might use 160Kbps or 256Kbps, while the simpler sounds are encoded at a lower 128Kbps. This produces a recording that optimizes both file size and sound quality.

There are drawbacks to VBR. File sizes are unpredictable, and some MP3 players can't play VBR recordings. For maximum compatibility, I prefer to record at a constant bit rate of 160Kbps. As for software, on Windows I use MusicMatch Jukebox from www.musicmatch.com, and on the Macintosh I use Apple's iTunes.

TUESDAY, FEBRUARY 26

MAC TIP

If you want to get serious about Mac programming (and we know you do), Metrowerks' CodeWarrior (www.metrowerks.com) is the way to go. It's not cheap, but most Mac programmers agree that it's the tool to use.

The program includes all the Java and C++ elements that you need. Metrowerks also sponsors free courses, including an introduction to Macintosh programming and developing.

For hobbyists, I recommend REALBasic from www.realbasic.com. It runs on Macintosh but can create programs that work on both Mac and Windows. You can try it free for 30 days.

Visit Apple's developer Web site (www.apple.com/developer/) for more news and cool resources.

GEEK SPEAK

Telematics refers to any integration of information and communication technologies. Telematics originally was an auto industry term in reference to the special automobile features including location tracking, vehicle control, and wireless communications.

WEDNESDAY, FEBRUARY 27

WEB TIP

Get Web Accessories for Internet Explorer, and you can speed up your online research enough to leave time for casual surfing. From any Web page, highlight a word or phrase on which you want to search for more information, right-click the mouse, and choose Web search. The selected words are immediately entered into a default search engine.

Search www.microsoft.com for "Web Accessories" to find the download page.

THURSDAY, FEBRUARY 28

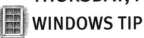

WINDOWS TIP

To trash a file without having to empty the Recycle Bin, perform the following steps:

1. Click the file to select it.

2. Hold down the Shift key and press the Delete key.

3. In the confirmation window, click Yes.

Now check the Recycle Bin. There's nothing there, and your file is gone.

This Month's Feature

COMPUTER GAMES BOTH SEXES LOVE

By Heather Kelley

As a female game developer and someone devoted to broadening the field of gaming to include more females, I am very interested in games that both males and females love. So, I've assembled a very biased list of 10 favorite wide-appeal games, in no particular order.

Besides simply being fun games, it's difficult to pinpoint what makes each of these games appeal to both women and men, but here are a few elements I considered:

- Offering the player a choice of violent or nonviolent gameplay
- Having an original visual style
- Featuring diverse casts of characters (male and female, human and animal, and supernatural)
- Incorporating mental challenges such as puzzle solving
- Having innovative gameplay mechanics

From these elements, you can see they aren't necessarily all about the twitch. Of course, a lot of chicks dig violent twitch games, and I play them when the mood strikes. But this list represents the games that most impact me as a developer; the games that make me want to do what I do. (By no means does this short list reflect all the games that might appeal equally to men and women, or all of my favorite games.)

Legend of Zelda Series (N64, Game Boy)

This game is the mother of all adventure series from master designer (if my industry could be said to have a master) Shigeru Miyamoto. You play as Link, a strange young man sent on quest after quest to fix the wrongs of your universe. Develop your skills at sword fighting, archery, and even horseback riding to meet physical challenges and fight dungeon enemies. One piece of advice: If you've never played a Zelda game before, play the two N64 games in order of their release; first play Ocarina of Time, and then play Majora's Mask.

Thief and Thief 2 (PC)

The Thief games are first-person games that are decidedly not shooters. Instead, developer Looking Glass pioneered the "sneak" style of gameplay. In both games you play as Garrett, a mercenary super-thief caught up in the factional power struggles of a gothic retro-futuristic world. Hide in the darkest shadows and avoid (or knock out) denizens (human and otherwise) as you silently steal valuables. I love the innovative audio design. What you hear and how much noise you make have direct impact on your success.

Spyro the Dragon (PSX)

As young, purple Spyro, you head-butt, run, flame, and fly your way through colorful fantasy worlds. This is PlayStation's answer to Zelda, and it's worthy of attention in its own right. It includes beautiful graphics and a great sense of control, and Spyro's downright cute, too.

The Sims (PC, Mac)

Start your own family inside the computer. Use your initial resources to build them a home and furnish it. Then take care of their needs for money, work, entertainment, and companionship—and, of course, their need to go to the bathroom. You decide how they live their lives. Developer Maxis (Electronic Arts) has done an amazing job of providing objects for this simulated world, down to the pet hamster. And what they haven't provided, you can get on one of the hundreds of Sims player sites.

Black and White (Multiple Platforms)

Many people consider this to be the next step in god-game evolution, and in game AI. As in most other god-sims, you are the deity in charge of a world, its inhabitants, lands, and resources. There are a couple of twists here, though. You can rule by benevolence or malice; the moral choice is up to you, and the world responds accordingly. Better yet, you raise and teach one of the world's creatures, essentially an animal demi-god who watches what you do and learns to repeat it.

Samba de Amigo with Maracas Controllers (DC) and Dance Revolution with Dance Pad Controllers (Arcade, PSX)

Rhythm and music games are a blast to play in mixed-gender groups, and, in my experience (generalization alert), they are the sole genre of games for which many women have the real-world experience to give them an edge over the guys. In both of these games, you move to the beat following the instructions from the screen. DDR is one of the original dancing games, converted from the Japanese arcade hit with an obsessive cult following. In Samba you use a pair of real maracas to shake to the rhythm. Both games reward skill with new songs and more challenging beats. Samba has the more interesting visual display: The frenetic, psychedelic, south-of-the-border fantasy world offers plenty for observers of the game as well as players. A caution: Neither of these is much fun to play without the special controllers, which you have to buy separately. On the upside, if you invest in the extra hardware, they're both great exercise.

Crazy Taxi (Arcade, DC, PS2)

The sole racer on my list gets a vote for its de-emphasis on reality and repetition and its emphasis on fun. You're a cabbie racing around an imaginary town that is strangely reminiscent of San Francisco. Your goal, naturally, is to pick up and deliver as many fares as possible within a time limit. Handling traffic, learning the neighborhood, and perfecting your starts and stops are some of the skills you need to develop to reach the pinnacle of your profession. If you have a chance to play Crazy Taxi in the arcade, don't pass it up.

Mario Party (N64)

There are three of these so far, all three combining the best of board games and mini-action (okay, twitch) games. Do not try to play these by yourself—they are called "Party" for a reason. Lead your Mario-world character around a game board, avoiding pitfalls and collecting points, while challenging your opponents to small, hyper games of skill.

Soul Calibur (DC)

As far as fighters go, this is my favorite. No gratuitous panty-shots or overly heaving chests. Just good, clean, butt-kicking fun. Fighting games usually give their female characters speed and agility over strength, and this game is no exception. The bladed weapons balance the characters' prowess even more. The Dreamcast version of this game is one of the most visually stunning games to appear for that platform. The next installment in this series is planned for PS2.

Heather Kelley is an award-winning game producer and designer with credits spanning PC and console games, smart toys, and internet games. She is co-chair of the Women In Game Development Committee of the International Game Developers Association. You can reach her at heather@igda.org.

LEO'S ESSAY

A LEVER TO MOVE THE WORLD

The ancient Greek scientist, Archimedes, once said, "Give me a lever and a place to stand and I will move the Earth." Today, you have that lever: the personal computer.

A lever amplifies the power of human muscle to accomplish otherwise impossible tasks. The computer amplifies the human mind to give it undreamt-of power and scope. With your computer you can converse with people all over the world. You can find nearly any nugget of information with just a few browser clicks. You can create works of art and enjoy the creations of others.

But nothing this powerful and complex comes without a price. In this case, the price is study. You wouldn't expect to pick up a violin and play it without practicing. You shouldn't expect to master the PC without spending some time learning how it works.

Fortunately, the computer is much easier to learn than the violin—and it doesn't sound quite so much like a screeching cat when you first start out. Begin by picking one program to master. New computers come with dozens of programs. Trying to learn them all at once would be like trying to learn a dozen foreign languages at the same time. Choose software in which you are interested and will likely use a lot, maybe a word processor or a home finance program. Start by skimming through the manual. Become comfortable with the basics, and then return to the manual to learn more advanced techniques. You might want to pick up a book or two to supplement the manual. You don't need to learn how to do everything. Just focus on the tasks you need the most. You don't have to know everything about the program; you just need to know how to use it to do what you want.

When you're proficient with one program, extending what you know to other programs will be easy. In time, you'll be a master of the computer, and with mastery comes power.

Reporters once asked Nobel Peace Prize winner Jody Williams, coordinator of the International Campaign to Ban Landmines, how she managed to make such a difference. She said that she couldn't have done it without e-mail. With the help of a computer, every individual has the power to change the world. Now go out and do your stuff.

FRIDAY, MARCH 1
LAPORTE SUPPORT

Q: How do I run Java files?

A: That's a simple question with a complicated answer.

Java is a programming language that is widely used on the Internet, chiefly because Java programs can run unmodified on nearly any computer. Java does require some support software to work on your system, but chances are good you already have everything you need.

All versions of Netscape Navigator and versions of Microsoft's Internet Explorer before 6.0 support Java right out of the box. You can run any Java program embedded in a Web page just by opening that page. All Macintosh computers come with Java support, too.

Unfortunately, Microsoft no longer provides Java support in Windows XP or versions of Internet Explorer 6 or later. If you're using XP and you visit a Web page with an embedded Java program, one of two things will happen. If the Web page has been updated to support the Java Plug-in standard, the browser will automatically download the files it needs. The Java program won't run on Web sites that still use the `<applet>` tag. In that case, you'll have to download the support files by hand.

You can get the necessary Java Runtime Environment, or JRE, for Windows XP free from Sun Microsystems at `java.sun.com/j2se/1.3/jre/download-windows.html`. It's a little over 5MB, but you need to download and install it only once.

The JRE also is required to run standalone Java applications on your computer. If you're using a program written in Java, it probably came with a JRE. If not, the program's documentation should explain how to download and install the additional files you need.

When the JRE is installed, you can run Java applications from the DOS prompt by typing `java` followed by the name of the java class file you wish to run. You also can use a program called Java Runner for Windows. It's free from `www.programfiles.com/index.asp?ID=8050`.

SATURDAY, MARCH 2
FOR GEEKS ONLY

Today's multi-gigahertz microprocessors run hot. Really hot. So hot, in fact, that they can burn themselves out in a matter of seconds unless they're properly cooled. (We know because it's happened to us.)

Be sure the fans on your computer are working. Check them from time to time for signs of wear, and clean out any dust that could reduce their efficiency.

When installing a new processor, don't forget to install a fan and heatsink. Be sure the fan has a good thermal connection to the processor. And always use a fan designed for the right processor. Using a fan designed for a Pentium on an Athlon can crack the processor.

For lots more information in CPU cooling, visit HardOCP at `www.hardocp.com/cooling.html`.

SUNDAY, MARCH 3

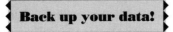

Back up your data!

PROTECT YOURSELF

Regular maintenance of your hard drive is important for the reliability of your system. That's why Windows makes it easy to access the three most important maintenance programs. Double-click My Computer, then right-click your hard drive and select Properties from the pop-up menu. Click the Tools tab; you see Error Checking, Backup, and Defragmentation.

Let's start with Backup. That's the one thing everyone should do every day. You don't need to back up the whole hard drive, just personal stuff like your checkbook, Internet bookmarks, and your great American novel.

You should also perform a weekly error check on the hard drive. Windows uses a program called Scandisk to find and repair mistakes in your directories. It's best to catch these early. Every month or so, run the thorough version of Scandisk to catch any flaws on the disk itself.

The final utility, Defragmentation, is less important. After months of use, the files on your hard drive can get disorganized. Defrag reorganizes them for faster access. You needn't run Defrag more than a few times a year.

MONDAY, MARCH 4

LAPORTE SUPPORT

Q: I periodically received warnings from Windows 98 telling me that I have Not enough stacks. *What are stacks and how do I ensure a full complement?*

A: Programs use stacks as temporary data storage. When a program runs out of stacks, it can generate an error. In most cases, you can't do anything to fix the problem—it's up to the software publisher to fix the bug in its program.

This raises an important issue. Computer users are often misled by program error messages into thinking there's something they can do to make things better. In fact, most of the time the message only means something to the programmer, if that.

If a program crashes, save your work, restart Windows, and hope it doesn't happen again. If the same program crashes frequently, check with the publisher to see if it offers an update. Sometimes it helps to re-install the program.

Error messages should really read `Something unexpected has happened and I can't go on. Awfully sorry about that. Please don't blame yourself.`

That'll be the day.

TUESDAY, MARCH 5

MAC TIP

Firewall software is an important weapon in your security arsenal. It keeps the bad guys from using the Internet to break into your computer.

If you're running Mac OS X, you already have built-in firewall capabilities. The easiest way to turn the firewall on is to download a script called Brickhouse from `personalpages.tds.net/~brian_hill/brickhouse.html`. It's $25 shareware. For other versions of Mac OS, I recommend Intego's NetBarrier ($60 from `www.intego.com`) or Sustainable Softworks' IPNetSentry ($35 from `www.sustworks.com`).

VIRUS ALERT

The Michelangelo virus activates tomorrow. This would be a good time to update your antivirus software (even though, as we'll learn tomorrow, Michelangelo isn't much of a threat any more).

WEDNESDAY, MARCH 6

TODAY IN COMPUTER HISTORY

In 1992, hysteria swept over the planet as newspapers, magazines, and television networks proclaimed that on March 6, the birth date of Renaissance artist Michelangelo, up to one quarter of American hard drives would be completely erased. This was the birth of the Michelangelo virus.

The media frenzy started through a coincidence. In January of 1992, one computer manufacturer claimed it had inadvertently distributed 500 PCs carrying the virus while another computer company issued a press release stating that from that point on it would bundle antivirus software with every PC it sold. The two events were completely unrelated, but apparently it was a slow news day and reporters tried to make a story out of it. By the time March 5 rolled around, the fever pitch had reached Y2K proportions. Even the respectable Wall Street Journal carried the headline "Deadly Virus Set to Wreak Havoc Tomorrow."

Why did the media go nuts? For one thing, John McAfee, the man behind McAfee Anti-Virus, told reporters that an estimated five million computers worldwide could lose their hard drives on account of the Michelangelo virus. (Take note that there were a lot of other ballooned predictions from other people.) As you can imagine, McAfee's prediction boosted his company's sales significantly.

When March 6 came, the virus struck only about 10,000 computers. Many members of the media claimed it would have affected far more if not for their reporting.

 ## WEB TIP

Webmasters, you can keep your Web site up to date with FTP Voyager for Windows. Its synchronization feature will update your Web pages automatically at the same time every day. FTP Voyager is $40 from www.ftpvoyager.com.

THURSDAY, MARCH 7

 ## WINDOWS TIP

What if your kitchen trash can asked you "Are you sure?" every time you tried to take out the garbage? If you're tired of getting the third degree every time you drag a file to the Windows Recycle Bin, here's how to turn off the warning permanently:

1. Right-click the Recycle Bin and select Properties.
2. Uncheck the Display Delete Confirmation Dialog box.
3. Click OK.

FRIDAY, MARCH 8

 ## LAPORTE SUPPORT

Q: I installed a game correctly, but when I click the icon to play the game I get this message: Needs DirectX 7.0 or later. *What should I do?*

A: DirectX is a set of tools and services Microsoft Windows provides for games and other demanding multimedia applications.

DirectX comes with all current versions of Windows, but some games require a newer version. You should be able to find a copy on the game's installation disc. If not, download the latest version for free from Microsoft at www.microsoft.com/directx.

SATURDAY, MARCH 9

FOR GEEKS ONLY

John "maddog" Hall is the executive director of Linux International (www.li.org), an open-source advocacy organization. He travels around the world speaking about the benefits of open-source, collaboratively created software, and has written such books as *Linux for Dummies*. He also happens to be the godfather of Linux inventor Linus Torvalds' children.

In a 1999 interview with IBM, Hall spelled out what people can do to become open-source freedom fighters. Here are his ideas:

- Use it.
- Tell your congressman about it.
- Review documentation.
- Join a user group.
- Tell your local government about it.
- Start a user group.
- Talk to your neighbor about it.
- Install it in your local library.

Hall adds, "We should all be Linux advocates, all the time. OK, you are allowed time off to eat, sleep, and go to an occasional movie, and you don't have to wear Linux underwear like I do…"

If you're curious, the nickname "maddog" is a Unix login name that originated during a time when Hall had a little trouble controlling his temper. By all accounts he's mellowed out, but the name remains.

SUNDAY, MARCH 10

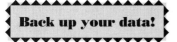

Back up your data!

PROTECT YOURSELF

One way to protect yourself while surfing the Web is to crank up your security settings. In Internet Explorer, click Tools, Internet Options, select the Security tab, and drag the slider to High. If the slider isn't visible, press the Default Level button to restore it.

Setting your security level to High disables features that the unscrupulous could exploit, but it also decreases your browser's functionality. For most users the Medium security is adequate.

Web-savvy users, try the Custom Level button to adjust the security for various elements such as ActiveX controls and cookies.

MONDAY, MARCH 11

LAPORTE SUPPORT

Q: Does constantly shutting down via the power button hurt the computer?

A: The safest way to shut down a computer is to give it the Shut Down command. In Windows this involves using the Start menu. (Yes, I know that makes no sense at all, but if they made computers easy to use, a whole lot of people like me would be out of a job!) Select Shut Down, and click OK. Most late-model PCs shut themselves off at this point.

If your computer doesn't turn itself off when you Shut Down, it's okay to use the power button when you see the "OK to shut down" message, but not before.

Power down a Macintosh computer by selecting Shut Down from the Finder's Special menu; with OS 8x and above, press the Power button on the keyboard to bring up the Shut Down dialog. Really old Macs have to be shut off manually.

People often wonder if it's better to turn off the computer or leave it on all night. I say turn your system off if you're not going to be using it for more than a few hours. It saves energy and doesn't harm the computer.

TUESDAY, MARCH 12

MAC TIP

The Network Utility program found in your Mac OS X Applications/Utilities folder offers many useful network diagnostic tools, including Ping. To give it a try, open Network Utility and click the Ping tab. Windows users can open a command-line window and type PING <server name> to do the same thing.

Ping is used to troubleshoot an Internet connection. It sends a signal to a remote system, waits for acknowledgment, and shows how long the round trip took.

You can use this information in several ways:

- Ping the IP address of a machine on your LAN to see if your network hardware is working.
- Ping a server by name, as in yahoo.com, to see if your Internet name resolution, or DNS, works. If you can see a numeric address but not a word-based address, your DNS settings are likely wrong.

- Ping a server to see how responsive it is. If it takes more than 500 milliseconds round trip, the remote server or the Internet itself is slow. If you see considerable packet loss, you have a poor connection.

Traceroute is Ping on steroids. It returns the names of the servers through which your packet traveled to reach its destination and how long each leg of the trip took. It's fun to see the places your data passes through on the way to its destination, and it can be useful information for diagnosing an Internet slowdown.

GEEK SPEAK

To *reboot* is to restart the computer. Rebooting the computer often is the first step in attempting to fix an otherwise healthy computer that is exhibiting random or minor malfunctions (that is, it's unusually slow, freezing frequently, or stuttering).

WEDNESDAY, MARCH 13

WEB TIP

Navigating Web sites that use frames can be confusing, especially if you'd like to send a link to someone or bookmark a page from a framed site. This is why Internet Explorer and Netscape Navigator both allow users to open a framed page in a new window:

1. Open any Web page with frames in either Internet Explorer or Netscape Navigator. (My Web page is a good example: www.leoville.com. There are two frames there, a navigation bar on the left and a content frame on the right).

2. Right-click any link inside the navigation frame and choose Open Frame in New Window from the menu.

The linked page appears in its own browser window, without the other frame.

If your browser is missing this handy feature, upgrade to the latest version.

THURSDAY, MARCH 14

WINDOWS TIP

If you have a mouse with a scroll wheel (like the Microsoft Intellimouse), try these scroll wheel + keystroke combinations in Internet Explorer:

- **Ctrl+scroll up/down**—Increase and decrease text size
- **Shift+scroll up/down**—Move back and forward through previously visited Web pages (like the Back and Forward buttons on the browser's toolbar)
- **Move the scroll wheel while pressing a mouse button**—Slow scroll up or down

These mouse key combinations work in many other Microsoft programs, too. Try them and see!

FRIDAY, MARCH 15

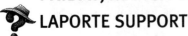

LAPORTE SUPPORT

Q: *I do not want my name to appear on the e-mails I send, only my e-mail address. Can you explain the procedure for making sure my e-mail address is the only personal information on my e-mails?*

A: The exact steps for doing this depend on which e-mail program you use. In general, you need to clear the name field in the e-mail account options.

If you use Microsoft's Outlook, select Accounts from the Tools menu and double-click the e-mail account you want to change. Click the General tab. In the User Information area, enter your e-mail address in the Name field. (Outlook requires something in that field.)

In Outlook Express, select Accounts from the Tools menu and do the same thing. Outlook Express allows a blank Name field, however, so you can just clear it.

SATURDAY, MARCH 16

FOR GEEKS ONLY

One of the unique things about Linux and Unix is the ability to spread work across multiple consoles. It might seem a trivial matter, especially when you come from a Windows-style environment. I mean, what use could having multiple consoles provide?

A *console*, in its basic definition, is simply a monitor and keyboard, analogous to the phrase *terminal*. In Linux you have what are termed virtual consoles (or console for short). A *virtual console* is another workstation or desktop (for you Windows and Mac OS people) to work in.

There is a great advantage when you run multiple programs in command-line mode. You can have several processes running, each on its own console. It helps keep you organized.

Accessing the Consoles

In most Linux distributions, the default number of consoles is set to four. You can access the consoles by pressing down on the Alt key and pressing one of several F keys (F1 through F7). For example, if you have two consoles, you would press Alt+F1 and Alt+F2 to access the consoles.

X Window

From within the X Window System, commonly known as X Window, add the Ctrl key as well to exit out of X Window and into another console.

To re-enter X Window from a command-line console, use the Alt+F7 key combination. If you go back to the console where you launched X Window, all you get is the script from the X server launch, not the actual X Window desktop.

SUNDAY, MARCH 17 (ST. PATRICK'S DAY)

AOL TIP

If you've recently visited a Web site but can't remember the Web address or URL, AOL can help you access it quickly. The AOL browser stores URLs for Web sites you've visited.

In the center of your toolbar where you enter the Web address, there's a pull-down menu on the right side (look for the down arrow). In AOL 5.0, the pull-down menu is on the left side. Click on that, and you'll see all the addresses listed. Click on an address and it will take you to that site.

If your list is getting too cluttered, you might want to clear it and start over:

1. Click My AOL in your toolbar.
2. Scroll down to Preferences.
3. Click Toolbar.
4. Click Clear History Now.

MONDAY, MARCH 18
LAPORTE SUPPORT

Q: I use CompuServe, and cartoons I download come as ART files. My e-mail friends say they can't read them. Can I convert these ART files to GIFs or JPGs?

A: When you visit a Web site on CompuServe (and its cousin, America Online), images on the page are compressed into a proprietary format called *ART*. The online services do this to save space on their servers and to speed up loading times. The compressed images don't look nearly as good as the originals—Web designers really hate that—and, as you've discovered, you might not be able to share ART files with friends who don't use AOL or CompuServe.

You can require CompuServe and AOL to use standard graphics formats by selecting WWW in your program's Preferences and unchecking the Use Compressed Images option. Your Web pages might load a tad slower, but the images are a lot clearer and easier to share.

To add insult to injury, when you save these graphic images from within AOL or CompuServe, they're saved in ART format, even though the filename extension says GIF or JPG.

Windows users can convert ART files using Internet Explorer 4 or later. Open the ART file in Explorer, right-click it, select Save Picture As and choose BMP in the Save As Type box. Then save the file. Convert the resulting .BMP file to JPEG using the Imaging program in the Start, Programs, Accessories folder.

According to AOL, no Macintosh programs can convert the ART format into a more common form.

TUESDAY, MARCH 19

MAC TIP

To change your desktop wallpaper in OS X, follow these steps:

1. Click the Desktop to make the Finder active.
2. Select Preferences under the Finder menu.
3. Change the wallpaper by pressing the Select Picture button.

By default, this opens the Desktop Pictures folder in the Library directory, but you can browse to anywhere on your computer to find a suitable JPEG or PICT file.

Incidentally, you can also use PDF files as desktop wallpaper—a good idea if you have any text in the image. A preview opens so you can look at your pictures before selecting one.

GEEK SPEAK

A *LAN* (*Local Area Network*) is a group of computers in relatively close proximity (for example, in the same office or in the same building) that are on the same network. If the computers are spread out geographically, it's called a *WAN* (*Wide Area Network*).

WEDNESDAY, MARCH 20

WEB TIP

Some versions of Netscape come with a pesky little feature intended to notify you when a new update of the Netscape browser becomes available for download. But all it seems to do is annoy people who'd rather update their browser themselves.

Follow these steps to turn it off:

1. Open Netscape.
2. Select Edit, Preferences.
3. Double-click Advanced and select SmartUpdate.
4. Uncheck the SmartUpdate field.

THURSDAY, MARCH 21

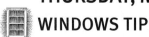

WINDOWS TIP

Do you know how full your hard drive is? To find out

1. Double-click the My Computer icon.
2. Right-click the C: drive.
3. Select Properties.
4. Repeat for other drives and partitions (D:, E:, and so on).

A colorful pie chart shows you how much space you have left. If your hard drive is getting bloated, shed some weight by deleting unnecessary files accumulated through normal computer usage.

FRIDAY, MARCH 22

LAPORTE SUPPORT

Q: Is it possible to get Windows 95, 98, or 2000 in Spanish?

A: ¡Claro que sié! Microsoft offers Windows in 31 languages, including Spanish. You might have a little trouble finding non-English versions of Windows in retail stores, so buy online at a site such as World Language Resources (www.worldlanguage.com, 800-900-8803).

International versions of Windows have the same features as the U.S. version with one exception: no Web TV software. If you have a TV tuner card in your computer, you'll have to find the software for it somewhere else.

For Spanish language support, visit Microsoft Mexico at www.microsoft.com/mexico. You also can find many books about Windows in Spanish.

SATURDAY, MARCH 23

FOR GEEKS ONLY

One TechTV viewer wanted to know if he could use an old machine as a dedicated MP3 jukebox for his car. Absolutely. We found a DOS-based MP3 player called DAMP (www.damp-mp3.co.uk/) that's perfect for the job. DOS is preferable to Windows because it's faster, smaller, and doesn't have to be shut down before you turn off the ignition.

For more information about playing MP3s in your car, visit www.mp3car.com/.

SUNDAY, MARCH 24

Back up your data!

PROTECT YOURSELF

Some online companies share your personal information with their advertisers or track your surfing habits. Always read a Web site's privacy policy before offering personal information.

You also can ask companies to stop collecting information about you. Members of the Network Advertising Initiative, including the biggest Internet advertising agencies, DoubleClick and Engage, have agreed to offer a single opt-out form to make it easier for consumers to protect their privacy. You can find the form at www.networkadvertising.org.

The Center for Democracy and Technology has also launched Operation Opt-Out to make it easier for people to get off mailing lists. Visit opt-out.cdt.org for more information. And whenever you you fill out an online form, be sure to uncheck the box requesting information from advertisers. Unless, of course, you like to hear from marketers.

MONDAY, MARCH 25

LAPORTE SUPPORT

Q: I accidentally deleted a program without uninstalling it. How do I remove it from the Add/Remove Programs list? It is really driving me crazy.

A: On Windows systems it's always best to remove software by using either the uninstaller that came with the program or the Add/Remove Programs control panel. If you merely delete the program's folder, you leave parts of the program strewn around your hard drive, wasting space and causing problems.

Furthermore, as you've noticed, the program's uninstall entry stays in the Add/Remove Programs control panel, even though selecting it results in an error. To remove the useless uninstall entry, use TweakUI.

Download TweakUI free from www.winmag.com/downloads. After you install it, open the Control Panels folder in My Computer, double-click TweakUI, click the Add/Remove tab, and then delete the obsolete entry.

Be careful with the Remove button, though. If you delete the Add/Remove Programs entry for an existing program, you might not be able to uninstall it later.

TUESDAY, MARCH 26

MAC TIP

Want to know what's running in the background on OS X? Open the ProcessViewer. It's in the Utilities folder inside your Applications folder.

You can see each process running, its owner (the person or process that launched it), its ID, and how much memory and CPU time it takes up. Click the More Info triangle at the bottom and get, yes, more info, including how much total processor time it has used.

TODAY IN COMPUTER HISTORY

On March 26, 1993, Apple announced that it would license to five other companies the use of its Newton (Apple's hand-held computer) technology. This represented the first time that Apple released a license, thus allowing the opportunity for "clones."

WEDNESDAY, MARCH 27

WEB TIP

Five Simple Ways to Speed Up Your Web Surfing

Here are a few simple tricks that I guarantee will greatly quicken your Web searching when using Internet Explorer. For many of these tricks to work, you must be using Internet Explorer 6 or later. If you're still using IE 5, download and install Web Accessories for Internet Explorer. You can find a copy at `www.microsoft.com/windows/ie/previous/webaccess`.

Tip 1:

There's a way to use the best search engine in the world, Google, from the convenience of the IE address box. Just be sure you've installed Web Accessories before implementing this golden trick.

After following these steps, you'll be able to type `goo` plus a search term in your Address window to perform a Google search, no matter where you are on the Web.

1. Go to Google and create a bogus search for `searchstring`.

   When the search completes, copy the long URL in the Address window. It should look something like this: `http://www.google.com/search?q=searchstring`.

2. Now, click the Quicksearch.exe item in your Links toolbar (again, it'll be there only if you installed Microsoft Web Accessories).

3. Click the New button.

4. Type `goo` in the Shortcut window.

5. Select Custom URL in the Search windows.

6. Paste the Google URL into the URL window.

7. Edit the URL, replacing `searchstring` with `%s`.

8. Click the Try It button to try your custom search. If it works, click OK, and then click Save to add the search to your Quick Search list.

Tip 2:

So, you're reading a Web page about new Toyota cars and want to learn more about a particular model from other sources on the Internet. If you have Web Accessories installed, highlight the word or phrase on which you want to search for more information, right-click the mouse, and choose Web Search. The selected words will immediately be entered into a default search engine. (Microsoft stripped this capability, called Smart Tags, out of IE 6 and Windows XP after considerable criticism. By the time you read this, they'll probably have put it back. It still works with IE5 when you've installed Web Accessories.)

Tip 3:

If you have a very slow Internet connection, you might want to prevent pictures from loading into your browser to speed the page loading process. Open the Links toolbar and choose Toggle Images.exe. No images will load until you run the executable again.

If you don't have Web Accessories installed, you can do the same thing by first choosing Tools, Internet Options, and then clicking on the Advanced tab. Scroll down to the Multimedia portion of the list, and uncheck the Show Pictures box.

You also might want to uncheck Play Animations and Play Video if you suffer from a very slow connection. You can always turn them back on when duty calls.

Tip 4:

It amazes me how many people still type in www, .com, and most ridiculous of all http:// when trying to get to a Web page. In most cases, you don't need to type that extra baggage. For example, if you're going to the TechTV Web site, all you need to do is type TechTV in the address box and press Ctrl+Enter. The http://, www, and .com will be added automatically. This doesn't work for .org, .net, and so on.

Tip 5:

If you have a slow Internet connection and, your intention when logging on is to head straight for a different site, you might consider getting rid of your home page so you don't need to wait for it to load. Go to Tools, Internet Options, and click the Blank button in the Home Page section. Click Apply, and Internet Explorer will load more quickly from then on.

THURSDAY, MARCH 28

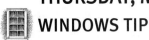

WINDOWS TIP

A driver is a small program that tells Windows how to use a specific device. Whenever you add a new piece of hardware, such as a sound card, to your PC, you need to install a corresponding driver in order to use the device.

Drivers are frequently updated to eliminate bugs and improve performance. To download and install a new or updated driver, follow these steps:

1. Connect to the Internet.
2. Right-click My Computer.
3. Click Properties.
4. Click the tab marked Device Manager. (In Windows 2000 and XP select the Hardware tab, and then click the Device Manager button.)
5. Double-click a listed device; a new window opens.
6. Click Drivers to find out what drivers you currently have installed on your computer.
7. Click Update Driver and Windows checks to see if you have the latest driver. If there's a newer driver available, it's usually a good idea to upgrade.

You also can find updated versions of drivers by visiting hardware manufacturers' Web sites.

FRIDAY, MARCH 29

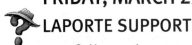

LAPORTE SUPPORT

Q: How can I remove a screensaver from the Display Properties list?

A: Windows shows a list of available screen savers in the Display control panel. To choose a screensaver, go to Start, choose Settings, and select Control Panel. Double-click the Display control panel and click the Screensaver tab.

Windows scans the Windows directory and its subfolders for files that end in .SCR and generates a list of screensavers.

To eliminate a screen saver from the list, find the associated .SCR file and delete it. Better yet, change the file extension from .SCR to .SCR.OLD. It will disappear from the list. To return it to the list, remove the .OLD.

Sometimes the .SCR file has a different name from the screen saver itself. Before you delete or rename a .SCR file, right-click on it and select Properties. The full screensaver name is listed next to Description.

SATURDAY, MARCH 30
FOR GEEKS ONLY

Windows users who are moving to Linux often wonder how to get programs to start up automatically when the computer is turned on. Linux provides plenty of places where you can start your own programs. The technique you choose depends on when in the boot process you want the program to run. For example, you can launch processes before any users have logged in by adding a line to the rc (run command) scripts. Or wait until X is running by putting the command in a window manager's startup folder. Here are a few useful techniques for getting your own processes to start automatically.

Tame the Daemons

Daemons and other processes that need to run the entire time the machine is on should be started at bootup—even before any user has logged in. As usual, there's more than one way to do that. On Red Hat systems, turn common daemons on and off by logging in as root and running `ntsysv` at the command line. If you're running X, you can use `tksysv`. Both programs can start or stop common services like Web servers, print services, cron, and so on.

Add It By Hand

If the program or service you want to start isn't in the default ntsysv list, you can add it by hand to `/etc/rc.d/rc.local`. This shell script runs after the other init scripts but before any users have logged in. This is where you'd commonly start a firewall or proxy server.

Start with the Command Line

You can also start a program when the command line shell is started. To start a program for all users, modify the `/etc/profile` script. (If you're not using bash as your shell, you should read the man pages for the shell you do use to see what configuration files it checks when it starts up. Use the command `man <shell name>` to read the manual pages for that shell. For example, tcsh checks the `/etc/csh.cshrc` and `/etc/csh.login` files instead of `/etc/profile`.)

A Startup Program for Every User

There's a startup program for each user, too. In the bash shell, modify the user's `~/.bashrc` file. (Note that tcsh uses the `~/.tcshrc` file.) You'd most commonly use these files to add command line aliases, modify prompts, and the like, but any shell command can be placed there.

SUNDAY, MARCH 31

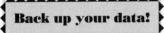

PROTECT YOURSELF

If you're tired of missing telephone calls while you're online, you might want to try Internet call waiting. Services such as Internet Call Manager (www.internetcallmanager.com), BuzMe (www.buzme.com), and Pagoo (www.pagoo.com) act as personal receptionists while you're online. BuzMe has an intuitive design and offers a call-management system with Caller ID, unlimited disk space for voice mail, and the retrieval of messages over a phone. It's only $5.95 per month.

One caveat: BuzMe automatically discontinues your voice messaging service with your telephone company. Because BuzMe's messaging service works through your PC, you don't receive phone messages unless you're dialed-up 24 hours a day or have an answering machine.

Pagoo advertises that they offer Internet call waiting, but what they really offer is an online messaging service. If a call comes through while you're online, Pagoo's software picks up the call. Seconds later, you can play the voice message on your computer. You are alerted to the call instantly, but you don't have the option to answer the call. It's only $4.95 a month.

Internet Call Manager works much like the others, but it offers a free trial so you can see if you like the idea before you sign up for the $5.95 a month service.

In all three cases you'll incur additional charges from your local phone company to add call-forwarding services to your line.

This Month's Feature

SEARCH THE INVISIBLE WEB

By Tom Merritt and Martin Sargent

Huge portions of the Internet are invisible to most search engines.

Some folks call this the invisible Web. Don't confuse the invisible Web with HTML pages that don't get indexed by the major engines. You can still find these pages by using specialty search engines sucha Artcyclopedia.com and Lawcrawler.com. We include a list of these at the end of this feature.

Search engines rely on programs called spiders, which only index HTML pages. Spiders can't index CGI scripts, PDF files, or information in databases. Various sources estimate you can find about 500 times more information in databases than in normal search engines.

DATABASE DIRECTORIES

These sites gather together online databases. You can't actually search the databases, but you can pinpoint just the databases you need:

- Direct Search (gwis2.circ.gwu.edu/~gprice/direct.htm), compiled by Gary Price of George Washington University, is a great resource for databases and for more information on the invisible Web.
- InvisibleWeb.com (www.invisibleweb.com) was created by Intelliseek, maker of BullsEye search software and ProFusion.

DATABASE SEARCH ENGINE

ProFusion (www.profusion.com) from Intelliseek searches more than 1,000 information sources, including the invisible Web. It works by formatting your search criteria to meet the specific requirements of each data source. Check out its features:

- Automatically searches across multiple sources and categorizes the results.
- Suggests alternative searches based on information it has learned.
- Allows searches by category, or by source within a category.
- Enables you to automate searches and enables alerts when search results change.
- Does not require specialized search skills.

SPECIALTY SEARCH ENGINES

Yahoo! and Google aren't always the best tools for finding information on a particular topic. Here's a partial list of some excellent specialty search engines that can help you find exactly what you're looking for.

Art

Artcyclopedia (www.artcyclopedia.com) is an amazing site. Artcyclopedia offers a database of works by 7,500 artists from the world's art museums and image archives.

Aviation

FlightSearch.com (www.flightsearch.com) has everything from aviation pictures and products to information on flight disasters.

Computer Games

There are several decent computer gaming directories on the Web, but these are the most helpful:

- Enfused (www.enfused.com)
- Gamez.com (www.gamez.com)
- GamePages (www.gamepages.com)

Computer Security

Go to SecureRoot (www.secureroot.com) and search more than 15,000 URLs for information about hacking, cracking, encryption, and anarchy.

Computer Programming

Are you a software developer? Want to learn more about programming? SourceBank (www.devx.com/sourcebank) has the goods.

Employment

Find postings from the Web's many job-listing sites on FlipDog (www.flipdog.com).

Fishing

Find everything from learning techniques to buying tackle on FishSearch.com (www.fishsearch.com).

Law

Trouble with the fuzz? Find legal information using these legal-oriented search engines:

- LawCrawler (findlaw.lawcrawler.com)
- Findlaw (www.findlaw.com)

Medicine

Feeling some symptoms? You might know about WebMD, but to broaden your search try a medical search engine. These specialty search engines find documents about particular conditions and medical issues:

- 9-11.com (www.9-11.com)
- CiteLine.com (www.citeline.com)
- MedHunt (www.medhunt.com)

Money

FinancialFind.com (www.financialfind.com) provides a comprehensive directory of financial information on the Internet.

Museums

MuseumStuff (www.museumstuff.com) has all you need to know about thousands of museums worldwide, nicely parceled into categories.

News

Moreover (www.moreover.com) is perhaps the best specialty search engine in any category. Moreover serves up headlines from more than 1,800 sources. Most important, the headlines retrieved are up to date.

Politics

OneWorld.net (www.oneworld.net) offers information on human rights and environmental issues worldwide.

Uncle Sam (www.google.com/unclesam) is your source for everything .gov. It's still the same Google you've grown to love, but results are limited to U.S. government Web pages.

Shopping

There are scores of comparison-shopping sites, but MySimon.com (www.mysimon.com) is the best. It finds the best price from some 1,600 online merchants.

Software

If you want downloadable software, try these sites:

- HotFiles.com (www.hotfiles.com)
- Tucows (www.tucows.com)
- Downloads.com (www.downloads.com)
- SoftSeek (www.softseek.com)

Search engines such as Google can't access much of the information hidden in documents and databases. To find this information, use a search engine that specializes in this *Deep Web*.

Try InvisibleWeb.com (www.invisibleweb.com) and Direct-Search (www.directsearch.com). They'll pull useful information out of databases for you.

You might want to try a service by BrightPlanet called LexiBot (www.lexibot.com). BrightPlanet claims that LexiBot can get at the roughly 550 billion documents in the Deep Web. According to BrightPlanet, regular search engines can find only 1 billion documents.

With 500 times more information to retrieve, LexiBot isn't too easy to master. The first time you take it for a test spin you might be confused. That's okay, because you have 30 days to play with it before you have to shell out $90.

Tom Merritt is Executive Web Producer at TechTV. Martin Sargent is a writer and guest host at TechTV.

SPRING CLEANING YOUR PC

Spring has sprung, and you know what that means. While the rest of the family attends to spring cleaning around the house, I'm planning to polish up the old PC. It sure beats whacking carpets.

If you're comfortable doing so, it's a good idea to open up your computer every year to clean out the accumulation of dust inside. (Not all computers open, however. iMac users, you get a free pass.) The dust can act as a blanket, causing critical components to overheat. Take care not to knock any cables loose while you're in there.

Turn your keyboard upside down and tap it vigorously. If a substantial amount of crumbs and debris pour out, you might want to stop eating while you browse the Internet. You also might want to pry off the key caps and use canned air to blow out any remaining gunk.

If you have a mechanical mouse, remove the ball and clean it with a gentle detergent. Use a cotton swab and a little bit of alcohol to clean off the rollers inside. Using a mouse pad will help keep the insides of your mouse clean. The new optical mice are sealed up and impervious to dust and dirt, so they require no maintenance. I recommend them.

I clean my monitor screen every few months or so, but if you haven't done so in a while, now's a good time. Don't use window cleaner on it, though. The solvents in most glass cleaners can eat through the coatings on your monitor, degrading the picture. I recommend an ammonia- and alcohol-free cleaner such as Klear Screen (www.klearscreen.com).

It's a nice feeling to do a little spring cleaning on your computer. The best part is, you have a perfectly valid excuse for not squeezing behind the refrigerator with a sponge this year.

MONDAY, APRIL 1 (APRIL FOOL'S DAY)

GEEK PRACTICAL JOKES

Infuriating, mystifying, maddening. Run Time Traveler on someone's computer and his or her Windows system clock will change to a different, random time every 30 seconds. The fun will end the first time he or she mouses over to the upper-left corner of the screen.

Download Time Traveler and other computer pranks from RJL Software (www.rjlsoftware.com). These guys are evil!

LAPORTE SUPPORT

Q: What's the difference between coaxial and s-video cables?

A: They're two different ways to move a video signal from one box (like a DVD player) to another (like your TV).

Coaxial can carry many types of video signals—RF or composite are the most common.

Both s-video and coaxial cables provide an analog signal. S-video sends separate signals for color and luminance, whereas coaxial cables deliver a composite video signal where the colors and audio are mixed.

S-video provides superior image quality on televisions, so you should use it whenever you can. S-video has grown in popularity as DVD players, gaming consoles, and video cameras capable of s-video output become more common.

TUESDAY, APRIL 2

THE TAX MAN COMETH

You have about two weeks to get your tax papers together. Go to www.irs.gov to learn about filing online or to download forms to print out. But don't wait until the 15th. The IRS servers become very busy as Tax Day approaches.

MAC TIP

Getting tired of the Wild Eep, Sosumi, and the other stock alert sounds on your Mac? Create your own sounds by recording snippets directly from your audio CDs:

1. Open the Monitors and Sound control panel.
2. Change the Sound Input setting to Internal CD.
3. Load the CD from which you want to record, and start playing it.
4. Open the SimpleSound utility (which you use to add and delete alert sounds).
5. Set the Sound menu to CD Quality.
6. Click the Add button.
7. Click the Record button when you hear the portion of the CD that you want to capture.

8. Name the captured sound.

9. Save it.

That's it. Now you have a new, CD-quality alert sound on your system for your personal use.

WEDNESDAY, APRIL 3

WEB TIP

To change the default Internet applications in Windows, open the Internet Options control panel and click the Programs tab. You can change each of your default Internet applications there.

On the Macintosh, open the Internet control panel. Click the E-mail, Web, and News tabs in turn and select the default program for each at the bottom of the window.

To make AOL the default, open the program, select Preferences from the My AOL menu, and click Associations.

THURSDAY, APRIL 4

WINDOWS TIP

Eliminate some unnecessary clutter on your Windows taskbar by removing the yellow speaker icon:

1. Right-click the speaker icon.

2. Choose Adjust and select Audio Properties.

3. Uncheck Show Volume Control on the Taskbar.

4. Click OK.

Don't worry, you haven't lost the icon for good. If you find that you just can't live without instant access to your volume controls, follow these steps to bring it back:

1. Click Start, Settings, and Control Panel.

2. Double-click the Multimedia icon.

3. Click the Audio tab and check the Show Volume Control on the Taskbar box.

4. Click OK.

FRIDAY, APRIL 5

LAPORTE SUPPORT

Q: *Although I shut down properly each time, the computer freezes as Windows 98 is shutting down. Is this a Microsoft bug?*

A: Nearly everyone who uses Windows encounters this bug sooner or later. It's a tough problem to fix because it can happen for so many different reasons.

When Windows shuts down, it asks all the open programs to shut down first. That gives you a chance to save your data. Windows waits for the programs to finish before writing out any remaining data to the hard drive and turning the computer off (or, on older machines, telling you it's okay to do so).

Unfortunately, programs don't always close properly, and Windows often is left hanging. If this happens to you, try closing all the running programs yourself first, disabling any programs that are running in the background, such as antivirus software, and then shutting down Windows. If you can figure out which program is stalling, you might be able to get a fix from its publisher.

Early versions of Windows 98 used something called Fast Shutdown that caused even more problems. Windows 98 users should run Windows Update (`windowsupdate. microsoft.com`) and be sure the Windows 98 Shutdown Supplement has been installed.

Shutdown Interruptus has so many possible causes that Microsoft has a Shutdown Troubleshooter on its Web site at `support.microsoft.com/support/windows/tshoot/ startup98`. In many cases, it's easiest just to back up your data, reformat the hard drive, and reinstall Windows. What a great way to kill a weekend.

SATURDAY, APRIL 6

FOR GEEKS ONLY

Midnight Commander is a GNU public license (which means it's free) file manager available for most Unix clones (including Linux), Windows 95/98, and the venerable OS/2 (does anyone even use OS/2 anymore?).

What makes it so special for Linux? If you're a Linux command line veteran, you know how fatiguing it can be to traverse the numerous directories typically found in a Linux machine. Typing and retyping, even with the use of the arrow keys to retrieve previous typed commands, takes time and is not very easy on the wrists.

Enter Midnight Commander. Although it's not the prettiest interface (think DOS shell circa 1987), Midnight Commander allows you to traverse and access files relatively easily. Just use the arrow keys to move the cursor to the file you want to manipulate. What's so great is that it still allows for command-line functions, so everyone from the Linux newbie to the Linux Jedi Master can use it.

Many recent Linux installations include Midnight Commander during the install. If you don't have it, you can get it at `canvas.gnome.org:65348/mc/download.html`. After it is installed, just type `mc` and away you go.

SUNDAY, APRIL 7

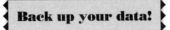

Back up your data!

PROTECT YOURSELF

A *virus* is a program that operates and propagates itself behind the user's back.

Although many viruses also can do damage to your computer's files, a program doesn't have to be destructive to be defined as a virus. It only has to be sneaky.

Viruses that do damage ("drop the payload") typically do so only when certain conditions are met. For example, the Michelangelo virus was programmed to do damage only on March 6.

Virus writers want their viruses to spread to as many computers as possible. They usually design viruses to replicate and send themselves out before doing damage.

MONDAY, APRIL 8

LAPORTE SUPPORT

Q: *I have a network at home (so I can use my DSL) and one at work. Can I use the same laptop in both places?*

A: You can, but you'll need to change the network settings at each location. You can do that manually with the Network control panel, but it's a lot easier to use a program to simplify the tasks.

Macintosh notebooks come with something called Location Manager that lets you create configuration sets for every place you use your computer. You'll find the Location Manager in the Control Panels folder under the Apple menu. There's also a Locations control strip module you can use to select configurations as you move around. In Mac OS X, use the Location command under the Apple menu.

Windows users can do the same thing with a $9 shareware program called NetSwitcher from www.netswitcher.com.

TUESDAY, APRIL 9

MAC TIP

Want to know how hard your computer is working? Launch the CPU Monitor in Mac OS X. You'll find it in the Application/Utilities folder. CPU Monitor can have different looks. Try Toggle Floating Window in the Processes menu.

CPU monitor also can display information in its icon in the Dock. Click Preferences in the CPU Monitor menu and select Display the "Extended" View in the Icon. Then, click OK.

If you notice that your CPU is always working at 100%, select Open Process Viewer from the Processes menu, and then sort the process list by % CPU to find the processor hog.

GEEK SPEAK

A *USB* (*Universal Serial Bus*) cable allows a computer user to easily install an additional device, such as a scanner or a CD-RW. The USB cable is plugged into the device and into the computer. That means you don't have to disassemble your computer to install a new device.

WEDNESDAY, APRIL 10

WEB TIP

Doctor HTML (`www.doctor-html.com/RxHTMLpro/`) offers several services designed to aid Webmasters:

- **Single Page Analysis** examines a page for spelling errors, verifies hyperlinks, and offers several HTML structure tests.
- **HTML Page Formatter** will take unstructured code from a Web page and reformat the text into nicely indented blocks. This makes it much easier to see when you are editing within a certain markup.
- **HTML Page Squisher** takes your HTML code and makes it as small as possible by removing any unnecessary characters. This reduced size makes for faster page loading times. One drawback is that the HTML code itself might lose its text formatting and not be as easily read.

You can get five reports for free. After that, prices vary depending upon how often you use it, but if you do any commercial Web design, it's a good investment.

THURSDAY, APRIL 11

WINDOWS TIP

Windows comes with a text editor called Notepad. There's a mini-word processor, too, called WordPad. You'll find both by clicking the Start button and navigating to the Programs, Accessories folder.

If you want something more substantial, try my favorite free Notepad replacement: NoteTab Lite from `www.notetab.com`.

FRIDAY, APRIL 12

LAPORTE SUPPORT

Q: *How do I change the message* `It's now safe to shut off your computer` *I get when my computer shuts down?*

A: The Windows shutdown graphic is stored in a file named `LOGOS.SYS`. You can create a replacement with any graphics editor, including Windows Paint.

Start by creating an image 640 pixels wide and 400 pixels tall. Do that in Paint by selecting Attributes from the Image menu and entering a width of 640 and a height of 400. When you have your image looking the way you want, squeeze the graphic horizontally by 50%. In Paint, use the Stretch/Skew command on the Image menu and enter 50 in the Stretch Horizontal box. Your image will look distorted, but don't worry. Windows will expand it back to normal when it displays it. Now, save the image in the Windows directory as a 256-color bitmap file named LOGOS.SYS. You should see your new message the next time you shut down.

If you want to change the Windows is Shutting Down window, do the same thing but name it LOGOW.SYS.

Do be careful with these files. A damaged graphic can cause difficulty shutting down. If you experience problems, just delete the modified files and Windows should return to normal.

If you're not artistically inclined, you can select from a wide selection of alternative shutdown messages (including some inappropriate for younger users) from www.jokewallpapers.com.

SATURDAY, APRIL 13
FOR GEEKS ONLY

If you use Linux, you're using GNU. So, what's GNU? It's not just a large African ruminant. GNU stands for *GNU's Not UNIX* and is pronounced "guh-new."

The GNU project was started 18 years ago by legendary programmer Richard Stallman in an effort to replace the expensive and proprietary UNIX software library with freely distributable equivalents. These days, most of the software you get with Linux and other UNIX variants is from the GNU project. In fact, Linux couldn't really exist without GNU. That's one reason Stallman wants everyone to start calling Linux, GNU/Linux. You can read about the genesis of the GNU project and its philosophical underpinnings at www.gnu.org.

One of the most important legacies of the GNU project is the notion that software ought to be free. Not free as in "free lunch" but free as in "free speech." When you get a program, whether you buy it or download it for free, you ought to have the information you need to modify the program to fit your needs. To do that, you need the programmer's original source code. GNU programs are licensed using the GNU Public License, or GPL, which requires that all programs come with the original source code and allows users to modify the software freely and distribute the modified versions, providing these versions are also licensed under the GPL. This notion is sometimes called *open-source software.*

Proponents of open source say you get better quality software and faster innovation if anyone, anywhere can work on a program. Open-source detractors say that the best software comes from companies that stand to make the most money from that software.

There's room in this world for both points of view. I, like many users, use both proprietary and open-source software. But it's nice to have the choice, and whenever possible, I choose GNU.

SUNDAY, APRIL 14

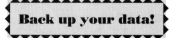
Back up your data!

 ## PROTECT YOURSELF

Nir Zuk, CTO of OneSource (http://www.onesecure.com) and considered by many to be the father of the modern firewall, contributed his expertise to this article. See http://www.techtv.com/callforhelp/answerstips/story/0,23008,2436994,00.html.

A firewall is hardware, software, or a combination of the two that prevents unauthorized access to your network.

Think of it as Internet customs and immigration. The firewall is the agent that checks each item entering or leaving the network. Each item must pass certain criteria to make it through. So, a hacker attempting to enter the network of California with a Florida orange would be stopped at the border.

There are three major types of firewalls. A *packet filter* looks at each packet entering or leaving the network and accepts or rejects it based on user-defined rules. Packet filtering is fairly effective and transparent to users, but it is difficult to configure. In addition, it is susceptible to tricks like IP spoofing. Most consumer-grade software firewalls, such as ZoneAlarm (www.zonealarm.com), are packet filters.

A *proxy server* (also known as *application gateway*) intercepts all messages entering and leaving the network. The proxy server effectively hides the true network addresses.

Proxies forward messages between clients and servers by appearing to the client (for example, a Web browser) as a server and appearing to the server (for example, a Web server) as a client. Hence, the client talks to the proxy, which then decides whether the communication should be forwarded to the server. If it does, the client contacts the server and forwards the messages to it.

Proxies can handle complex protocols (which packet filters cannot) because they implement both a client and a server for each protocol. The drawbacks are reduced performance and a limited number of supported protocols. Hardware routers, such as the Linksys Broadband Router (www.linksys.com), usually act as proxy servers.

Stateful inspection combines the speed and broad protocol support of packet filters with the security and support of complex protocols of proxies. It does it by inspecting all the traffic, looking for security-related information, and using this security-related information to make smart decisions regarding which traffic should be accepted and rejected. High-end commercial firewall systems, such as Checkpoint (www.checkpoint.com), often use this more sophisticated technique.

In practice, many firewalls use two or more of these techniques in concert.

MONDAY, APRIL 15

LAPORTE SUPPORT

Q: *Can you recommend a Web-based e-mail service that works with Outlook Express?*

A: Outlook Express can't understand the language, or "protocol," that most Web-based e-mail services use (with the exception of Microsoft's own Hotmail). So you need a bilingual service: one that speaks both its native Web protocol and something called POP (Post Office Protocol). Most e-mail programs, like Netscape Messenger, Outlook Express, and Eudora, use POP to retrieve mail.

There are more and more bilingual Web-based e-mail services these days. My favorite is Yahoo! Mail, mail.yahoo.com. For a list of others, visit www.emailaddresses.com and click on the POP3/MAPI Mail link on the left.

Macintosh owners using Mac OS 9 or later can use Apple's free mac.com service to receive e-mail with Outlook Express but not send it. Visit www.apple.com and click the iTools tab at the top.

TUESDAY, APRIL 16

MAC TIP

From time to time, you can use ProcessViewer as a handy way to restart the Dock. For example, sometimes the "poof" of disappearing icons leaves little puffs of smoke on the screen. To clear them, or any Dock weirdness, kill the Dock process. It will restart automatically:

1. Open ProcessViewer (in the Utilities folder).
2. Click the Dock item.
3. Select Quit Process from the Processes menu.

The Dock will close and reopen, cleaning itself up in the process.

GEEK SPEAK

Bandwidth is the amount of data that can be transmitted in a fixed amount of time. For digital devices, the bandwidth usually is expressed in bits per second (bps). For analog devices, the bandwidth is expressed in cycles per second, or hertz (Hz).

WEDNESDAY, APRIL 17

WEB TIP

To change the size of the text on a Web page in Internet Explorer, choose Text Size from the View menu. If the text is still too small, you can override the designer's font size choices using the Accessibility settings. Open Internet Options from the Tools menu. Click the General tab, and click the Accessibility button. Check the Ignore Font Sizes box, and then click OK.

THURSDAY, APRIL 18

WINDOWS TIP

If your desktop is cluttered with icons, follow this simple tip to clean it up:

1. Right-click on an empty part of the desktop.
2. Select Arrange Icons and click Auto Arrange.
3. Your desktop icons automatically arrange in orderly rows.

Any new icon you add will appear in one of the rows.

FRIDAY, APRIL 19

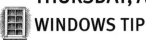
LAPORTE SUPPORT

Q: *When I close MS Word, it always says* `Changes have been made that affect the global template, NORMAL. Do you want to save those changes?`. *How can I make it stop?*

A: The first thing to do, and do it immediately, is to check your system for viruses. If you don't have an up-to-date antivirus program and you're using Windows, visit `housecall.antivirus.com`. It can detect a Word macro virus online. Macintosh users should pick up a copy of Symantec Norton Anti-Virus, `www.symantec.com`.

Word Macro viruses often store themselves in the Normal template, where they automatically will be opened every time you create a new Word document. One symptom of infection is a Normal template that is being changed abnormally often.

SATURDAY, APRIL 20

FOR GEEKS ONLY

Richard Stallman is founder of the GNU Project, a movement launched in 1984 to develop a free operating system. (See April 13.) Here's Stallman's definition of "free software":

- You have the freedom to run the program for any purpose.
- You have the freedom to modify the program to suit your needs. (To make this freedom effective in practice, you must have access to the source code, as making changes in a program without having the source code is exceedingly difficult.)
- You have the freedom to redistribute copies, either gratis or for a fee.
- You have the freedom to distribute modified versions of the program, so the community can benefit from your improvements.

An estimated 20 million computers now run some form of GNU/Linux. Far more than a programmer and open-source advocate, Stallman is a politically active humanitarian concerned with many of the world's woes. His site, `stallman.org`, provides a glimpse into the psyche, politics, and life of this strange cat.

SUNDAY, APRIL 21

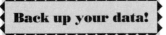

Back up your data!

PROTECT YOURSELF

To make sure your family's different Instant Messenger accounts stay separate, be sure your IM software doesn't automatically log you in when you start the computer.

Yahoo! Messenger: To change your login preferences, select Change User from the Login menu. Uncheck the Automatically Login item. You also might want to uncheck Remember my ID & Password to preserve your privacy.

AOL Instant Messenger: In the buddy list, go to the My AIM menu, select Edit Options, and choose Edit Preferences. Click the General tab. Uncheck the boxes next to the Automatically Sign On When AIM Starts and Start AIM When Windows Starts options.

Now when the machine boots, it will ask for your ID before starting up either of these services. And your kids won't get messages from your friends and vice versa.

MONDAY, APRIL 22

LAPORTE SUPPORT

Q: I received e-mail telling me that the government is trying to pass a bill that will make people pay a nickel for every e-mail they get! Do you know if this is true?

A: Good for you for asking. It's most emphatically not true. In fact, this hoax has been making the rounds of the Internet for more than two years now. Like a lot of Internet rumors, this story gets passed along by well-meaning folks who don't take the time to check it out.

The e-mail tax proposal has been debunked by everyone from the U.S. Postal Service (www.usps.gov/news/press/99/99045new.htm) to members of Congress.

Whenever you get one of these messages, do some research before forwarding it. I recommend a visit to Hoaxbusters, a service of the U.S. Department of Energy at `hoaxbusters.ciac.org`, or Don't Spread That Hoax at `www.nonprofit.net/hoax/default.htm`.

TUESDAY, APRIL 23

MAC TIP

You can set the QuickTime System Preferences panel to automatically update QuickTime:

1. Open the System Preferences.
2. Click QuickTime.
3. Press the Update tab.
4. Check the Check for Updates Automatically option to have QuickTime look for updates.
5. Press Update Now to check for updates right now.

If you click the third-party button and press update now, QuickTime will look for plug-ins and other third-party software. However, I tried it and it doesn't seem to do anything.

GEEK SPEAK

FireWire is a high-speed serial connection that's most often used to connect video cameras and hard drives to computers. Apple invented and named FireWire, but it's now an open standard designated by the mellifluous "IEEE 1394." There was a movement to dub the technology HPSB, for high performance serial bus, but it never took off. FireWire's maximum throughput is 400 megabits, or 50 megabytes, per second.

WEDNESDAY, APRIL 24

WEB TIP

Not every site is as nice as TechTV, providing printer-friendly versions of its articles. Save ink and cut down your printing time by choosing not to print Web background images. In Internet Explorer, do the following:

1. Select Internet Options from the Tools menu.
2. Go to the Advanced tab.
3. Scroll down to Printing, and uncheck Print Background Colors and Images.
4. Click OK.

In Netscape, follow these steps:

1. In the File menu, select Page Setup.
2. Uncheck Print Background. Click OK.

Be sure the box is checked if you later decide you do want to print a background image.

THURSDAY, APRIL 25

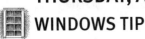

WINDOWS TIP

Sometimes, Windows is smarter than you think. Just like a pet dog, Windows picks up certain habits if you do them over and over and over again.

Take, for example, the automatic insertion of "Shortcut to" when you name a shortcut. If you keep removing "Shortcut to," Windows eventually will understand that you don't like this. After you remove this eight times, it will stop adding this text in the future.

Why do this?

1. You can already tell it's a shortcut because of the shortcut box above the icon.
2. More than one "Shortcut to" title clutters up the desktop.
3. You can't jump from icon to icon by pressing the S key because all shortcuts begin with *s*.

FRIDAY, APRIL 26

LAPORTE SUPPORT

Q: I'm changing ISPs. Is there a way to redirect people to a new e-mail address when messages go to my old address?

A: Some Internet service providers will provide a forwarding service for a small monthly fee. If yours won't, you'll have to notify all your friends by hand. That's one of the main reasons people are reluctant to change ISPs.

You can avoid the problem in the first place by using a mail forwarding service. Companies such as Bigfoot (`www.bigfoot.com` and Yahoo! Mail (`mail.yahoo.com`) can set up a free e-mail address that automatically sends incoming mail to your current ISP. Give out the free address to friends. Then, if you change ISPs, all you have to do is change the forwarding address and your mail automatically will follow you.

SATURDAY, APRIL 27

FOR GEEKS ONLY

WinLinux is a version of Linux designed for the Windows user who isn't ready to make a whole-hearted commitment to the way of the penguin.

WinLinux offers a relatively easy introduction to the operating system, without messy partitioning or arcane command-line entries. The installation and hardware configuration is done completely from within Windows.

Linked with Windows

WinLinux runs on the Windows file system. This is nice because, unlike most other Linux distributions, which require a Linux file system, WinLinux doesn't require you to partition your hard drive. Installing WinLinux is a relatively uncomplicated affair, much like installing an application within Windows.

WinLinux also simplifies installation because it can use the Windows Device Manager to figure out what hardware you have installed and automatically add the appropriate drivers.

If you're interested in Linux, but don't want to hassle with creating a dedicated Linux partition on your hard drive, try WinLinux.

Constraints

I don't recommend WinLinux for experienced users, however. Most Linux mavens will ultimately feel constrained by the Windows file system. If you're a Linux pro, or plan to be one, bite the bullet, repartition your hard drive, and go with a more serious Linux distribution. I like Linux-Mandrake (www.linux-mandrake.com) best. And these days the installation is pretty darn easy, even for novices. Incidentally, if you are new to Linux I recommend you use a spare PC or separate hard drive if you have one. Chances are you'll crash or break something within the first 48 hours of installing Linux. That's not a bad thing—learning anything involves making mistakes. But you'll want to contain the damage to a non-mission–critical machine.

SUNDAY, APRIL 28

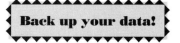

Back up your data!

 PROTECT YOURSELF

From the point of view of users, one of the best things about high-speed Internet connections is that they're always on. No more waiting for the modem to squeak and squeal its way online.

Unfortunately, from the point of view of Internet providers, that's one of the worst things about high-speed access. They'd prefer to be able to control your bandwidth consumption a little more closely. That's why many DSL providers have started using PPPoE, or point-to-point protocol over Ethernet.

PPPoE allows your ISP to split its connectivity into multiple channels. It can put more customers on the same line, keep track of use, and have more control over how bandwidth is allotted.

A PPPoE connection requires users to install PPP dialers, just like in the bad old modem days. But even if you're stuck with PPPoE, you're not stuck with the software your ISP provides you with. DLS guru John Navas, `cable-dsl.home.att.net`, recommends the free RASPPPoE dialer from `user.cs.tu-berlin.de/~normanb`. He says it's faster and more reliable.

You also can use a hardware-based PPPoE dialer. Many broadband routers, such as the Linksys Etherfast router, offer built-in PPPoE support.

Some ISPs might tell you that PPPoE is safer because you're not always online. It's not true. As with any other high-speed connection, you should always run a firewall with PPPoE.

MONDAY, APRIL 29

LAPORTE SUPPORT

Q: In Excel (Office 97) I password protected a worksheet and then forgot it. I've tried copying and pasting, renaming, but nothing works. How can I get around that?

A: Not very easily. An Internet search for "Excel and password" will find numerous Excel password removal programs and service bureaus. But there are limits to what they can do.

The passwords in earlier versions of Excel were fairly easy to crack, but the latest versions of Excel store their passwords using RC4 encryption, an industrial-strength scrambling technique that can't be hacked. The only way to find the password is to try every possible combination. This brute-force method would be impossibly time consuming by hand, but often can be accomplished by computer in just a few days.

The task is much simpler when the password is a common English word. Password cracking programs try all the words in the dictionary first. One program I found at `www.lostpassword.com` claims to be able to try millions of words per minute. At that rate it wouldn't take long to find a password that's in the dictionary.

If the password is a nonsense combination of letters, numbers, and punctuation longer than 10 characters, the program could take quite a long time and might never find the answer. That's why it's always best to use random characters in any password.

If you have trouble remembering your passwords, use a password storage program like Password Keeper from `www.gregorybraun.com`.

TUESDAY, APRIL 30

MAC TIP

Mac OS 9 has a folder in the System Folder called Startup Items. Any alias in that folder automatically will be opened when the system starts up. Mac OS X has no such folder, but you still can get files to autolaunch when you boot up:

1. Open the Login system preferences file.
2. Click the Login Items tab.
3. Click Add to add items.
4. Click the Hide box if you don't want to see the program launching.

Each user has his or her own set of startup items.

GEEK SPEAK

DVD stands for *digital video disk* or *digital versatile disk,* depending whom you ask. It looks like an ordinary CD, except it stores more data. DVDs can hold 4.7 gigabytes of data per side—enough to hold a feature-length film or an entire basement worth of *National Geographic* magazines.

This Month's Feature

MAKE YOUR MONITOR LAST

By Mike Nadelman

Use these tips to maintain the life of your monitor:

- Turn off your monitor, and then shut down your system. If you turn on your system, turn on the monitor last. If you use a power strip, it's okay to turn them off simultaneously.
- Adjust the screen so that the picture does not extend past the visible frame around the CRT. For example, I like to leave a thin black edge around the screen image.
- Protect the monitor from excessive heat. Clutter, exposure to direct sunlight, and dust increase the internal temperature in the monitor.
- Be careful when connecting the monitor interface cable to the computer. A bent or broken pin on the cable could result in an expensive repair. Don't over-tighten the screws on the connector.

A few common monitor problems are easily fixed:

- Broken or bent pins on the interface cable
- Loss of single or multiple colors
- Minor focus problem
- Flat line or vertical line on the display
- Out-of-synch, rolling, or herringbone image

There also are more difficult repairs that will cost you more money to fix:

- Burning smell or smoke coming out of the monitor
- Liquid spilled into monitor
- No power, or acts as if power switch is not working
- Severe focus problem
- A dropped monitor that shows noticeable frame damage

If you experience any of these problems, you should take your monitor to a repair shop. Of course, if the cable has a bent pin, simply replace the cable yourself. Most repair shops offer free initial testing to verify the cause of the problem.

Determine whether the monitor is worth fixing. If the repair cost is more than the cost of a new monitor, don't fix it. Simply buy an affordable replacement.

Test your monitor

We use special test equipment to check monitors for compliance. You can download and run a few of these testing programs from our Web site (www.computer-repair.com/monitortesting.htm).

Warning

Hazardous voltages exist in monitors even when they are unplugged. Do not open your monitor to make repairs yourself. Take your monitor to qualified personnel for internal adjustments and repairs.

Mike Nadelman is president and founder of Advanced Computer Solutions in San Francisco.

LEO'S ESSAY

SEND THIS MESSAGE TO EVERYONE YOU KNOW

Stop me if you've heard this one. Congress is about to pass a tax on Internet traffic! The FCC plans a tariff on modem use! Bill Gates will pay me $1000!

Sound too good to be true? Well, it is!

I get urgent e-mails like this every day from well-meaning Chicken Littles. I bet you do, too. But these messages are almost always bogus. They're e-mail hoaxes that spread like wildfire because people don't think before passing them along. In a way they're a kind of virus, wasting Internet bandwidth and your time. I know the people who pass along these warnings are trying to do the right thing, but it's just another form of spam and it's time to stop the insanity.

When you get an urgent message promising something wonderful or warning of impending doom, don't immediately pass it along to everyone you know. Before you press the forward button, do a little research. Pay a visit to the Internet hoax page sponsored by the Department of Energy at `http://hoaxbusters.ciac.org`. If it's listed there, it's bogus. And they're almost all bogus. Trust me.

No one is giving away the Nieman-Marcus chocolate chip cookie recipe. There is no Good Times virus. And Craig Shelford is just fine and you can stop sending him greeting cards now. (He received more than 16 million.)

Next time you get one of these messages, relax, take a deep breath, and press the Delete key. Your friends will thank you for it.

WEDNESDAY, MAY 1

WEB TIP

May is Internet Explorer Shortcut month. Every Wednesday, learn four new hotkeys that save your wrists (evil mouse clicking!) and speed up your Web surfing.

Four handy keyboard shortcuts for Internet Explorer:

- **F11**—Toggle between full-screen and regular view of the browser window.
- **Alt+Home**—Go to your home page.
- **Up Arrow**—Scroll toward the beginning of a page.
- **Down Arrow**—Scroll toward the end of a page.

THURSDAY, MAY 2

WINDOWS TIP

To launch programs faster, program a hotkey—either a function key or a combination of Ctrl+Alt+*shortcut key*—to open applications for you:

1. Find the icon of the program for which you'd like to create a hotkey, and right-click it. (The icon can be the original program icon or a shortcut to it.)

2. Choose Properties from the menu and be sure you're in the Shortcut tab.

3. Place your cursor in the Shortcut key field, pick a function key or a key combination you would like to assign to the program, and press it.

4. Click OK.

If you would like to do even more with hotkeys, download the free Hotkeys program from `members.nbci.com/PostcardWare/hotkeys.htm`. Hotkeys not only help you launch applications, but also let you reboot your computer, log off Windows, and more with just a keystroke.

FRIDAY, MAY 3

LAPORTE SUPPORT

Q: What's the difference between copying a file, saving a file, and backing up a file (using Windows Backup utility) to a storage device other then the hard drive?

A: The difference is mostly semantic. In all three cases you make a copy of a data file. And, in the words of Martha Stewart, that's a good thing.

When you save or copy a file, you create an exact duplicate. That's the best kind of backup, because you can easily verify that you have a good copy by opening it.

Backup programs automate the process, but they typically copy all your data into one large file. You need the backup program to restore your files. Backup programs verify the contents of the backup, so you can be reasonably sure you've got a good copy.

The key to any backup procedure is to do it religiously, at least weekly, and to make multiple copies in case one is lost or goes bad. Furthermore, it's very important to keep some of those copies off site, where they'll be safe in case a major disaster such as fire or flood strikes.

SATURDAY, MAY 4

FOR GEEKS ONLY

Help! The LILO (Linux Loader) boot disk I created while installing Red Hat Linux is broken! How can I fix it? Can I make another without re-installing?

The boot disk acts as a safeguard in case something happens to your computer and your hard drives become inaccessible. This can result from a bad installation, a virus, or a hard drive error. When disaster strikes, the boot disk enables you to access your hard drive and initiate file repairs.

You can create a new working Linux boot disk from DOS:

1. Run a program called RAWRITE on the Linux CD. RAWRITE is located in the dosutils folder on the root directory.

2. RAWRITE asks what image you want. (There's an images subdirectory in the dosutils folder—boot, sup, rescue.img.) You want the BOOT.IMG. Type in D:dosutilsimagesboot.img (or whatever the letter for your CD-ROM is). This formats a floppy and creates the disk for you.

SUNDAY, MAY 5

PROTECT YOURSELF

Have you ever heard of a helpful virus? They exist. In May, 2001, the Cheese Worm created headlines by invading Linux servers that had been compromised by hackers and patching the security hole. A similar anti-worm worm was released to ferret out Code Red infections in Microsoft Web servers.

Programs such as these raise interesting ethical questions. Their effect is purely benign, even helpful. They fix problems instead of creating them. But they do invade systems without their owners' consent. Is it ever okay to break into someone's house? What if it's to fix a leaky roof? The jury's still out, but I bet this isn't the last we've seen of helper viruses on the Net.

MONDAY, MAY 6

LAPORTE SUPPORT

Q: How do I get rid of items on the Windows 98 Quick Launch taskbar without deleting the programs themselves?

A: The Quick Launch taskbar is one of the more useful features in Windows. I use it to display miniature icons for the programs I use most often. Turn it on by right-clicking the taskbar and selecting Quick Launch from the Toolbars list.

To add a new item to the Quick Launch toolbar, right-click a program or document icon, drag it to the toolbar, and then select Create Shortcut(s) Here from the pop-up menu.

To remove an item, drag it off the taskbar and into the Recycle Bin. That deletes the shortcut, but not the program.

TUESDAY, MAY 7

MAC TIP

In Mac OS X, system preferences control the appearance of your date and time settings, network settings, Internet settings, and more.

A padlock is displayed at the bottom of many system preference panels. Click it to prevent people from making changes to the system. After you lock an item, you must enter the system administrator password to make any changes. This is a handy way to keep novice or malicious users from tampering with the system.

GEEK SPEAK

MIDI (Musical Instrument Digital Interface) communicates musical information from one electronic device to another, "telling" a device how to create the sounds. For example, one could compose a song using the saxophone sound on one synthesizer, send it through the computer, and then play that same song and sound through another keyboard.

WEDNESDAY, MAY 8

WEB TIP

Use these four handy Internet Explorer keyboard shortcuts:

- **Home**–Jump to beginning of page
- **End**–Jump to end of page
- **Ctrl+F**–Bring up dialog box to search for a word or phrase in current page
- **Ctrl+R**–Refresh page

MAY

THURSDAY, MAY 9

WINDOWS TIP

The keyboard shortcut to close open files, programs, and even Windows itself is Alt+F4.

To shut down Windows, click the desktop and press Alt+F4.

To close a program, click in the program's window, save your data, and then press Alt+F4. In some cases this only closes the topmost window. After you've closed all the open windows, a final Alt+F4 usually will close the program itself.

FRIDAY, MAY 10

LAPORTE SUPPORT

Q: When I scroll through Web pages using the arrow at the bottom of the scroll column it goes too fast. Can I adjust the scrolling speed?

A: Unfortunately, Windows doesn't offer a way to slow down page scrolling. That's too bad, because on today's hyper-speed computers, pages often scroll too quickly to control.

If you have a mouse with a wheel you might be able to scroll at different speeds by clicking the wheel. Then the scroll speed can be controlled by the mouse's position. (That's one of many reasons to invest in a wheel mouse. My favorite is the Microsoft's Intellimouse Optical, which sets you back about $50.)

You can get a similar effect on mouse devices with only two buttons with a shareware program called DragAndScroll. You can download it from www.kagi.com/OwnerWorld/dnscr.htm. DragAndScroll is free to try and about $15 to buy.

On the Macintosh you can slow the speed of the scroll with SmartScroll from www.marcmoini.com. It's free to try, $12 to buy.

SATURDAY, MAY 11

FOR GEEKS ONLY

I have two hard drives. One is a 6.3GB Western Digital, the other is a 100MB Seagate. I want to install Linux. Will there be enough space on my 100MB hard drive to install Linux, or at least the boot files?

The Linux kernel is small—just a few megabytes—but the whole Linux operating system (of which the kernel is a part) is a lot bigger. Although a 100MB hard drive can hold and run Linux, if you want to run multiple applications you're probably going to need more space.

We recommend that you put Linux on a hard drive with at least 2GB total space, as some Linux applications are just as large as some Windows applications.

(Note: You can allocate space from both drives. Linux needs space, but it doesn't necessarily mind where the space is.)

Incidentally, it's possible to fit an entire working Linux system on a floppy disk. Visit the Linux Router Project, `www.linuxrouter.org`, to see how (and why).

SUNDAY, MAY 12

Back up your data!

PROTECT YOURSELF

Firewalls and antivirus programs both protect your computer, but they do it in different ways.

An antivirus program scans for evil little beasties on your system and keeps them from doing any damage. You can get computer viruses in your e-mail, by downloading files, or by trading software with friends with infected computers. A firewall acts as a barrier to potentially hostile traffic from the Internet. It prevents bad guys from breaking into your computer and blocks unauthorized data from leaving your machine.

Computer viruses are so common that everyone who spends any time on the Net needs an antivirus program. Windows users can download AVG free from `www.grissoft.com` or run a free scan from the Web at `housecall.antivirus.com`. For Mac users, I recommend Norton Anti-Virus for Macintosh. It's $63 from Symantec, `www.symantec.com/nav/nav_mac`. Be sure to update your software monthly—new viruses crop up all the time.

Modem users probably don't need a firewall, but a firewall's a must-have for folks with full-time connections to the Internet, like cable modems and DSL. I recommend ZoneAlarm for Windows. It's free from `www.zonealarm.com`. The best Macintosh firewall is Intego's NetBarrier. It's $75 from `www.intego.com`.

MONDAY, MAY 13

LAPORTE SUPPORT

Q: For weeks my newspaper has run an ad from someone seeking "Adobe Photoshop, any version." This seems like a blatant request for pirated software. What's the scoop?

A: It's not necessarily piracy. Many companies allow purchasers of their software to resell it. In most cases the original owner must delete all copies of the software from his or her own machine and transfer all CDs and manuals to the new owner.

Other restrictions might apply, as well. For example, some companies allow software to be resold only once. And buyers might not have the same support and upgrade rights as the original owner.

The rules vary, even within Adobe's own product line. The only way to be sure if software can be resold is to read the End-User License Agreement. The rules for transfer of the software can be found buried somewhere in the fine print.

TUESDAY, MAY 14

MAC TIP

The Mac OS X dock can contain miniaturized versions of the windows for currently running applications. To try it out, open Internet Explorer, and then click the yellow button in the upper-left corner of the window to miniaturize that window. The dock preserves the contents of the window so you can read it. If it's too difficult to read as is, turn on magnification for a better look:

1. Click the Apple menu.
2. Select Dock.
3. Click Turn Magnification On.

Modify the degree of magnification by selecting Dock preferences from the same menu.

TODAY IN COMPUTER HISTORY

On May 14, 1944, legendary Director George Lucas (best known for his *Star Wars* series) was born in Modesto, California. Mr. Lucas continues to be a pioneer in the field of cinematography, digital special effects, and animation.

WEDNESDAY, MAY 15

WEB TIP

Try out these four Internet Explorer keyboard shortcuts:

- **Ctrl+N**—Open new browser window
- **Ctrl+W**—Close current window (good for cleaning up pop-ups)
- **Tab**—Move forward through the items on a Web page, the Address bar, and the Links bar
- **F1**—Display Internet Explorer Help or, in a dialog box, display context Help on an item

THURSDAY, MAY 16

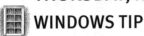

WINDOWS TIP

Ever wanted to stop a print job after catching an error in a huge text document? Ever wanted to change the print order to move a document from the bottom of the list to the top? By using the print queue of your printer, you can do both these tasks.

The next time you send a job to the printer, pay attention to the Printer icon in the system tray. Double-click this icon to open the Print Queue dialog box.

To purge any document from the queue, follow these steps:

1. Highlight the document.
2. Press Delete, or go to Printer and choose Purge Print Documents.

To change the print order, follow these steps:

1. Position your pointer over the document you'd like to move, and click and hold the left mouse button.
2. While holding down the left mouse button, move the document up or down the list.

You also can get to the Print queue from the Start menu. Choose Settings, Printer, and then double-click the printer whose queue you want to manage.

FRIDAY, MAY 17
LAPORTE SUPPORT

Q: Can a Web site change my Internet settings? On three occasions, my IE home page has been redirected to another site without my permission.

A: It's theoretically possible for a Web site to sneakily modify your browser's start page, but it's such a reprehensible act that most sites don't do it.

If, in your wanderings down the dark alleys of the Internet, you've run into sites that do hijack your home page, you can't do much about it but put things back as they were and resolve never to go there again.

The same thing sometimes happens when you install new programs. Software publishers claim they do it as a convenience to users. I say it's an intrusive practice that ought to be stopped. To modify an old motto to fit modern times, a man's home page is his castle. Hands off!

Fortunately it's not too hard to restore your original home page. In Netscape, open Preferences from the Edit menu, click the Navigator section and change the URL in the Home page Location text box. If you use Internet Explorer on a Mac, open Preferences from the Edit menu, click Browser Display, and enter the new URL in the Home Page Address text box. In the newest versions of both browsers you can just surf to your preferred start page and drag the mini-icon in the address window to the Home icon on the button bar.

SATURDAY, MAY 18

FOR GEEKS ONLY

Macmillan ships a shrink-wrapped version of Quake II for Linux. But if you already own Quake II for Windows, you might not want to spend $50 for a Linux version. Well, you don't have to. You can use the data from your Windows disk in conjunction with a free Linux version of the game engine from Id Software to get QII running on your Linux box. Here are the steps. (You can read all this in greater detail in the Linux Quake How-To at `www.linuxgames.com/quake/`.)

Be sure you have version 2.0.24 or later of the Linux kernel. You also need a machine with enough oomph to run QII (a P166, 32MB of RAM, and 25MB to 400MB of free disk space, depending on how you install the Quake data). Quake II can use the X Window server, but it runs best in console mode using the SVGAlib (1.2.10 or better). If you want sound, be sure your sound card works in Linux.

Get the Linux QII Linux binaries from Id Software (`ftp.idsoftware.com`). They're also mirrored at other sites. The RPM files install at /usr/local/games/quake2. You can copy the Quake II data files from the QII CD-ROM to your disk using the following commands:

```
cd /usr/local/games/quake2
cp -r /mnt/cdrom/Install/Data/*
```

Then delete the unnecessary Windows files as follows:

```
rm -f /usr/local/quake2/*.dll
rm -f /usr/local/quake2/quake2.exe
rm -f /usr/local/quake2/baseq2/gamex386.dll
```

Or, if you already have the relevant files on your Windows partition, you can save space by making a symbolic link to them as follows:

```
cd /usr/local/games/quake2
ln -s /win95/games/quake2/baseq2 (or the path to your baseq2 folder)
```

For this to work, of course, you have to mount your Windows partition every time you want to play Quake.

Now install the Linux binaries by switching to root and RPMing them:

```
su root
rpm -Uvh quake2-xxxxx.i386.rpm
```

The RPMs are for Red Hat Linux. If you're using another version, check the How-To for details.

Now you're ready to try your installation. Exit to the console and type

```
cd /usr/local/games/quake2
./quake2 +set vid_ref soft
```

Quake II should run using software rendering. If you want to take advantage of your graphics accelerator, you'll need to install some additional libraries. The How-To has details and links.

Quake runs great on Linux, especially if you have an accelerated graphics card. Enjoy!

SUNDAY, MAY 19

AOL TIP

There's a software product called AOL Mail for Palm Organizers that allows you to take your e-mail with you wherever you go. Even better news is that it even works with the Macintosh.

You can download the software for free, but you'll need a Palm modem to access your mail—it won't connect through a TCP/IP.

With AOL Mail, you will not be able to view images, hyperlinks won't work, and you don't have the ability to upload or download attachments. It's just a quick fix (until you return to your computer) with text-only e-mails.

To download AOL Mail, go to AOL keyword Anywhere. You'll also find instructions for installation and some information about surcharges.

MONDAY, MAY 20

LAPORTE SUPPORT

Q: I have data on disks I created with Windows 3.1. How do I use them with my Windows 98?

A: You can use them just as you did in Windows 3.1. The floppy disk format for DOS and Windows hasn't changed in more than a decade.

When you have trouble reading a vintage floppy, it's likely that the disk itself is damaged. Floppy disks are not particularly hardy. It's common for them to fail after just a few years. I recommend transferring any data on disks to a hard drive as soon as possible. For long-term archival storage, nothing beats burning that data onto a CD or DVD.

TUESDAY, MAY 21

MAC TIP

When you install Mac OS X, it asks if you want to set up an iTools (itools.mac.com) account. Say yes. iTools is a suite of online tools that Apple first began offering with Mac OS 9. It includes a free Mac.com e-mail address and iDisk (20MB of free storage).

When you create an iTools account, an iDisk icon appears in your file browser. Click the icon to mount the iDisk. It appears on the desktop just like a local hard drive. You can copy files to it, but you'll also find files on it. Open the software folder to access a number of useful programs from Apple and others. Apple automatically updates this software and it does not count toward your 20MB limit.

GEEK SPEAK

A *WAN* (*Wide Area Network*) is a network in which the computers are connected over a distance. Whereas a *LAN* (*Local Area Network*) relies upon cables for connection, a WAN uses telephone lines and satellites for communication purposes.

WEDNESDAY, MAY 22

WEB TIP

Check out some more Internet Explorer shortcuts:

- **Shift+Tab**—Move back through the items on a Web page, the Address bar, and the Links bar
- **Alt+Right arrow**—Go to the next page
- **Alt+Left arrow or Backspace**—Go to the previous page
- **Shift+F10**—Display shortcut menu for a link

THURSDAY, MAY 23

WINDOWS TIP

In Windows, another way to make the current window bigger or smaller is to double-click the title bar at the top of the window.

FRIDAY, MAY 24

LAPORTE SUPPORT

Q: Is there a way to interconnect a laptop with a PC for transferring files?

A: This is a task every laptop-lugging road warrior faces sooner or later. How do you get all that work you did on the road back into your desktop PC?

If both computers run Windows 95 or later, you can use a direct cable connection to share files between desktop and laptop. The Windows Help file walks you through the process. Select Help from the Start menu and click the Index tab. Enter Direct Cable Connection for details. You can order the special cable you need from most computer stores or buy online at www.1pt.com.

Macintosh computers with built-in Ethernet ports can share data using a crossover Ethernet cable. Crossover cables are also available at most computer stores. For details, search your Mac's online Help Center for "Using Ethernet to transfer files."

Most Macintosh notebooks also support something called *target disk mode*. Connect the notebook to your desktop using a SCSI or FireWire cable, and then press and hold the T key as you turn on your Powerbook. The Powerbook shows up as a hard drive on your desktop Mac. FireWire target disk mode works with standard 6-pin to 6-pin FireWire cables. SCSI target disk mode requires a special SCSI disk adapter available from Apple.

For the occasional transfer of a few small files, it's often easiest to just e-mail them to yourself.

SATURDAY, MAY 25

FOR GEEKS ONLY

When I'm installing Linux, it wants me to install a driver for a SCSI card. My card is a Promise Technology, Inc. Ultra66 card, but my driver is not in the installation. Can you tell me what to do?

The problem probably is in your card. The Promise Technology Ultra66 card is not a SCSI card. It is an IDE controller card, featuring the UltraDMA/66—an ATA (AT Attachment) protocol. So trying to find or install Linux-based SCSI drivers is not the solution.

Linux recognizes almost all IDE controllers, which probably includes Promise's board, but these boards aren't necessarily seen automatically. Because you have two IDE connectors in addition to the existing two, you need to tell Linux that they're there. (Linux automatically probes only the first two IDE interfaces, the ones that reside on the motherboard, during the installation.)

To get Linux to see them, enter a command at the boot: prompt. The details for this can be found at the Red Hat compatibility site (`http://www.redhat.com/corp/support/hardware/index.html`).

In general, finding drivers for Linux can be a time-intensive task. Unless a peripheral manufacturer creates a Linux driver for its products, it is usually up to the Linux community to create and support device drivers. Most drivers are reverse-engineered DOS or Windows drivers created by Linux enthusiasts. This means that unless someone feels a need to create a Linux driver for a product, you're out of luck unless you do it yourself.

This is starting to change, however, as the computer industry comes to see Linux as a viable alternative OS. Companies such as Creative Labs are offering Linux drivers for their products. Although this will make things easier in the future, right now it is still difficult when you need the appropriate driver for your new WhizzyBang 2002 card.

Some places to begin a Linux driver hunt are Red Hat (`www.redhat.com`), Freshmeat.Net (`www.freshmeat.com`), Linuxapps (`www.linuxapps.com`), and Linux newsgroups.

SUNDAY, MAY 26

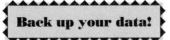

Back up your data!

 ## PROTECT YOURSELF

In the past, creating a successful computer virus was a purely technical achievement. Some viruses hid on the boot sector of a floppy disk, some appended themselves to other programs, and some even survived a computer reset by storing their code in the computer's BIOS settings. But they didn't need much help from users. Those days are long gone.

With the advent and widespread use of automated virus scanning tools, it has become difficult to try to append onto other programs without being detected. Thus, the next generation of e-mail viruses was born.

Where boot sector viruses were previously written in machine language by hardcore techno-geeks, e-mail viruses require someone with people skills, too. Think of it as a problem in marketing. E-mail virus writers face the challenge of devising an attachment compelling enough for people to open. After you've gotten them to click, they're yours.

A virus is spread more quickly if it has an interesting subject line or message body. That's all it takes to create the next I Love You or Anna Kournikova.

As a security conscious computer user you have one primary task: Don't be seduced by the virus creators. Resist the urge to double-click that sweet-sounding attachment. If you want them to smile, open that file. But to stop hackers dead, use your head. *Don't open attachments!*

MONDAY, MAY 27 (MEMORIAL DAY)

To learn more about American wars and the veterans who fought in them, visit the History Channel's Memorial Day exhibit at `www.historychannel.com/exhibits/memorial/ memorial.html`. Veterans can connect with each other in the forums.

 ## LAPORTE SUPPORT

Q: Is it possible for a hacker to hack my computer while I'm reading the NYTimes.com or while writing e-mail? If so, what can I do to stop him?

A: When they asked the outlaw Willie Sutton why he robbed banks, he said "Because that's where the money is." Hackers usually aren't bank robbers, but they do share similar motivations. Unless your hard drive contains documents of particular interest, I wouldn't worry about hackers too much.

Of course, I don't worry all that much about car thieves, either, but I always lock my car door. It's probably better to be safe than sorry, and protect yourself from hack attacks with a firewall. For Windows machines I recommend ZoneAlarm. It's free for personal use from www.zonelabs.com. The best firewall for Macs is NetBarrier from Intego, $74.95 from www.intego.com, (305) 868-7920.

To test your firewall and learn more about online security, visit Steve Gibson's excellent Shields Up site at grc.com.

TUESDAY, MAY 28

MAC TIP

The dock feature in Mac OS X is also a context switcher. Use these commands to switch between applications:

- Press Command+Tab to cycle through open applications.
- Command+Shift+Tab moves through the applications in the other direction.
- Option+click an icon in the dock to hide the current application window and switch to the clicked application.

GEEK SPEAK

A *dumb terminal* is a computer workstation that consists of only the monitor (screen), keyboard, and perhaps mouse. The actual computer, to which the terminal is connected, is in a different location and often connects to several other dumb terminals.

WEDNESDAY, MAY 29

WEB TIP

Give the last set of IE keyboard shortcuts for the month a try:

- **Ctrl+Tab or F6**—Move forward between frames
- **Shift+Ctrl+Tab**—Move back between frames
- **Page Up**—Scroll toward the beginning of a document in large increments
- **Page Down**—Scroll toward the end of a document in large increments

THURSDAY, MAY 30

WINDOWS TIP

The next time you find yourself in need of Windows- or program-specific help, try these shortcuts:

- Press F1 if you're working in a program and you need an answer fast.
- For general Windows help, hold down and release the Windows key+F1.

FRIDAY, MAY 31

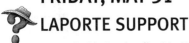

LAPORTE SUPPORT

Q: *I just subscribed to WebTV. Are there any programs that allow me to listen to music over the Internet?*

A: WebTV (now the MSN TV service) supports music in several formats. Of these, the most popular is RealAudio. For a listing of more than 10,000 RealAudio broadcasts, visit `realguide.real.com/music`. Some support for the Windows Media Player is also available. A directory of Windows Media programming can be found at `windowsmedia.com`. You might not be able to play everything you see in these guides, but most of the listings should work.

If you have WebTV Plus, you can use Beatnik, a program designed to add sound to Web pages. To get an idea of what Beatnik can do, visit `www.beatnik.com` or the WebTV Plus walkthrough at `www.beatnik.com/support/walkthrough-webtv`.

WebTV also can handle MIDI. MIDI tunes sound a little cheesy because they rely on WebTV's built-in synthesizer for playback. For a list of WebTV compatible MIDI sites visit `www.net4tv.com/voice/story.cfm?storyid=934`.

The Ultimate WebTV Search site, `www.webtvsearch.com`, also has a music category with quite a few RealAudio and MIDI links.

This Month's Feature

TOP 10 E-BOOK TIPS

By Regina Lynn Preciado

E-books can save your back, improve your grades, and increase your knowledge. You can sneak them under the covers after lights-out more easily than the traditional flashlight. They also can cost you a few hundred dollars up front if you want true portability. And do you really want to spend more time staring at pixels?

Of course you do. Here's what you need to know:

- **You need a computer, a PDA, or an e-book handheld, but not all three**—E-books come formatted for Adobe Acrobat eBook Reader, Microsoft Reader, PDAs, Web browsers, or special e-book devices. The software is free. The hardware is not. Barnes and Noble (`www.bn.com`) has a handy chart that helps you decide whether you need to buy an e-book device.
- **You can download e-books almost anywhere you can buy bound books online**— Powells.com, BarnesandNoble.com, and Amazon.com all sell e-books. If you're tired of mainstream fare, explore smaller e-press catalogs such as BookLocker (`www.booklocker.com`), Serial Books (`www.serialbooks.com`), or Crossroads

Publishing (www.crossroadspub.com), which (begin gratuitous plug) published TechTV Executive Producer Tom Merritt's e-novel, *Boiling Point*.
Yahoo!'s e-bookseller list
(dir.yahoo.com/Business_and_Economy/Shopping_and_Services/Books/Booksellers/Electronic_Books/) and Google's e-book section
(directory.google.com/Top/Business/Industries/Publishing/Publishers/Electronic/E-Books/) offer dozens of other options.

- **E-books are only slightly cheaper, if at all, than wood pulp**—Public-domain classics are often free—visit the Gutenberg Project (www.promo.net/pg/) to find them—but expect to spend some dough on modern titles. E-publishing reduces paper and shipping costs while it adds coding expenses. Plus, there's that pesky author royalty, those few cents per copy. You think e-books grow on trees?
- **You can carry a lot of e-books without adding weight to your luggage**—Your PDA or RCA REB e-book reader can hold a dozen titles. Your carry-on luggage can too, but only if you leave your clothes at home. Microsoft Reader gives you server space for your library.
- **For now, you can't transfer an e-book from Palm OS to Pocket PC**—Although an industry standard (www.ebxwg.org) is on the way, at press time you could trade e-books only if both reading devices share the same format.
- **E-books are great for reference**—You can annotate, highlight, bookmark, and search e-book text. Try that with Grandma's encyclopedias from 1966.
- **You can download a full range of fiction and non-fiction**—Publishers are doing their best to bring you more than just reference material. Sci-fi and romance novels seem to do particularly well in digital sales.
- **E-books have the same quality as print**—The only way specialty e-publishers can compete with the big guys is to set high editorial standards. These smaller publishers often let you read a chapter online before you download.
- **If you've written the great American novel, submit it**—Writers overwhelmed, disgusted, frustrated, or ignored by the Bertelsmannian behemoths now have another chance to get their work in front of readers. Many e-book publishers post writers' guidelines on their sites.
- **You can buy e-books at the mall**—Waltz into a Barnes and Noble, plug your e-book device into a console, and download like crazy.

TIPS FOR ASPIRING E-BOOK AUTHORS

From Mighty Words (www.mightywords.com) CEO Chris Haskell:

- Write well. Make it fascinating and unique so readers love you. That was the secret for unknown authors J.K. Rowling and John Grisham.
- Be prepared to promote your own work tirelessly.
- Take advantage of the medium. Do what you can't do on paper. Make it short. Make it timely.

- Make it easy to read. If you think Palm owners will buy your title, make the page sizes small. Pick clear fonts.
- Pick topics that are not covered in books. The book industry needs to print a lot of copies to cover the setup costs. You could write an e-book; one with an audience of 500 in mind.
- Make your e-book available in a standard format, like Adobe's PDF. There are more than 200 million computers with PDF reader already installed.

Freelance writer Regina Lynn Preciado lives in Los Angeles with her dog, Jedi.

THIS ELECTRIFYING SEASON

The summer storm season is here. After small children bearing peanut butter sandwiches, lightning is one of the biggest threats to your computer.

I remember a phone conversation with a friend a few years ago. We suddenly were disconnected by a powerful lightning strike near her house. She later told me that the resulting power surge had not only fried her computer and modem, it had killed half her kitchen appliances, too.

When an electrical storm is on its way to your neck of the woods, roll up the car windows, take in the laundry, and disconnect your computer. It's a good idea to power down and unplug everything, even if you use a surge suppressor. The megawatts carried by a lightning bolt can pass right through even the best suppressors. You also should disconnect your modem—lightning can sneak in through the telephone lines, too. According to the latest research, it's not helpful to hide under your bed.

For advance warning of severe thunderstorm activity in your area, subscribe to American Power Conversion's Lightning Notification Service at `lightning.apcc.com`. The U.S. Weather Service also provides storm warnings at `weather.gov`.

SATURDAY, JUNE 1

FOR GEEKS ONLY

Internet security sites such as ShieldsUp (grc.com) warn about open ports. But what is a port, and why is an open port bad?

Ports are not physical connections; they're software connections. Think of them as the software equivalent of an electrical plug and socket. The socket is created by a program. It opens the port and begins listening for traffic. To close the port, close the program. If you discover an open port you didn't know about, you've got to find the program that opened it. An open port means a potential vulnerability in your system.

Ports are numbered from 0 to 65355. Most common Internet tasks have dedicated ports. For example, Web traffic travels over port 80, telnet uses port 23, e-mail port 110. Microsoft's NetBios uses Port 139 to share files.

Some processes, such as FTP, assign port numbers dynamically. As long as both ends of the conversation agree on the port number to use, the conversation can continue. It's like CB radio. If you are broadcasting on channel 6, nobody hears you unless they are listening to channel 6.

If you want to look up a port number, try Metadigm's nifty port number utility (www.metadigm.co.uk/support/portnum.shtml). The master list of assigned port numbers is maintained by IANA at www.iana.org/assignments/port-numbers.

SUNDAY, JUNE 2

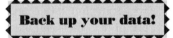

Back up your data!

PROTECT YOURSELF

A *firewall* is a system that monitors incoming and outgoing communications and filters traffic based on rules. A firewall can be made up of multiple devices, or it can be as simple as a piece of software running on a single computer.

The firewall typically is configured to block suspicious-looking packets of data based on the rules programmed into it by the firewall administrator. For example, it can block pings and port scans, making a system practically invisible on the Internet.

Firewalls have traditionally served as the first line of defense between the Internet and privately owned systems. If configured properly, they can block most types of network attacks. Firewalls have historically been deployed to defend corporate assets, but recently, many companies have started to sell personal firewall software targeted at home users who are connected to the Internet around the clock through broadband cable or DSL connections.

Although firewalls are powerful blocking tools, remember that anything intentionally allowed through the filter rules can be just as damaging as the blocked traffic. For example, most firewall rules typically allow Web browsing and e-mail access, but what if someone sent a virus as an attachment to an e-mail message? A firewall would not typically block this type of attack.

MONDAY, JUNE 3

LAPORTE SUPPORT

Q: How do ISPs afford local telephone numbers for subscribers all over the nation?

A: Internet service providers are not like you and me. They buy phone lines wholesale, and the more they buy, the less it costs per line. That's why so many small, local ISPs are being snapped up by big nationwide providers. It's cheaper to run a big operation.

ISPs and online services like America Online don't need as many lines as you might think. They usually buy only one line for each five to ten customers. That's because subscribers are never all online at the same time. Of course, the fewer lines an ISP owns, the greater the chance of busy signals. A good ISP keeps the user to phone line ratio well below 10 to 1.

The total cost for equipment and phone lines is usually just a few dollars a month per subscriber. ISPs spend much more providing their customers with technical support. A single tech support call can end up costing them $20 or more. That's why some free ISPs charge for tech support, and all ISPs work hard to minimize the amount of help their end users need.

For many companies, the biggest expense, by far, is acquiring new customers. In 1999, America Online spent $800,000,000 on sales and marketing—nearly one fifth of its total revenue. That's a whole bunch of free floppies.

TUESDAY, JUNE 4

MAC TIP

To virtually eliminate an item's desktop icon, press Command+Shift 4 to take a snapshot of your desktop and follow these steps:

1. Open the snapshot with SimpleText.
2. Select an icon sized amount of your desktop color.
3. Copy the selected area.
4. In the Finder, select the icon you want to hide.

5. Select Get Info from the File menu.

6. Click in the upper-left box with the icon and paste the copied color.

The Finder uses this little smidgen of color as the icon, making the file or folder just a floating name. If you have a complex pattern on your desktop you might have to play with the icon to get it just right.

GEEK SPEAK

A *hub* is a central device that connects a group of computers or networks. Unlike a router, a hub is a passive device that merely serves as a connector.

WEDNESDAY, JUNE 5

WEB TIP

You don't need to buy a guide to find out when your favorite television show is airing. Most local cable listings are accessible online.

With most sites that offer TV listings, it's as easy as entering your zip code and then choosing the cable provider. Most likely, there's only one company providing cable in your area. Cable listings are usually displayed in a nice, easy-to-read grid.

You can print channel lineups for future reference and search in creative ways. For example, you can find out what's on channel 36 for the entire week. Or you can run a search for programs airing at 7 p.m. for the entire week.

Popular TV listings include Yahoo! TV Coverage (tv.yahoo.com/), ZAP2it (www.zap2it.com/), and TV Guide Online (www.tvguide.com/).

THURSDAY, JUNE 6

WINDOWS TIP

If you've ever accidentally turned off a PC without going through the required shut down, then you've experienced ScanDisk. This program detects and fixes hard drive errors after an improper shut down.

To use ScanDisk, follow these directions:

1. Single-click the Start button, mouse-over Programs, Accessories, System Tools, and then click ScanDisk.

2. Under the type of test, click Thorough.

3. Click Start to begin scanning your hard drive.

4. Uncheck Automatically Fix Errors if you'd like to specify how ScanDisk repairs errors it finds.

FRIDAY, JUNE 7

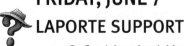

LAPORTE SUPPORT

Q: Can I download drivers for my ancient Mac 5200 using my PC?

A: You can easily download files for your Mac on your Windows PC. Just remember that although a PC cannot read a Mac disk, Macs can read PC disks. So start with a PC-formatted floppy disk.

Download the files on your PC as usual. (A great source for old Macintosh drivers is the Macintosh Driver Museum, www.macdrivermuseum.com). Then, copy the downloaded files to the floppy. Be sure not to modify the files in any way on the PC.

Now insert that disk into your 5200 and copy the files to your hard drive. You might need to use StuffIt Expander to decompress the drivers before you can install them.

SATURDAY, JUNE 8

FOR GEEKS ONLY

Can you use a free ISP with your Linux computer? Unfortunately, probably not. Free ISPs use software that feeds ads to your PC, and that software is Windows compatible. You can use any paid ISP though.

Be sure that your modem works. Go to http://www.linmodem.org to get more information about using a modem in Linux. We also have a Linux Superguide at http://www.techtv.com/superguides/linux/ that addresses a lot of Linux issues.

SUNDAY, JUNE 9

Back up your data!

PROTECT YOURSELF

We've all heard of knowledge workers who suffer from carpal tunnel syndrome and other repetitive stress disorders. But computers do not, by themselves, cause injury. It's what we do, how we do it, and for how long we do it that creates the potential for injury. The most common problems related to computer work occur over time, and they can be avoided or reversed if not neglected.

The basic types of injuries associated with computer work include the following:

- Tendon inflammation
- Tendonitis in the wrist or forearm
- Epicondylitis ("tennis elbow")
- Nerve compression
- Carpel tunnel syndrome
- Muscle fatigue
- Backache
- Visual discomfort

To avoid computer-related injuries

- Be sure you have enough space on your work surface
- Keep your keyboard/mouse/trackball at elbow height
- Adjust your chair; sit back
- Take frequent mini-breaks
- Adjust the monitor so you can see characters clearly

MONDAY, JUNE 10

LAPORTE SUPPORT

Q: *What is the point in having both IE 5 and AOL installed at the same time if I only use AOL?*

A: No point at all. AOL comes with its own browser, a customized version of Internet Explorer. If you're content with that browser, there's no need to install another.

On the other hand, AOL does work with other browsers. All you have to do is run AOL, minimize its window, then run the other browser. People often do that to take advantage of features that aren't available in AOL's version of Internet Explorer; sometimes they do it because they like another browser better.

TUESDAY, JUNE 11

MAC TIP

The first thing we do when we buy a new Mac is to turn off the voice that reads pop-up windows. If you find that woman as annoying as we do, go to the Mac OS 9 Speech control panel and follow these steps:

1. Click Voice.
2. Move down to Talking Alerts.
3. Unclick both boxes.

If all you need is a nicer voice telling you what to do, select another voice by going back to the Voice screen. In Mac OS X you can select the voice by opening System Preferences, clicking the Speech button, and selecting Text-to-Speech.

VIRUS ALERT

A few of the viruses that might activate today include

- Eraser
- Alliance
- Mercy
- Junkface

As always, it is important to have your virus protection up to date.

WEDNESDAY, JUNE 12

WEB TIP

Studios often put hidden extras called *Easter eggs* on their DVDs to give viewers an added bit of fun. Easter eggs can be anything from a funny outtake to a hidden trailer for an upcoming movie to a completely different cut of the movie you're watching. Usually these gems are hidden within the menus and title screens of your DVD.

The Web contains many sites aimed at helping movie buffs find and execute these Easter eggs. Two such sites include DVD Review (`www.dvdreview.com/html/hidden_features.shtml`) and `codes.ign.com`.

THURSDAY, JUNE 13

WINDOWS TIP

If your desktop icons are too big or too hard to see, you can quickly change their size:

1. Right-click an empty area of your desktop and choose Properties.
2. Open the Appearance tab.
3. Find Icon in the Item drop-down menu.
4. Change the size and press Apply to see how your icons look with the new size. Don't be afraid to repeat this step and experiment with different sizes.
5. When you're satisfied with your icon size, click OK.

FRIDAY, JUNE 14

LAPORTE SUPPORT

Q: It seems to me that I have eliminated a great deal of spam I used to get by deleting cookie files. Could this be true?

A: Ever since *60 Minutes* did its story on browser cookies these little preference files have been blamed for everything from ring around the collar to global warming. I don't know about global warming, but you can't blame cookies for your junk e-mail woes.

Cookies are small text files that Web sites store on your hard drive. They're just like the preference files created by other programs you use—and relatively benign. Sites use cookies to save information between your visits, things like how many times you've been to a site, your preferred typeface, and your site login and password.

A Web site cannot use cookies to discover your e-mail address. It only knows your address if you volunteer it. A site could use a cookie to save your address, but it's much more likely to save it in its own database. Cookies are too fragile to be useful for that sort of storage.

It is true, however, that after you give your address to a Web site, it can be sold to junk e-mailers. That's why the best way to avoid spam is to be very judicious about giving out your address. I rarely give out my main e-mail address online. Instead, I use an address I created on one of the free Web-based e-mail sites like `mail.yahoo.com` or `www.hotmail.com`. I don't mind if those accounts fill up with spam.

SATURDAY, JUNE 15
FOR GEEKS ONLY

One viewer who wanted to install a UNIX clone asked me the difference between Linux and Hurd and FreeBSD.

All three are UNIX-like operating system kernels. FreeBSD is the oldest, and the most like UNIX. In fact, it's the direct descendent of one of the two original flavors of UNIX, the Berkeley System Distribution, or BSD. If it's true UNIX goodness you're looking for, stick with FreeBSD.

Linux was created by a Finnish graduate student in 1991 because he was dissatisfied with an operating system he was using called minix. The student was named Linus, so he called his version of minix, Linux. Linux has become insanely popular, and is very similar to FreeBSD. Both are essentially UNIX clones. System programmers will notice significant differences, but end users probably won't. Because Linux is so popular, it is very well supported and works with the widest variety of hardware.

Both FreeBSD and Linux come with vast amounts of software originally created by the GNU project. As we mentioned in April, GNU is an attempt to replace the proprietary and expensive UNIX operating system with a freely distributable alternative. The GNU project duplicated most of the common applications that came with UNIX, but was slow to come up with the most important piece: an operating system kernel. Eventually, the GNU project decided to use the open source Mach kernel developed at Carnegie Mellon. The Hurd is a project to provide the additional services that Mach needs to work with GNU. The Hurd, as the youngest of the three kernels, is the least ready for primetime. It's still pretty buggy and many features are missing.

Visit these sites for more information:

- **GNU Hurd**—`http://www.gnu.org/software/hurd/hurd.html`
- **FreeBSD**—`http://www.freebsd.org/`
- **Linux**—`http://www.linux.org`

SUNDAY, JUNE 16

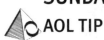

AOL TIP

You finally got an e-mail from that long-lost friend you've been wondering about, and he sent his address and phone number so that you can really keep in touch this time. But when you tried to reply to his e-mail, you accidentally hit Delete. Don't worry, all is not lost. With AOL 5.0, you have 24 hours to retrieve e-mail that has been deleted.

Here's how to retrieve deleted e-mail:

1. Click on the Mail Center icon in your toolbar.
2. Select Recently Deleted E-mail.
3. Choose Keep as New or Permanently Delete.

MONDAY, JUNE 17

LAPORTE SUPPORT

Q: How do I remove Quicken Download Manager from my system tray?

A: Intuit's Quicken is the long-time champ of money management programs. The Quicken Download Manager automatically installs in the Windows versions of Quicken 99 and 2000.

The Download Manager runs all the time, waiting for you to get online. You can tell it's running because a little red Q appears in your system tray. During idle moments online, it downloads financial data from the Net that it displays the next time you run Quicken.

If you'd prefer to download this data manually, turn off the Download Manager. To do so temporarily, just right-click the red Q in the System Tray and select the Close command from the Download Manager menu.

If you want to permanently ban the download manager, open Quicken. In Quicken 99, select Internet Connection from the Online menu and choose Options. In Quicken 2000, point to Options on the Edit menu and select Internet Options. After the Internet Connection Options window opens, check the Don't Use Background Downloading option and click OK. Close Quicken and restart your computer; the little red Q should be gone.

TUESDAY, JUNE 18

MAC TIP

It happens to everyone: a program freezes. As bothersome as this can be, there is often a way to exit the program.

Try pressing the Option, Command, and Escape keys at the same time. Exit the program in question when the prompt comes up. Continue by saving any open files and then stop working. Count yourself lucky and reboot. During the reboot you have to wait for a disk check.

TODAY IN COMPUTER HISTORY

On June 18, 1993, after 10 years with the company, John Sculley resigned as president of Apple Computer. Mr. Sculley later filed a lawsuit claiming that he had been wrongfully dismissed. Michael Spindler, nicknamed "The Diesel," succeeded Sculley to become the new president of Apple Computer.

WEDNESDAY, JUNE 19

WEB TIP

If you hate standard fonts and yearn for something different, customize. In your browser, you have the option to change the way your text is displayed:

1. Click Tools.
2. Select Internet Options.
3. Click the Fonts button at the bottom of the window.

You can now change the font for pages that do not have a font specified.

To customize your default browser font in Netscape, follow these steps:

1. Click Edit.
2. Select Preferences.
3. Click on Appearance.
4. Choose Fonts.

THURSDAY, JUNE 20

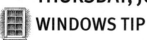

WINDOWS TIP

Why waste power by leaving your computer running full bore when you're away? Before you go to lunch, teach your computer how to go to sleep:

1. Open the Power Options control panel.
2. Choose a power scheme. The various settings determine how long your computer waits before going to sleep.
3. Click OK.

If your system supports power management, you also might have a Suspend entry in your Start menu that you can use to put your machine to sleep instantly, but be careful. Not all machines wake up from sleep mode gracefully. If you experience instability after waking your system up from Sleep mode, it would be better to shut the system down entirely when you're not using it.

FRIDAY, JUNE 21

LAPORTE SUPPORT

Q: How do I save the slide presentations such as PowerPoint shows to a CD so they can play back on the TV with a normal DVD or CD player?

A: PowerPoint presentations can only be played back with the help of a computer. To get one to work in a DVD player you'd have to make a movie out of it first, and then record the movie to VideoCD. Even then only some DVD players are able to play the resulting disc. I haven't discouraged you, have I? Okay, here's how to make a VideoCD with your CD recorder.

Start by turning the presentation into a video. The Office 97 disk comes with an application that can do this: Microsoft Camcorder. Microsoft doesn't include Camcorder with Office 2000 due to compatibility problems with newer hardware. Some shareware programs work just as well, though, including Hypercam from www.hyperionics.com (free to try, $30 to buy) and Camtasia from www.techsmith.com (free to try, $149.95 to buy). On the Macintosh you can do the same thing with a program called ScreenMovie from www.macdownload.com. It's also free to try and $30 if you want to keep it.

Use one of these programs to record the screen while you're running through the PowerPoint presentation. The next step is to turn that AVI or Quicktime file into a VideoCD. VideoCD is an antique format that never caught on here in the States. Most computer CD-ROMs can play homemade VideoCDs, as can some DVD players.

Now you need to convert the video into the proper MPEG format. On Windows, I use the free avi2vcd from www.mnsi.net/~jschlic1/. Mac users can use Cleaner 5 from www.terran.com but it costs $599. I don't know of any free solutions for the Mac.

After converting the video you can lay it to disc using your CD burner and a VideoCD compatible program. The most common of these is VideoCD Creator, which comes with Roxio's Easy CD Creator Deluxe, $89 from www.roxio.com, 1-866-280-ROXI. Roxio's $99 Toast 4 Deluxe for the Macintosh will also work.

SATURDAY, JUNE 22

FOR GEEKS ONLY

The Screen Savers' Top 5 List strikes again, this time with the five most geeky letters in the English alphabet:

5. **K**—Basic memory unit. 64K. 10K, which if you ask me, is way too far to run. And who can even begin to work on their hard drive without a heaping bowl of Special K?

4. **I**—We have Apple to thank for this. With the iBook and the iMac, this simple vowel will always be firmly entrenched in the annals of techdom.

3. **X**—There's something just inherently techie about this letter. That camera has a 35X zoom. Oooh, I have a DivX. Heck, even the "X-Files," with all its technological connections, wouldn't be as sophisticated sounding as The V-Files.

2. **E**—For electronic. E-mail. E-commerce. Egad, we have way too many gizmos in our lives.

1. **C**—Being that computers are indeed the center of many of TechTV viewers' universes, how could the most widely used programming language, C, not be at the top of the list?

SUNDAY, JUNE 23

Back up your data!

PROTECT YOURSELF

To stay safe on the Net, don't turn on services unnecessarily. File sharing is the biggest problem. If you don't have a reason to use file sharing, turn it off. Don't run an FTP or a Web server unless you have a reason. These services open ports and make your computer accessible to bad guys.

Be stealthy and don't name your computer something obvious. I don't put my personal name or anything associated with me on the computer. Otherwise, if people sniff my network (this is very easy to do) and find out my name, they have more reason to attack. Don't put your name or address in your computer.

When you're on the Internet, hide your IP address. If you're using ICQ, make sure you use the security feature and turn off your IP address. You can use a program such as Freedom from Zero Knowledge, `www.freedom.net`, to hide your IP address from all comers.

MONDAY, JUNE 24

LAPORTE SUPPORT

Q: My 14-year-old asked me to sign a parental consent form to allow him to get paid to surf the Net. Why would they pay anyone to surf the net? What's the catch?

A: The only catch is that your kid might make more money by mowing lawns than surfing the Web. He'd definitely get more exercise. Several dozen sites offer to pay people to browse the Internet. What they're really paying you for is watching advertisements. When you sign up, you download a program that displays ads on your screen the whole time you're online. Advertisers pay for your eyeballs and the site passes a little of that money along to you. Very little. The software also tracks your "interests and preferences" as you surf. Considering how teenagers feel about privacy, that might be enough to get your son back delivering papers where he belongs.

TUESDAY, JUNE 25

MAC TIP

Under the Apple menu in the upper left corner of your screen is a handy application called the Apple System Profiler.

This program goes through your system and inventories all your hardware and software. It's a great way to check out exactly what you're running, freeze your system in time, or send details to a confused tech support person. You can turn any element of this handy utility into a clipping file.

Just place your cursor over some element—memory overview, for example—and click and drag that element from the Apple System Profiler window to the desktop. You can cut and paste this information into an e-mail message or text file.

Under Mac OS X you'll find Apple System Profiler in the Application/Utilities folder.

GEEK SPEAK

A *client/server* is a network design in which one computer, called the server, stores information (data, software, and so on) and another computer, called the clients, can access that information.

WEDNESDAY, JUNE 26

 WEB TIP

Web mail is not all that secure. You should realize that right from the get-go. Still, a few precautions can lower the risk of someone breaking into your Web-based e-mail:

- Don't use dictionary words or personal names as your password. Random letters and numbers work best. Try typing the keys above the letters of a memorable word or using the first letters in each word of a memorable phrase. It's also a good idea to add punctuation and mix up the letter case.
- Many services use a secret question to retrieve forgotten passwords. Someone can discover your birthday or mother's maiden name. Make up fake birthdays or names instead.
- Every passing day makes your password less secure. Change your passwords frequently. The more often you change them, the more secure they are.
- Most Web-based mail systems give you an option that lets you automatically log in without entering a password. This option is convenient, but it might let strangers read your e-mail. If other folks use your system, be sure your e-mail service prompts you for a password every time you log in. You should also clear your browser's cache after checking your mail on public machines.

THURSDAY, JUNE 27

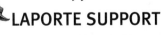 WINDOWS TIP

You are planning a trip to Hawaii. You have several browser windows open while you surf for the best hotel rates and flight fares. You have your e-mail program open to ask friends where to find the best beaches. You also have Word open so you can chart your itinerary. How do you move from window to window, program to program, without using your mouse?

It's toggle time:

1. Press Alt and hold it down.
2. Press Tab at the same time.
3. When the dialog box appears, continue to press Tab.
4. Release Alt after you Tab to the window you desire.

FRIDAY, JUNE 28

 LAPORTE SUPPORT

Q: *My 16-year-old son asked me if he could put MP3 files on his personal Web page, and I told him no. Isn't it illegal to do so?*

A: Gee whiz, Mom. You're no fun at all! (But you might be right.)

There's an epidemic of music piracy online, thanks to MP3—an audio format that makes it possible to store high-quality music in a fairly small file. MP3s might force a revolution in the way music is distributed, but until then, posting something you don't have the rights to is just plain wrong.

Not all MP3s are illegal, however. Some artists are more interested in having their music listened to than in getting paid for it. If your son really wants to put music on his site, show him the Internet Underground Music Archives (`http://www.iuma.com`). He'll find thousands of songs there that he can link to his page.

SATURDAY, JUNE 29

FOR GEEKS ONLY

TechTV host Scott Herriott appeared on The Screen Savers television show to share his list of the Top Five Movie Robots, ever. If you don't agree with this list, write to him at `scott@techtv.com`.

Scott's Top 5 Movie Star Robots

Robocop was excluded due to his cyborg status (human/machine combo), and Schwarzenegger's out 'cause it was too obvious. Otherwise, here are my picks:

5. **Robby the Robot**—What I like best about this clanky, semi-globular hunk of junk from the sci-fi classic *Forbidden Planet* are the rotating rings on the side of his head. One sticks straight out, the other bends up at a 90-degree angle. Why? Did he fall? Is he hard of hearing on one side? Whatever the case, he was a forerunner of the *Lost in Space* robot, and for that, we should all be thankful.

4. **Maria from Fritz Lang's *Metropolis***—Let's face it, she's just hot. I'm fairly certain that Madonna was inspired by her.

3. **Gort from *The Day the Earth Stood Still***—This pinnacle of stoicism kicked some major booty. His lack of peepers made him even creepier. You felt as though he could explode at any moment—a trait, I believe, every robot should have.

2. **Jean Claude van Damme**—'Nuff said.

1. **C3PO and R2D2**—No, it wasn't a tie. But because these wimpy and cutesy droids were apparent soul mates, I couldn't bear to separate them. I put them in the number-one spot cause I didn't want to deal with loads of negative e-mail from *Star Wars* geeks.

Thanks for sharing, Scott. And Klaatu Barada Nikto, to you, too.

SUNDAY, JUNE 30

Back up your data!

PROTECT YOURSELF

Windows 95 came with a handy Emergency Recovery Utility (ERU) that backs up files in case of damage to your system.

If you're still using Windows 95, you might want to install ERU from the Windows 95 installation CD:

1. Go to the Windows 95 CD directory named Other/Misc.
2. Drag and copy the folder named ERU to your C:/ drive (or other hard drive of choice).
3. Double-click the new ERU folder on your hard drive.
4. In the ERU directory, locate the file ERU.inf.
5. Right-click the ERU.inf file.
6. Click Install on the menu that pops up.

If you've upgraded to Windows 98 or Me, you can do the same thing with a free utility by Gerhard Broeske. Download your copy from `home.nexgo.de/gerhard.broeske/announce1.html`.

Windows NT/2000/XP users can create an emergency repair disk using the Backup program. You'll find it in the Accessories/System Tools folder under the Start menu. Run Backup and select Create an Emergency Repair Disk from the Tools menu.

This Month's Feature

GEEK ON THE GO

By Becky Worley and Jennifer Gross

We take our laptops on business trips, visits with the family, and even long vacations. As known computer geeks, we usually are called upon during these trips to help someone else fix a computer that's misbehaving, so we like being prepared.

BECKY'S LIST OF TRAVEL ESSENTIALS

Here's what to bring if you want to have a stress-free computing experience on the road.

- **Extra batteries for the laptop**–Schlepping an extra battery will buy you two more hours of word processing on the plane. I try to imagine hauling my laptop and components as the substitute for going to the gym on travel days. I also keep a set of AA batteries, and many handhelds require AAA batteries, so I try to keep a fresh set in the bottom of my purse.

- **Floppy and CD drives**—If you bring the floppy and leave the CD drive, you'll need to install a program using a CD. If you bring the CD and leave the floppy drive, you'll need to transfer a document using a floppy. This is a form of Murphy's law.

- **Power adapter for a car's cigarette lighter**—Many new airplanes have cigarette-lighter power adapters under the seats. I bought an adapter at Radio Shack for $79. Of the many types available, I felt most comfortable using the type that converts electricity to a regular, 110-volt, household-type outlet.

- **Cat 5 cable**—I've found myself in hotels that have a strange lamp with an extra phone jack and an RJ-45 jack. For a fee, I can plug my cat 5 cable into the RJ-45 jack and connect to the hotel's network. Always having an extra bit of cat 5 cable has bought me Internet connectivity four times faster than if I'd left that cable at home.

- **Dongle or extra phone cord**—Two laptops ago my modem used a dongle to connect to the wall jack. I lost the dongle not once, not twice, but three times. If your laptop modem needs a dongle, order two.

- **Mini USB mouse**—It looks like a piece of sushi, but the mini-mouse by Atek makes mousing on the road a lot easier. I hate the touchpads on laptops and I sometimes tire of the eraser-head pointing devices, so it's nice to have a USB, plug-and-play mouse on hand. The Atek mouse costs $50, but it is optical and has a great feel considering its teeny form factor.

- **USB networking kit**—Belkin (and some others) make direct connection USB kits. This elegant way to connect two PCs avoids the instability of DCC and the hassle of setting up an Ethernet network. The Belkin kit costs $55, and the software install and configuration are easy. If you needed to share documents or printers while on the road, this is an easy solution.

- **Klear Screen cleaner**—I'm a multi-tasker. While consuming a Cinnabon from the O'Hare Airport food court, I decide to watch a DVD on my laptop. The cinnamon roll is not only huge, but it's unwieldy—next thing you know, sticky bun on the LCD of my laptop. Warning: Don't use alcohol to clean an LCD; the protective oils that coat the screen will be stripped away. I have used the products from Klear Screen, but any specifically identified LCD cleaning towelettes will do.

- **Copy of your windows CD with product key**—When I first traveled with my new laptop, I shut the cover without shutting down the computer. It wasn't the brightest thing in the world, but who knew it would trash my OS? I couldn't reboot. I was stuck with a seven-pound weight in my bag for the rest of the trip. Even worse, all my contacts thought I'd be available via e-mail; instead, I was incommunicado.

If I'd had a copy of my windows CD and product key, I could have reinstalled the OS to get back up and running. Your EULA (end user license agreement) allows you to make and keep one backup copy of your windows CD for personal use. I don't like to travel with my original Windows CD, but if you don't have a CD burner, the original is better than nothing.

- **Boot disk**—In the case described above, my computer wouldn't boot into Windows, so I needed to boot from my emergency start disk. Once booted, I would have used the Windows CD to reinstall my OS if needed.
- **Tool Kit**—Whenever I travel, I run into someone having a computer problem. My family saves up computer questions until I show up. So if you are a known computer geek, take a tool kit in case you have to open a case or reset a jumper. Regardless, you look cool when you have a set of tools specifically for computers.

JENNIFER'S TIPS FOR TAKING YOUR LAPTOP ANYWHERE

If leaving your laptop at home isn't an option when you go on vacation, pay attention to the following tips. You'll learn how to protect your data, access your ISP on the road, and guard your PC against theft and damage.

- **Power up in Europe**—Don't forget to purchase an electrical outlet adapter for your notebook to adjust for the difference in voltage.
- **Leave a copy of your data at home**—Extreme heat, jostling, vibration, and moisture can damage your notebook, and you could lose data. That's why it's crucial to back up before you travel. Also be sure to leave a copy of your important data at home.
- **Protect it from theft**—Notebooks are popular targets for thieves. Don't let yours out of your sight at the airport, and don't leave it in the car unattended. You also can throw thieves off the scent by keeping yours in an inexpensive carrying case that doesn't look like your typical notebook bag. Also write down your notebook's serial number and keep it handy (but not with the computer), so you can report it to police if it gets stolen.
- **Protect it from damage**—You might love sunshine and loud music, but your notebook does not. Before you travel, find out how to protect your laptop from the heat, resonating noises, and other damaging dangers.

Becky Worley is a host on TechTV's program Call for Help. Jennifer Gross is a freelance writer and former Call for Help associate producer.

YOU DON'T HAVE TO BE WIRED TO LOVE FREEDOM

I love computers, but at this time of the year it's important to remember that the wise men who created our nation didn't have any of the benefits of today's technology.

There was no air conditioning in the Pennsylvania State House when the Founding Fathers gathered in the sweltering summer heat of 1776. No deodorant, either. But on a positive note, no one had to tell Ben Franklin to turn off his cell phone and pager.

CNN wasn't in Philadelphia to cover the events, and no pundits debated the pros and cons of independence on Larry King Live.

The Declaration of Independence was handwritten with quill pen on sheepskin parchment. It took a full day to print and many days more to distribute it to all the states. The document itself wasn't even signed until August 2. What do you expect? There was no e-mail. No fax service. No spell checkers. Which might explain why the Declaration begins, "When in the courfe of human events."

But I wonder if Jefferson's prose would have been any clearer had he used a word processor? Would George III been more understanding if Ben Franklin had flown to London to deliver a PowerPoint presentation on independence?

As we celebrate 226 years as a nation this month, it's worth remembering that there are some things technology can't improve. Life, liberty, and the pursuit of happiness don't necessarily require a 19-inch monitor. And sometimes a quill pen is more powerful than any gigahertz processor.

MONDAY, JULY 1

LAPORTE SUPPORT

Q: Is it better to have a single drive (C:) or a drive divided into several partitions (C:, D:, E:)?

A: Dividing a single, physical drive so that it appears to consist of several smaller drives is called *partitioning*. It's like putting up partitions to divide a single large room into several smaller living areas.

Partitioning is neither better nor worse for your drive—it's just a way to organize your computer. Some users create individual partitions for the operating system, programs, and documents as a way to keep them all separate. Plus, if one partition is damaged, you still might be able get to the data on the other partitions.

I keep my Windows swap file on a separate partition to keep it from getting mingled with other data, reaping a small benefit in performance and reliability.

Advanced users often partition so that they can use multiple operating systems on the same drive, for example, Windows 98, Windows XP, and Linux.

Almost all operating systems offer some way of managing partitions. Windows comes with an antique DOS program called FDISK (it's in the c:\windows\command folder). MacOS comes with a program called Drive Setup.

There's one drawback to using either of those two programs: They erase all the data on your drive in the process of partitioning it. That means you either have to start with an empty drive or make a full backup before you begin.

If you're serious about partitioning, I recommend buying a program that creates and resizes partitions without erasing data. The best is Partition Magic from Powerquest (www.powerquest.com). It costs about $70.

For most users, modifying a disk's partitions is completely unnecessary and even risky. Unless you have a specific reason to re-partition and really know what you're doing, I strongly suggest leaving your disk as is.

TUESDAY, JULY 2

MAC TIP

Mac OS X has BSD UNIX as its underlying operating system. That means it has all the features of a true UNIX OS. Except for one thing: The root account is disabled by default.

The login you create when you install Mac OS X is an administrator account, which gives you most of the capabilities that a root account has. But for absolute power over your system, you still need to log in as root. Here's how to turn on root access:

1. Go into Applications, Utilities folder, and select the NetInfo Manager application.

2. Select Security from the Domain menu and click Authenticate.

3. After you have entered an administrator password you can select Security from the Domain menu again and click Enable Root User.

4. Be sure to give this account a secure password.

You should continue to use your normal user account most of the time, but from now on, when you need to log in as root, you'll be able to.

GEEK SPEAK

HTML (*HyperText Markup Language*) is a language used to create pages that Web browsers can read. HTML was invented in 1989 by physicist Tim Berners-Lee. He was looking for a way for his colleagues at CERN to collaborate on papers over the Internet.

WEDNESDAY, JULY 3

 WEB TIP

Scirus.com is a search engine designed specifically for locating science-related articles and sites. It only searches science-focused sources. Furthermore, it not only turns up results available for free on the Web, it can give you information on articles that exist on pay-for-access sites. For these pay-for-access articles, Scirus gives you the article's title, author, and source, as well as a few lines from the article to give you an idea what it's like. If you're working from a university or similar institution, you can often access these normally restricted articles for free.

You can search for both free and access-controlled material, or restrict your search to one or the other. You can also restrict your search to various subject areas. A handy feature of the site is that any of these search customizations can be saved and restored on your next visit.

The engine's advanced search features are the same robust ones you'd expect from today's engines. The site Scirus lives on has a very clean and navigable design, so there are no distractions and you can begin your search right away. Help sections, advanced search, and general information about the site are all just one click away from the main page.

THURSDAY, JULY 4 (INDEPENDENCE DAY)

 WINDOWS TIP

You need to know what kind of video card you have to get new or updated drivers. To find out what kind of card and chip you are using:

1. Open the computer and find the card. Look at the main chip on the card, and look for the chip label. It should tell you what kind of chip it is.

2. The card should have a label on it that states the name of the card.

3. If you can't find a label, the card should have an FCC number on it. Record the FCC number, and look it up on the FCC site at `http://www.fcc.gov/oet/fccid/`.

After you identify the chip or card manufacturer, visit the manufacturer's Web site for the drivers.

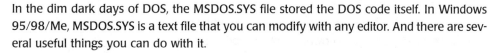

LAPORTE SUPPORT

Q: When I print anything from the Net, information on the right and left of the page is cut off. It works okay when I print e-mail. How can I fix this?

A: The difference between an e-mail message and a Web page is in the formatting. Web designers apply many rules to get a Web page to look just so on the screen. Unfortunately, sometimes a page that looks great onscreen is not so hot on the printed page. But you can take some steps to get that page printed right.

First, reduce your margins. Click Page Setup under your browser's File menu. Enter smaller numbers in the left and right margin boxes. Most printers cannot print all the way to the edge of the page, but if you enter left and right margins of 0, your browser resets them to the smallest values the printer can handle.

If that doesn't do the job, try printing those pages in landscape mode. Turning the page sideways gives you a lot more width. Select Page Setup from the File menu again, then select Landscape orientation.

Some browsers, like Internet Explorer 5 on the Mac, enable you to reduce the page before printing. Select Page Preview from the Print menu and click Shrink Pages to Fit before printing.

SATURDAY, JULY 6

FOR GEEKS ONLY

In the dim dark days of DOS, the MSDOS.SYS file stored the DOS code itself. In Windows 95/98/Me, MSDOS.SYS is a text file that you can modify with any editor. And there are several useful things you can do with it.

You'll find MSDOS.SYS in the top directory of the C: drive, but if Windows is set to hide invisible files, you won't be able to see it. Open My Computer, select Folder Options from the Tools menu, click the View tab, and select Show Hidden Files and Folders. Now you should be able to spot the file nestled in the C:\ directory. Right-click it, select Properties, and turn off the Hidden and Read-only attributes. Now you can edit the file in Notepad.

Don't mess with the seemingly random stuff at the end of the file. MSDOS.SYS has to be more than 1,024 bytes long for compatibility with other programs. Leave that part alone, and focus on the Options section, where you can actually do some cool stuff.

YOU DON'T HAVE TO BE WIRED TO LOVE FREEDOM

For example, the Boot Directly into Safe Mode option does just that—it forces your machine to boot directly into Safe Mode. This might be helpful if your function keys aren't working, or if you're having hardware problems.

To turn it on, set the value to 1:

```
BootSafe=1
The default is OFF:
BootSafe=0
```

SUNDAY, JULY 7

Back up your data!

PROTECT YOURSELF

Computer not working? Before you throw it out the window or use it for an anchor, take the time to go through some basic diagnostic maneuvers. Who knows, it might still be the wonderful toy (or tool) it once was.

Check Your Drivers

The absolute first thing to do after you have verified that you have power is to make sure you have the latest drivers installed (assuming the computer is booting).

Check Your Peripherals

If you get the BIOS (sign-on screen at startup, your monitor, video card, CPU, and RAM are most likely okay.

If you don't, go through this checklist:

- Be sure the monitor is plugged in and has power.
- Verify that your power supply is working.
- Try swapping video cards (also try using a PCI card, if you are using AGP, and vice versa).
- Try swapping RAM.
- Try swapping CPUs.
- At this point it's down to the motherboard. Try swapping it with a unit you know is good.

If Your Computer Won't Boot

If the BIOS signs on just fine but the computer complains that it can't find the operating system, try the following:

- Be sure the hard drive IDE/SCSI power connectors are good.
- If you are using SCSI, be sure during boot you see the drive's SCSI ID number and that the SCSI device is set as your boot drive.
- Go into your BIOS and be sure that under boot options, the hard drive you are using is selected, either IDE or SCSI (also select Boot From Floppy).
- Try booting from a known good boot disk (floppy). If it boots from the floppy and you can use DOS commands to navigate around, check the hard drive directories. Make sure the necessary startup files are there. If you get no response from the hard drive, then you either have a power problem, a bad cable, or the drive itself is bad.
- Try using a different power connector for the hard drive.
- Try using a new IDE or SCSI cable.

Check Your Video Setup

If the system boots but your display is funky, check the video card setup:

- Be sure the card is fully seated in the AGP or PCI socket.
- Sometimes the contacts on the card and the socket get dirty. Pull out the card and clean the contacts with a pencil eraser. Use compressed air to blow dust out of the socket.
- Booting from a DOS boot disk tells you if the video card works. Borrow a card from a friend and try swapping it.
- If you can, try swapping all your stuff except the motherboard into a friend's case. If it works fine with your friend's motherboard, you have figured out your problem.

Test Your RAM

Use a program such as Gold Memory (www.goldmemory.cz) to test your RAM.

MONDAY, JULY 8

LAPORTE SUPPORT

Q: I copied some Word 97 files to a disc at work and worked on them at home. When I opened the files from the same disc at work, the computer said I had a virus: W97M/Marker.gen. Does my computer at home have the virus, or is it the computer at work?

A: It's not always easy to follow the chain of infection of any virus. Researchers still debate the origins of the devastating influenza epidemic of 1918. Some believe it came from China. Others are convinced it began in Iowa. No one knows if humans got it from pigs, or the other way around. The same problems exist in tracking down the source of computer viruses.

Just because your work computer was the first to find the virus doesn't mean it originated at home. Word macro viruses spread when you open an infected document. The macro is copied to the computer's hard drive and spreads quickly to other Word files. By now, Word documents on both computers are probably infected.

The W97/Marker virus is commonly spread via e-mail, although you could have been infected by a Word file given to you on a disk. It's not a particularly destructive virus. The worst side effect is that it disables the macro virus protection in Word. It might also delete files in your Word startup folder. For complete information on the virus and its effects, visit the Symantec Anti-Virus Research Center, `www.sarc.com/avcenter/venc/data/ w97m.marker.gi.html`.

TUESDAY, JULY 9

MAC TIP

Three different kinds of programs can run under Mac OS X.

- *Classic applications* are apps designed for Mac OS 9. They run only under the Classic environment—essentially a protected Mac OS 9 mode. When a Classic app is running, the Mac OS 9 menu bar displays onscreen. If a Classic application crashes, it can bring down the entire environment, but Mac OS X usually continues undamaged. (Microsoft Office 2001 is an example of a Mac OS 9 Classic app.)
- *Carbon applications* are usually Mac OS 9 apps that have been modified to run under Mac OS X. They run in Mac OS X native mode and can take advantage of Mac OS X features such as the Aqua user interface and protected memory. But Carbon is not intended for use in new Mac OS X apps. It's primarily a bridge between the old Mac OS 9 API and Mac OS X.
- *Cocoa applications* are fully native Mac OS X apps. They take advantage of all of Mac OS X's features. Mac OS X works best with Cocoa apps. (Omniweb is an example of an application written from scratch for Mac OS X using the Cocoa API.)

VIRUS ALERT

As always, the world is full of viruses, including today's Angela virus in Word 6.x/7.x. Check your antivirus program to be sure you have the latest virus definitions.

WEDNESDAY, JULY 10

WEB TIP

Looking for a good deal on a Web host? How about free? There are plenty of companies and groups who will host your Web site at no charge.

The big free hosts, like Geocities and Tripod, support themselves with advertising. Along with a free Web page you get their ugly ads, but they have fast servers and easy Web design tools, and they're simple to get started with.

If you'd prefer to avoid the ads check your Internet service provider. ISPs such as AOL, Earthlink, AT&T, and Verio provide space for small personal Web sites at no extra charge.

If you run a non-profit or charitable organization there are many companies that will support your work with free Web hosting. For example, groups that help deaf people can create free sites at www.deafvision.com/nonprofit/. Yahoo lists many similar services. Search for "non-profit Web hosting."

Some Web hosts give you free space without imposing their ad banners on your site. Doteasy, www.doteasy.com, gives you ad-free Web space as long as you use them to register your domain for a very reasonable $15 per year. If you planned to pay for a custom domain name anyway, this sounds like a pretty good deal. Microworld offers free space with no banners at www.microworld.com as does Brinkster, www.brinkster.com.

For an up-to-date list of free Web hosts with reviews, visit www.100best-free-web-space.com or www.clickherefree.com.

THURSDAY, JULY 11

WINDOWS TIP

If you're using Windows 98 or later, the simplest way to free space on your hard drive is to run the Disk Cleanup utility. Open My Computer, right-click your hard drive, select Properties from the pop-up menu, and then press the Disk Cleanup button. Place checks next to the items you want to clean up, and then click OK.

You also can use Disk Cleanup to remove unused programs. On the More Options tab, click Clean Up under Windows Components. To remove a component, clear its check box. Uninstall unused applications by clicking Clean Up Under Installed Programs on the More Options tab.

When you clear the cache, check to be sure that it can't grow to more than 20 megabytes. There's no need to waste disk space with a larger cache, and Internet Explorer for Windows can sometimes reserve hundreds of megabytes. You'll find the cache settings in the Internet Options control panel.

FRIDAY, JULY 12

LAPORTE SUPPORT

Q: *Is there a way to use all my addresses in Outlook to make a mass mailing in Word?*

A: What you want to do is called a *mail merge*. You merge the contents of an address database, in this case Outlook's address book, with a form letter to create custom letters.

To do this in Microsoft Office, open Word and select Mail Merge from the Tools menu. Press Create to create your form letter, then press the Get Data button and select Use address book. One of the choices is the Outlook address book.

SATURDAY, JULY 13

FOR GEEKS ONLY

Here's a nifty little Linux command: cal. Type `cal` on a Linux/UNIX command line, and it displays a calendar (Gregorian) for the current month.

Want to display the entire year? No problem. Just type in the year:

```
cal 2001
```

Typing `35` displays the year 35, not the year 1935. Type in the full year for anywhere between 1 and 9999.

Want to display a different month of this, or any year, say, January of 2001? Type this:

```
cal 1 2001
```

July of 1969? No sweat. Type the following:

```
cal 7 1969
```

SUNDAY, JULY 14

Back up your data!

PROTECT YOURSELF

Here are some fundamental questions you need to answer before designing a security policy for your firewall:

- **What servers do I have running on my network?**—You need a list of those servers so you know which ports to open.
- **Do I need to poke holes for complex protocols?**—If you are using a packet filter (such as ZoneAlarm or the Linksys broadband router), you need to allow access for protocols such as FTP, RealAudio, and online gaming.
- **What is my policy regarding outbound connections?**—Allow outbound connections for the major Internet services such as Web browsing and e-mail, but don't allow unlimited access to other services. Telnet, for example, is notoriously insecure. Outbound traffic on an obscure port is often a sign that you have a Trojan horse virus running on your system.
- **Which approach should I take: Block any access that's not explicitly approved, or allow any traffic that's not specifically blocked?**—The first case is the safest and

most often used. All access to your system is blocked unless you've given explicit approval. Allowing all traffic that's not explicitly blocked makes it much easier to use the Net, but it's too risky for most situations.

After you answer these questions, building the security policy is just a matter of programming firewall rules for the allowed inbound and outbound protocols. Do not forget to add a last rule to block all traffic—unless you have chosen the dangerous "implicit accept" approach.

MONDAY, JULY 15

LAPORTE SUPPORT

Q: On a digital camera, what does 2x optical or 3x optical mean? Is the higher optical number better?

A: It's all about the zoom. A higher number means you can zoom in closer.

Ads for digital cameras often refer to two kinds of zoom: optical and digital. Optical zoom uses the lens itself to bring the picture in closer, just like a telephoto lens on a 35mm camera. Digital zoom uses software to enlarge the image.

There's a big difference in quality between the two techniques. Optically magnified images look just as good as unmagnified images. Digitally enlarged images are fuzzier, and the higher the zoom, the worse the picture.

If you're in the market for a digital camera, compare optical zoom specifications and ignore the digital numbers.

Incidentally, you see the same kinds of specs when you shop for a scanner. Scanner resolutions are usually quoted both optically and digitally. As with cameras, you should ignore the inflated digital specs and consider only what the scanner's optics can do without software help.

TUESDAY, JULY 16

MAC TIP

Microsoft has turned its flagship word processing program into a Cuisinart for writers. It slices, it dices, it practically makes julienne fries.

But sometimes you just as soon not have all those fancy features. If you just want to write without Word looking over your shoulder, turn off its automatic correction features. Open the AutoCorrect item under the Tools menu. Uncheck everything. Make sure to click each tab and uncheck the items in there, too. Of course, if there are any automated features you like, leave them checked.

To turn off spelling and grammar checking, select the Spelling and Grammar item from the Tools menu, click the Options button and uncheck the relevant items.

Finally, turn off the helpful little paper clip guy. Under the Help menu select Hide the Office Assistant. Notice how much more peaceful you feel?

TODAY IN COMPUTER HISTORY

July 16, 1951 is Dan Bricklin's birthday. Dan invented the first spreadsheet program, Visicalc, for the Apple II in 1979.

WEDNESDAY, JULY 17

WEB TIP

IRC is the oldest and most popular form of chat on the Internet. You can join an IRC chat room by downloading a client and logging in to an IRC server. I recommend mIRC for Windows from www.mirc.com, and Snak for the Macintosh (www.snak.com). Both pages have excellent introductions to IRC. Read them before you log on.

Thousands of IRC servers all over the world host as many as 80,000 people chatting at once. Many of these servers are organized into loose networks.

When you launch your chat client you're asked to create a nickname and choose a network to join. Most clients then log into a server on that network. Each network hosts hundreds of chat rooms or "channels." Type /list to get a list of channels, and /join plus the channel name to begin chatting on one. A good place to start is the #newbies channel.

One word of warning, though. IRC is a little like the Wild West and there's no sheriff in town. Most rooms are not moderated, and anything goes, so it's no place for children. It's a favorite hangout for software pirates, malicious hackers, and even pornographers. When you're in IRC, your Internet address is easily accessible, opening you to hack attacks. And unless you really know what you're doing, never download files from strangers on IRC.

But IRC is also great fun and enables you to meet lots of wonderful people online. It's also a great place to get help and information on a wide variety of subjects. If you take sensible precautions, IRC can be one of the best things to do online.

THURSDAY, JULY 18

WINDOWS TIP

If you find Internet Explorer too complicated, take a look at MSN Explorer, Microsoft's attempt to put a friendly, easy-to-use face on the Internet. MSN Explorer bundles the most used Internet functions, Web browsing, e-mail, instant messaging, and multimedia into a single program. It's a free download from explorer.msn.com. You can use MSN Explorer with any Internet service provider, but you must use Microsoft's Hotmail service for your e-mail.

MSN Explorer is pretty, but it's simple. It doesn't have many of the features that are common in more powerful programs, and that includes e-mail spell checking. If you're a weak speller, you have two choices. You can use a third-party spell checker like QuickSpell, about

$25 from `www.fornada.com/html/quickspell.html`, or you can use Outlook Express to access your Hotmail account.

To set up Outlook Express so that it uses Hotmail, select Accounts from the Tools menu, press the Add button, and select Mail. Enter your name, press Next, then enter your Hotmail e-mail address. Outlook Express recognizes it as a Hotmail account and configures itself accordingly. You're still able to use MSN Explorer, but when you want to create e-mail with the benefit of spell checking, you can use Outlook Express.

FRIDAY, JULY 19

LAPORTE SUPPORT

Q: I'd like to add sound to particular folders or files. Is there a way to "associate" a WAV file to a folder opening or file access?

A: In Windows you use the Sounds control panel to associate a sound with an onscreen event. Open My Computer, double-click the Control Panel folder, and then open the Sounds control panel inside.

To play a sound whenever a folder opens, select the Start Navigation event, and assign a WAV file to it. Make sure it's a sound you like: Internet Explorer also plays the sound whenever you click on a link.

To play a sound any time you double-click a file, assign a WAV file to the Open Program event.

Associating sounds with events is a little trickier on the Macintosh. Users of System 8.1 and earlier can use a free program called SoundMaster from `xi6.com/soundmaster.html`.

With Mac OS 8.5 and later, use the Appearance control panel to install sound sets. You can create these yourself using SoundSet constructor from `www.channel1.com/users/cg601/ssc/`. To get a sound whenever you open a folder, attach it to the Window opening event in the Window Sounds section. For a sound when you open a file, associate it with the Launch application event in the Finder Sounds section.

SATURDAY, JULY 20

FOR GEEKS ONLY

Remember that `MSDOS.SYS` file? Here's another fun tweak. (See July 6 for a refresher on how to find the file.)

As you might know, when you start up Windows 95/98/ME you can press the F8 key as the operating system is loading to bring up the Startup menu. The Startup menu lets you choose different Windows modes (Normal, Safe Mode, Command Prompt Only, and so on). It can be tricky to press F8 at just the right time, though. Here's how to make the Startup menu show up every time you start Windows.

Add the following line to the [Options] section:

```
BootMenu=1
```

If there's already a line for BootMenu, set it equal to 1 to turn on the boot menu or 0 to turn it off.

But what if you don't want Windows to sit waiting for input at the Startup menu forever? Add this line to the [Options] section:

```
BootMenuDelay=
```

The number after the = sign is the number of seconds to wait for input before continuing with a normal Windows startup. The default value is 30 seconds, but I like to use a shorter value like 5 seconds. That gives me enough time to make my selection without slowing down the boot process too much.

For more information on the MSDOS.SYS file and its commands visit support.microsoft. com/directory/article.asp?ID=kb;en-us;Q118579.

SUNDAY, JULY 21

 **AOL TIP**

Are you tired of the advertising offers that pop up every time you start AOL? You can use AOL's Marketing Preferences settings to stop the insanity. Here's how to change your Marketing Preferences:

1. Click My AOL in your toolbar.
2. Choose Preferences.
3. Click Marketing (or type in the keyword Marketing Preferences or Choice).
4. On the right side of the page you will see six different categories to choose from, including e-mail, telephone, and mail. Go through each one of those and set the preferences to say whether or not you wish to receive "special offers" from AOL.

Check these marketing preferences regularly—AOL resets them from time to time.

For more information, check out the keyword Privacy. In the Privacy Policy, AOL says that it "may use information about the kinds of products you buy from AOL to make other marketing offers to you, unless you tell us not to" and they "give you choices about how AOL uses your personal information."

While you're at it, you might also want to take a look at keyword TOS (Terms of Service) and read the Member Agreement and Community Guidelines.

MONDAY, JULY 22

LAPORTE SUPPORT

Q: In the good old days, the PRTSCR key printed out exactly what was onscreen. Can you do this with Windows 98?

A: Ah, yes; the good old days. Back when Wham! ruled the airwaves, Ferris Beuller was still skipping school, and the Print Screen key actually printed the screen.

George Michael might be playing nostalgia tours these days, and Ferris is probably a partner in a lucrative law practice, but the PRTSCR key is still where it always was, at the top of your PC keyboard to the right of the F12 key. And believe it or not, PRTSCR still does something. It just doesn't print out the screen any more.

In Microsoft Windows, pressing the PRTSCR key copies an image of the screen to the clipboard. From there you can paste it into Microsoft Paint or any other graphics program and print it.

Press Alt+Prtscr to copy an image of just the topmost window to the Clipboard.

Misty-eyed Macintosh nostalgists will be glad to know that they can still copy the current screen image to a file in Mac OS 9 by pressing Command+Shift+3. Command+Shift+4 lets you select a region of the screen for saving. In Mac OS X you'll have to use the Grab utility.

Who says nostalgia ain't what it used to beWham?

TUESDAY, JULY 23

MAC TIP

If you switch back and forth between Mac OS X and OS 9 and routinely save files to the desktop, you might see that the files you saved in Mac OS 9 aren't on your Mac OS X desktop, and vice versa. To get to these files, you need to access the Desktop folder for each operating system. Here's how.

Under Mac OS X

To access your Mac OS 9 desktop files, open the Desktop Folder located at the top level of your Mac OS 9 boot drive.

Under Mac OS 9

In Mac OS X, each user has his or her own Desktop folder. To find a particular folder:

1. Go to the top level of the drive that holds Mac OS X and open the Users folder.
2. Find the appropriate user. Each user will have a folder. For example, if your name is Patrick, find the Patrick folder and open it.
3. You'll find the Desktop folder inside.

GEEK SPEAK

A *database* is a computer file containing structured data. Database files usually consist of multiple records, and each record is composed of several fields. The database file is arranged so that it's easy to retrieve any field from any record. For example, an address book database would contain multiple address records. Each record would contain name, address, city, state, country, and zip code fields.

WEDNESDAY, JULY 24

 ## WEB TIP

Many people ask me whether I recommend Internet Explorer or Netscape. I'm going to get angry e-mails no matter which I choose, so let me start by saying that there's no right answer to this question. It's like asking if I prefer chocolate or vanilla. The beauty of a personal computer is that it is personal. There's no one to tell you what to do.

As it turns out, I like both chocolate and vanilla, and I use both browsers. I do slightly prefer Microsoft's Internet Explorer on Windows and Macintosh OS 9. It seems more reliable, and its support of Internet standards is more complete than Netscape's. On the other hand, when I'm using Mac OS X, I use a shareware browser called Omniweb. It's free to try from `omnigroup.com/products/omniweb/`.

There's a third browser that's not as well known as Netscape or Internet Explorer but well worth trying. It's called Opera. You can download a version for nearly any operating system from `www.opera.com`.

I suggest you try all three browsers and stick with the one that suits you.

THURSDAY, JULY 25

TODAY IN COMPUTER HISTORY

Today in 2001, W32.Sircam.worm wreaked havoc on the computing world. This e-mail worm was particularly insidious, sending copies of itself and a random file from the infected computer's hard drive to all addresses in the victim's address book. When recipients opened the attachments, they experienced everything from minor Windows annoyances to actual deleted data and corrupted `.dll` files. That's why you should *never* click an attachment you're not expecting, even if it appears to be from a friend.

Oh, and don't forget to update your antivirus definitions today.

 ## WINDOWS TIP

Here's how to remove the arrows from shortcut icons in Windows. Download TweakUI from Microsoft at `www.microsoft.com/ntworkstation/downloads/PowerToys/Networking/NTTweakUI.asp`. Follow the instructions for installing the program, and then open the TweakUI control panel. Click the Explorer tab, and select the arrow style you prefer for your shortcuts: normal, light arrow, none, or custom.

FRIDAY, JULY 26

LAPORTE SUPPORT

Q: *My school received donated Macintosh 6100/66 computers with 500MB drives (they're marked). The computer only sees 40MB useable. How do we make the rest of the drive useable?*

A: The Power Macintosh 6100 came with a 500MB hard drive, so it should be able to see the whole thing. I verified this at www.everymac.com, a useful database of the specifications of every Macintosh ever manufactured.

I'd guess that those hard drives were partitioned at some point and that some of the partitions are invisible. Run the Apple System Profiler and click the Devices and Volumes tab to see how big those drives are supposed to be.

To recover the missing drive space, boot from a Mac OS 9 system disk and run Apple's Drive Setup program. Delete any partitions you find and reinitialize the hard drive to use all 500MB.

SATURDAY, JULY 27

FOR GEEKS ONLY

You spend a lot of time looking at the gray toolbars in both Windows and Internet Explorer. Now you can change the color to reflect your personality.

Here's a Registry hack that tells Windows to sample a bitmap image file for the background of your Explorer toolbars.

A word of warning though. As always, take care when modifying your Registry. Changes are saved instantly and it's possible to muck up your Registry to the point where your system won't start at all. If you do have a problem after working on the Registry, boot to DOS and, from the C:\ prompt type SCANREG /RESTORE to revert to a previous copy of the Registry.

To install a customized Explorer background:

1. Open the Registry Editor. (Click Start, select Run, type regedit in the blank field, and press Enter.)

2. Open the directory folders to the path (in the left window pane)
   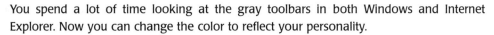
   HKEY_CURRENT_USER\Software\Microsoft\Internet Explorer\Toolbar.

3. If the right window pane doesn't have an entry called BackBitmap, right-click an empty space in the right window pane, click New, and select String Value. Enter BackBitmap as the value and press Enter.

4. Now double-click BackBitmap and type in the path of the bitmap image file you would like to use as the background (example: `C:\windows\clouds.bmp`).

5. Close the registry editor. Relaunch Windows or Internet Explorer to see the changes take effect.

SUNDAY, JULY 28

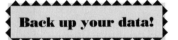

Back up your data!

PROTECT YOURSELF

Plenty of details about you are available to anyone who knows where to look online. All an unscrupulous person needs to steal your identity is an Internet connection and $50 to $100 to find your full name, street and e-mail addresses, phone number, Social Security number, driving record, bankruptcy reports, tax returns, and more.

Services such as A1-Trace USA, the American Information Network, and Discreet Data Systems sell personal info that has long been available to those in the know.

Unfortunately, because much of this information is a matter of public record, you can't keep all of it under wraps. The best way to protect yourself is to maintain a low profile on the Web: Watch what you say in newsgroups and public online forums. Such posts are archived for long periods of time—sometimes forever—and can be easily accessed from sites like groups.google.com.

If you suspect that your identity has been stolen, notify your banks, creditors, credit bureau, post office, and other pertinent agencies immediately. The U.S. government runs an excellent Web site to help people who are victims of identity theft at `www.consumer.gov/idtheft`. It's worth reading even if you haven't had a problem.

For more information about protecting your privacy online visit the Electronic Privacy Information Center (`www.epic.org`), Privacy Rights Clearinghouse (`www.privacyrights.org`), and the Public Interest Research Group (`www.pirc.org`) .

MONDAY, JULY 29

LAPORTE SUPPORT

Q: How can I change the name under Registered To in my Systems Properties. My ex put his name in there and I got the computer.

A: Windows hides the name of the registered user in the System Registry. The best way to change it is to use a free utility called Tweak Revisited, which you can download from `www.jsware.net`. Not only can you use it to change the name of the registered user, it also helps manage cookies, customize the Windows startup screen, and a whole lot more.

TUESDAY, JULY 30

MAC TIP

The Finder's file browser in Mac OS X has a handy toolbar at the top. You can add icons to it by dragging files and folders to the toolbar:

1. Open the browser, click the View menu, and select Customize Toolbar.
2. Drag the icons you want to the toolbar.
3. Drag the ones you don't need off at the same time.
4. Press Done when you're finished.

GEEK SPEAK

A *docking station* is a fixed piece of hardware to which a portable computer can connect. The docking station usually contains more resources than its portable counterpart can maintain, such as network connections or additional drives.

WEDNESDAY, JULY 31

WEB TIP

You might have noticed that some Web addresses begin with *www* and others don't.

The *www* is the name of a computer located at a particular dot-com address. For example, when you type in www.techtv.com, you're accessing a computer named www at the Internet location techtv.com.

Traditionally, computers on the Net are named to indicate what they do. The www means "this computer serves World Wide Web pages." It's one way users can know what kind of site they're going to before they press return.

There are no computer naming requirements, though. Our Webmaster could just as easily have named the computer fred, but wouldn't you feel silly typing in the address fred.techtv.com?

This Month's Feature

FANTASY FOOTBALL ONLINE

by Patricia Moore

Fantasy Football is a modern form of football "pool" in which you choose (read: bet on) a football team and expect (read: hope) that your team will win. The unique aspect of this game is that you play the role of a team coach or manager. You build a team of players by mixing and matching quarterbacks, wide receivers, running backs, defensive linemen, and so on. How they play in real life determines how well your fantasy team fares.

Now that Fantasy Football has been adopted into the online community, it is easier than ever to let your favorite NFL stars earn you the status and prestige that you deserve.

Where to Play Online

Many different sites offer varying levels of Fantasy Football support, from the home Web sites of individual football enthusiasts to large sports organizations. Unless you personally know the coordinator (read: bookie), it is probably a good idea to stick to the better-known sites, which generally have a higher level of accountability and integrity.

A few of these sites include

- Yahoo! (http://fantasysports.yahoo.com)
- ESPN.com (http://games.espn.go.com)
- NFL.com (www.nfl.com/fantasy)
- CBS Sportsline.com (http://fantasy.sportsline.com)
- Stats.com (www.stats.com)

Picking Your Team

When building your team, research the most recent statistics and/or expectations of both rookie and veteran players. Read sports publications such as *The Sporting News* (www.sportingnews.com) and the local newspapers of each team. For example, the *Miami Herald* contains detailed statistics of the Miami Dolphins, and can be found online at www.miami.com/herald/content/sports.

Of course, the World Wide Web is full of comprehensive football sites, including NFL.com (www.nfl.com), Superbowl.com (www.superbowl.com), and Pro Football Weekly (www.profootballweekly.com), which contain useful as well as not-so-useful information on teams and players. Don't forget to check the injury roster at www.footballinjuries.com.

Follow the NFL Weekly

After you've picked your team, your job is to watch football. Watch *lots* of football. As far as I know, research has yet to be conducted to disprove the theory that cheering for your football team from your living room couch actually can affect the outcome of the game. Some even believe that throwing cheese doodles at the TV has a negative effect on the opposition. Hey, it can't hurt.

Although the coordinator of your Fantasy Football League keeps track of each member's statistics, pay attention to how your team is doing. Visit the Web site that hosts your league. You also might want to keep your own statistical record for peace of mind.

Yeah, But What's in It for Me?

Many of the Fantasy Football Leagues play for money. Be sure to understand the winning delivery policies at the beginning. Different percentages of the pool might go to the overall winner, second and third place, division champions, unique or outstanding individual players, pity-prizes, and so on. Sometimes, payments are doled out weekly, but more often get distributed at the end of the season.

Money is not the only reward for playing/winning this game. (In fact, sometimes there's no money involved at all.) Winners may reap weekly bragging rights, the honor of throwing a Super Bowl party, or countless other expressions of personal satisfaction for a job well done.

Patricia Moore is a freelance writer based in California.

AH, WILDERNESS

Every year in August, my family packs up and heads into the wilderness for a week of camping. I can imagine it already: the pine-scented air, birds singing next to a gurgling brook, hearty campfire songs and roasted marshmallows, the utter lack of electricity, phone lines, and computers. The horror! The horror!

My wife thinks it's good for me to get away from technology for just one week a year. She also thinks I should do 10 sit-ups every single morning. How could such a sweet person be so cruel?

I guess Mrs. Laporte doesn't understand that I use my computer to get away from it all. When I boot it up, I take a vacation, leaving the perils and frustrations of everyday life behind, to bask in the perils and frustrations of Windows XP.

No doubt she mistakes the muffled curses and manic pounding that emerge from under my office door at these times for signs of unhappiness or frustration. Nothing is further from the truth. I am seldom more relaxed than when I am forced to remove five screws for the tenth time to open my case so I can get my network card working with my sound board. These moments are balm to heal my fractured soul.

What no one who hasn't actually owned a computer can ever hope to understand is that we love these beige spawns of Satan. The whine of their cooling fans blends in perfect harmony with the throbbing in our temples as we grind our teeth while trying to convince USB to co-exist with DUN. What can a cool mountain lake offer that compares to the limpid hue of the Blue Screen of Death? How can a sunset compete with the rainbow glory of a freshly burned CD?

So go ahead. Run away to the fields and streams of your miserable little camping adventure. I will draw the blinds, turn up the MP3s, and pound my keyboard until my wrists tingle. That is all the vacation that I need. And may I remind you that no one ever got skin cancer from overexposure to the glow from a computer monitor?

THURSDAY, AUGUST 1

WINDOWS TIP

Here's a simple tip that lets you hide all the icons on your desktop. Why would you want to do this? Neat freaks hide icons to keep their desktops tidy. Privacy freaks hide them to make it harder for snoopers to navigate their computers. Pranksters do it to baffle the easily confused.

Before you apply this tip be sure there are other ways to launch your applications, such as the Start menu. And since we're modifying the Windows Registry, reread the warning in the January 26 entry. Ready? Here we go:

1. Start the Registry Editor.
2. Go to HKEY_CURRENT_USER\Software\Microsoft\Windows\ Current Version\Policies\Explorer.
3. From the menu select Edit, New, DWORD value.
4. Name the value NoDesktop.
5. Double-click NoDesktop and give it the value 1.
6. Close the Registry Editor and reboot your computer.

To restore the icons on the desktop, change the value of the NoDesktop Key to 0.

FRIDAY, AUGUST 2

LAPORTE SUPPORT

Q: I want to get a DVD drive for my 433MHz Celeron PC. Should I go with a hardware or software decoder?

A: Video on DVDs is stored in a compressed format called MPEG-2. Decompressing MPEG-2 files takes a fair amount of processing power. Some slower computers can't do it on their own; they might require additional processing help in the form of a DVD hardware decoder card. The card contains a digital signal processor, or DSP, designed for decoding MPEG-2 video. It does the work your CPU can't.

Computers running faster than 500MHz generally have enough oomph to decode the DVD without any help. If your DVD drive comes with a software DVD player, give it a try. If the video and audio stay in synch, and you don't notice any stuttering or dropped frames during the movie, you don't need a hardware decoder.

On the other hand, if you can't get good performance with a software-only player, go with a hardware decoder. We recommend the Sigma Designs Real Hollywood Plus (www. sigmadesigns.com/products/hollywood_plus.htm). Hardware decoders have one advantage over software decoders. They usually come with an output port for a TV set. So if you plan to watch the DVD playback on a television, it might be worth $50 for a hardware decoder card.

SATURDAY, AUGUST 3

FOR GEEKS ONLY

Most people get their first experience with karaoke at bars, weddings, and the occasional company function. Although professional karaoke DJs use expensive specialized equipment, the basic premise is pretty simple: All you really need is a way to mix a singer's voice with an instrumental background. And if the singer can watch the lyrics scroll by over some cheesy video, all the better.

You can easily turn your computer into a karaoke system with just a little software and a karaoke disc, either CD or DVD, depending on the kind of drive installed in your system.

If you plan to use a CD-ROM drive, it must support either VCD or CD/XA format discs. Check the manufacturer's Web site if you're not sure. All newer CD-ROM drives should work.

You'll find many karaoke titles on VCD at Web sites such as www.allvcd.com. To play these discs back, use VCD player software such as Global's DiVX player, free from www.divxity.com.

If you have a DVD drive, you also can play back VCD discs but stick with DVD karaoke. The picture quality is much better (I'll withhold judgment on the actual video itself). You can use the DVD playback software that came with the drive. You'll find DVD karaoke discs online at sites such as www.karaokewow.com and www.singingstore.com.

For the truly cheesy, try MIDI karaoke— that's karaoke music played back using your computer's onboard synthesizer. The Computer Karaoke Homepage at www.teleport.com/~labrat/karaoke.shtml has a complete collection of MIDI karaoke titles and players, and even tells you how to make your own.

One of the better MIDI players out there is vanBasco's Karaoke Player v2.5 (www.vanbasco.com). This free player supports KAR (Karaoke) files, as well as MIDI. It includes a player, a tempo/pitch control, a piano, and a graphical representation of MIDI output. It also supports lyric sheets.

Now that you've got the music playing, it's time to mix your voice in. You'll need a microphone with a mini-jack connector. Plug the connector into the mic jack on your sound card. You'll have to enable the mic input on the sound card by launching the mixer. Open the Volume Control application in the Accessories folder under the Start menu. From the Options menu, choose Properties, and select Recording. Check the box under Microphone and adjust the level about halfway up. Now put on "Don't Cry for Me Argentina" and blast away.

If you get really serious about this karaoke thing, you might want to buy a karaoke mixer, which you plug into your sound card. That makes it much easier to mix the music and your voice.

SUNDAY, AUGUST 4

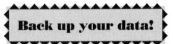

Back up your data!

PROTECT YOURSELF

Keeping sensitive information away from prying eyes is important. If you have that kind of information (bank accounts, contact information, and so on) on your computer, here is one way to add a little more security to your data.

For quick and dirty encryption that will thwart the casual snoop, use the password protection in your file compression software. We'll use WinZip as an example (it's $29 from www.winzip.com but you can download a free trial version from the site).

How To Create the Archive

1. Open WinZip.
2. Click New to create a new archive.
3. Name the file and click OK.
4. In the Add dialog box click the Password button.
5. Enter your password, and then add to the archive all the files you want to protect.

Be sure to delete the unprotected originals of the files. You will need the password to access the files in future.

Two Important Caveats

- The contents of the archive can still be viewed without knowing the password, but they cannot be extracted. You might want to rename your documents with nondescript names.
- The password is not unbreakable. It makes it more difficult to get your data, but if someone is determined to get in, he can. You might want to consider PGP for greater security. PGP encrypts files using a technique that can't be broken by anyone short of the CIA. You can download a free copy from www.pgpi.com.

MONDAY, AUGUST 5

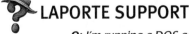

LAPORTE SUPPORT

Q: I'm running a DOS game in Windows 2000. It works okay except for the sound. How can I get it to work?

A: You need a DOS sound card emulator. Go to the Utilities section of W2kgamer.com at `http://www.win2kgamer.com/utils/`. Download the SoundFX 2.1 DOS Sound card emulator. The software enables Windows 2000 to play sounds for DOS games.

TUESDAY, AUGUST 6

MAC TIP

If an application dies in Mac OS X, you can force it to quit by pressing Command+ Option+Esc just as you would in Mac OS 9. Unlike Mac OS 9, however, you get a list of running applications and the chance to force any of them to quit.

Because Mac OS X is a much more stable operating system, you can usually continue using the computer even if an application has crashed.

Unix gurus might be interested to note that you can get a much more complete listing of running processes by using the Process Viewer in the Applications/Utilities folder. You can also use the UNIX `top` and `kill` commands in the terminal application, if you prefer.

GEEK SPEAK

Freeware is a term for software that is available free of charge. The creator often retains the copyright and may restrict use and redistribution.

WEDNESDAY, AUGUST 7

WEB TIP

One of our TechTV viewers noticed pornographic images in her temporary Internet files folder. Other people in her office noticed the same thing. She wondered how those files got there and whether she could track Web usage on the machine.

Chances are, someone is surfing the Web after normal business hours. It's a common occurrence in offices.

To prevent people from using your computer, you need to lock it down with a password. Talk to your office's IT department to see if you can get your computer password protected.

Meanwhile, you can get rid of those files by emptying your browser's cache. Even if you use only one browser, check all the browsers installed on your system, just to be sure.

To delete cache files in Netscape:

1. Open Netscape.
2. From the Edit menu, select Preferences, click the Advanced tab, and click Cache.
3. Click the Clear History button.
4. Click the Clear Cache button.

To delete cache files in Internet Explorer:

1. Launch Internet Explorer.
2. From the Tools menu, choose Internet Options and click the General tab.
3. Click the Delete Files button (under Temporary Internet Files).
4. Click the Clear History button (under History) .

THURSDAY, AUGUST 8

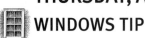

WINDOWS TIP

You can monitor resource use in Windows 95/98/Me using the System Monitor program.

To access the System Monitor:

1. Click the Start menu and point to Programs, Accessories, System Tools.
2. Select System Monitor.

System Monitor is not installed by default. If it's not in your System Tools folder, you can install it using the Add/Remove Programs control panel.

To get an idea of your memory demands, you can have System Monitor track your usage. Here's how:

1. Under the Edit menu, select Add Item.
2. Under the Category window, select Memory Manager.
3. Under the Item window, select Swap File Size. Click OK.
4. Under the File menu select Start Logging and select a place to save the log file.

Now let it purr away in the background for an afternoon of work. System Monitor records your memory demands as you work.

Windows NT/2000/XP users can monitor resource use using the Performance tool in the Administrative Tools control panel. Right-click on the graph and select Add Counters to monitor a variety of system parameters.

FRIDAY, AUGUST 9

LAPORTE SUPPORT

Q: *Can you recommend a way to keep the cyberporn from my 8-year-old daughter's eyes? I know about programs for Windows, but I have a Mac G4.*

A: The Learning Company makes the best Web filtering program for Windows and Macintosh. It's called CyberPatrol. Download a trial version for free from www.cyberpatrol.com.

But you should know Web blocking software is not perfect; adult content occasionally sneaks through. When it comes to Internet safety, there's no substitute for parental supervision. I recommend keeping the computer in a public area of your home (such as the living room or family room) so you can keep an eye on what's going on. Supervise its use by children under 12. And make sure you teach the older kids the basics of online safety. Material to help you is available at GetNetWise (www.getnetwise.org).

SATURDAY, AUGUST 10

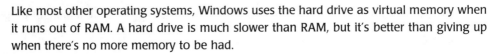

FOR GEEKS ONLY

Like most other operating systems, Windows uses the hard drive as virtual memory when it runs out of RAM. A hard drive is much slower than RAM, but it's better than giving up when there's no more memory to be had.

Windows allocates space on the drive for virtual memory in something called a *swap file* (in Windows NT/2000/XP it's called a paging file). It's almost always best to let Windows manage the size and location of your swap file, but if you have more than 256MB of RAM or you're running low on disk space, you can manually change the settings.

In Windows 95/98/Me:

1. Open the System control panel.
2. Click the Performance tab.
3. Click Virtual Memory.
4. Select the Let Me Specify My Own Virtual Memory Settings option.

In Windows NT/2000/XP:

1. Open the System control panel.
2. Click the Advanced tab.
3. Press the Performance Options button.
4. Press the Change button.

At this point you can change the location and size of your swap file. Microsoft recommends setting your swap file to 1.5 times the amount of RAM you have. However, if you have more than 256MB of RAM you should be just fine with a swap file of 200MB. If you set the minimum and maximum file size to the same amount, Windows will create a permanent swap file of static size; otherwise, it will resize the file as needed. Static files are faster.

If you have a huge amount of RAM, you might be tempted to disable virtual memory altogether. Don't. Even with gigabytes of RAM, Windows always needs a little bit of swap file. You can reduce it to 20MB or so, though.

SUNDAY, AUGUST 11

PROTECT YOURSELF

You can test your own antivirus software. The European Institute for Computer Antivirus Research (EICAR) has developed a simple way to test nearly any antivirus program on the market.

Open Notepad and type the following text into it as a single line (no spaces):

```
X5O!P%@AP[4\PZX54(P^)7CC)7}$EICAR-STANDARD-ANTIVIRUS-TEST-FILE!$H+H*
```

Be sure not to add any extra text. Save the file as aseicar.com, and then scan it with your antivirus program. It should report infection by the following:

```
EICAR-STANDARD-ANTIVIRUS-TEST-FILE
```

This is not a real virus and poses no threat to your system, but you should probably remove it after testing to avoid scaring yourself or others in the future.

This test merely verifies that your antivirus is working properly. You'll still need to perform regular updates to ensure that it will detect the latest viruses.

MONDAY, AUGUST 12

LAPORTE SUPPORT

Q: How does an optical mouse work?

A: A modern optical mouse is equipped with a small silicon light sensor, a light-emitting diode or LED, and a microprocessor. The light from the LED bounces off your desk and the sensor records variations in the patterns on the surface, sampling it 1500 times a second. The microprocessor calculates the mouse's speed and direction based on those variations.

Because nearly every surface has some pattern, an optical mouse works nearly everywhere, so you don't need a special mousepad. It won't work on a mirror, however—the reflections confuse the microprocessor.

Optical mice work great and because there are no moving parts, they're much more reliable. I recommend, and use, Microsoft's IntelliMouse Optical and the Apple Pro mouse.

You can find out more about optical mice by visiting these sites:

- Microsoft IntelliMouse Optical at `http://www.microsoft.com/products/hardware/mouse/optical.htm`
- Apple Pro Mouse at `http://www.apple.com/mouse/`
- How the Mouse Works at `http://www.howstuffworks.com/question631.htm`

TUESDAY, AUGUST 13

MAC TIP

If you run Mac OS X and frequently use Classic applications, you might want to automatically launch Mac OS 9 when you first start up. Follow these steps:

1. Open the Classic panel in System Preferences.
2. Check the Start Up Classic on Login to This Computer box.

There are some other handy features here, too. You can stop or restart the Classic environment, and if you click the Advanced tab, you'll find additional start-up options and a sleep timer.

GEEK SPEAK

Telecommuting is the act of working from a location other than the place of employment, often from one's own home. When telecommuting, the person uses the telephone, computer, fax, and/or modem to communicate with the employer and other colleagues.

WEDNESDAY, AUGUST 14

WEB TIP

The spinning globe or AOL icon in the upper-right corner of your browser window is called the *throbber*. I kid you not. Here's how you can replace the throbber in Internet Explorer with one of your own design.

Open an image editor—Microsoft Paint will do—and create a square image. When you're finished editing, create two versions of it: one 38×38 pixel version and a smaller 22×22 pixel version. Save both files as bitmap (.BMP) files.

Now download these three tools from Access Codes Software (`accesscodes.hypermart.net/download.html`):

- Internet Explorer Personalizer
- Animated Bitmap Creator
- Animated Bitmap Viewer

You can use the Animated Bitmap Creator and Viewer to create animated versions of your images, and then install them with the Internet Explorer Personalizer. The Personalizer comes with replacement animations if you don't want to create your own. All three programs are free.

THURSDAY, AUGUST 15

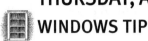

WINDOWS TIP

You can configure Windows to launch your favorite applications every time it starts up. In fact, there are several ways to do this.

- Any shortcut in the Programs\Startup folder under the Start menu automatically executes when you boot into Windows. Add a shortcut here for any program you want to load at boot. Removing shortcuts from this folder is just as easy. Just right-click them and select Delete.
- The registry key HKEY_CURRENT_USER\Software\Microsoft\Windows\ CurrentVersion\Run can also contain the names of programs that run automatically on start up.
- In Windows NT/2000/XP, startup items can be added to HKEY_LOCAL_MACHINE\ Software\Microsoft\Windows\CurrentVersion\Run.
- In Windows 95/98/Me, startup items can be added to the Run= key of the C:\WINDOWS\WIN.INI file or to the old DOS start up files AUTOEXEC.BAT and CONFIG.SYS.

In Windows 98/Me you can run the Microsoft System Configuration Utility to control startup items in all of these locations. Click Run under the Start menu and enter MSCONFIG, then click OK. Click the Startup tab to see a list of all the programs that currently launch when Windows starts up. To disable any program, uncheck it.

You also can use the freeware Startup Cop to control items that launch at startup. Download a copy from www.zdnet.com/downloads/stories/info/0,10615,77594,00.html. It has many useful additional features. Or, take the minimalist approach with Mike Lin's excellent Startup Control Panel from www.mlin.net.

FRIDAY, AUGUST 16

LAPORTE SUPPORT

Q: When I start my computer, it gives me two beeps and then stops functioning. What do the two beeps mean?

A: If your computer beeps once when it's starting up, that's good. But if it beeps several times and just sits there, that's bad. Your system has failed the *Power On Self Test* or *POST*. Something is so catastrophically wrong with the system that it can't even display an error message on the screen. All it can do is beep at you.

To decipher the beep code, check your motherboard manual or the manufacturer's Web site. If you know who made your system's BIOS, you might find help at Eric's BIOS Central, www.bioscentral.com. Eric lists the beep codes for many systems.

Here are some of the common codes for systems with an AMI BIOS:

- **Two short beeps**—A memory parity error has occurred in the first 64KB of RAM. You probably have a bad RAM chip (or your RAM is missing or loose).
- **Five short beeps**—The system CPU has failed.
- **One long, three short beeps**—A fault has been detected in memory above 64KB.
- **One long, eight short beeps**—The video adapter is either missing or defective.
- **One long beep**—POST has passed all tests. Your system is fine. (That's the beep you hear most of the time when your system starts up.)

If your computer beeps insistently the next time you turn it on, don't despair. In many cases these problems can be easily fixed by reseating your RAM or video card.

SATURDAY, AUGUST 17

FOR GEEKS ONLY

To check free space in Linux (or other UNIX clones), use either the disk free command, `df`, or the disk usage command, `du`. Both list files and directories in 512 byte blocks by default.

The `df` command reports free disk space on all mounted file systems or a given name. The name can be a device name (usually a specific HD, CD-ROM, or Zip drive), directory mounting point (`/usr` or `/var`), or directory name (`/root/desktop`), such as the following example:

```
df -c /sbin
```

You have the following options:

- **-a**—Displays usage
- **-b**—Displays sizes in bytes
- **-c**—Displays grand total of all arguments
- **-k**—Displays sizes in kilobytes
- **-r**—Displays "cannot open" message if file or directory is inaccessible
- **-t *type***—Shows files only of type
- **-x *type***—Shows files not of this type

The `du` command displays the disk usage on a directory and its subdirectories. For example:

```
du /sbin
```

Command options include the following:

- **-a**—Displays usage for all files not just subdirectories
- **-b**—Displays sizes in bytes
- **-c**—Displays grand total of all arguments
- **-k**—Displays sizes in kilobytes
- **-r**—Displays "cannot open" message if file or directory is inaccessible
- **-s**—Displays grand total for each named directory
- **-x**—Displays usage of files in current file system only

For more information on these commands type `man du` or `man df` at the command prompt.

SUNDAY, AUGUST 18

AOL TIP

When you install America Online's software it will ask you, "Would you like this copy of the AOL software to be your default Internet application for WebPages, newsgroups, and e-mail?" If you only use AOL, answer yes. If you use any other ISP in conjunction with AOL, it's best to say no. If you answered yes by mistake, here's how to put things right:

- **Browser**—If you want any other browser to launch when you double-click Internet shortcuts, use my instructions from June 19th to restore the default browser.
- **E-mail**—You need to use AOL to read AOL mail, but if you want a different program to launch when you click mail to links on Web pages, you'll have to use the Internet Options control panel to set a different default e-mail package. Open the Control Panel, and then click the Programs tab. Select your e-mail program from the drop-down menu next to E-mail.
- **Newsgroups**—While you're there you can also change your settings for newsgroups.

MONDAY, AUGUST 19

LAPORTE SUPPORT

Q: My desktop and laptop computers might be unplugged for 10 days or so while I'm on vacation. What would be the effect? What might be lost? Would I have to reinstall Windows 98?

A: Fear not. Your data will be perfectly safe. Unless you plan to store the computers on top of a giant magnet, that is.

Depending upon the season, it's probably a good idea to unplug the computers and modems from the wall, in case a thunderstorm hits while you're away. Otherwise, enjoy your vacation. Windows 98 will be waiting when you come back.

TUESDAY, AUGUST 20

MAC TIP

In 1964 at the World's Fair in New York City, AT&T first showed off its Picturephone. People marveled at the notion that you'd be able to see as well as hear callers. Today that vision is finally a reality. Using an inexpensive camera hooked to your computer, you can make video phone calls for free anywhere in the world. All you need is an Internet connection and video conferencing software.

The best known video conferencing package is Microsoft's Netmeeting. It comes free with every copy of Windows. But what about Macintosh users? Never fear, Poor Leo is here!

My favorite video conferencing program for the Mac is iVisit from Eyematic Interface, www.ivisit.com. IVisit doesn't have all the bells and whistles that come with Netmeeting, but it's a very capable program. And because there's a version for Windows, too, Mac users don't have to limit themselves to calling other Macintoshes.

GEEK SPEAK

An *IP address* (*Internet Protocol Address*) is a number that identifies a computer on a TCP/IP network—typically, the Internet. Every computer on the Internet has a unique IP address in the form of four numbers ranging from 0–255 separated by dots, for example 192.168.1.1.

To view your IP address in Windows 95/98/Me, connect to the Internet. Click the Start menu, select Run, enter winipcfg, and click OK.

WEDNESDAY, AUGUST 21

WEB TIP

You've found the funniest image on the Web, but you can't be bothered going to the site every time you need to laugh. Don't have a mirthless day; instead save that image as wallpaper:

1. Surf to the image in your browser.
2. Right-click on the picture.
3. Click Set as Wallpaper (or Set as Background).

That's it. Your wallpaper is automatically changed.

THURSDAY, AUGUST 22

WINDOWS TIP

Direct memory access (DMA) gives your hard drive the ability to access memory directly, without going through the CPU. It can help speed up tasks that are disk intensive, such as accessing databases.

To activate DMA in Windows 98:

1. Right-click My Computer and select Properties.
2. Click the Device Manager tab.
3. Click Disk Drives. Then select your hard drive and click the Properties button.
4. Click the Settings tab. Check the DMA check box if it is not checked.
5. Click OK and restart Windows.

If the check box is grayed out, your motherboard chipset doesn't support DMA. If you have problems booting, reboot in safe mode and turn off DMA.

To activate DMA in Windows 2000/XP:

1. Right-click My Computer and select Properties.
2. Click the Hardware tab, and then select Device Manager.
3. Click IDE ATA/ATAPI controllers.
4. Right-click an IDE channel and select Properties (your hard drive is probably on the primary IDE channel).
5. Select the Advanced Settings tab.
6. For Device 0 and Device 1 under Transfer Mode, select DMA if Available. Click OK.
7. Click OK and restart Windows.

Don't turn on DMA if you are using an extremely old hard drive. You want to stick with the PIO mode 4 or the default setting. You can turn on DMA for other devices like CD-ROM drives, but be careful. DMA may cause data buffer problems when used in conjunction with a CD-RW or CD-R.

FRIDAY, AUGUST 23

LAPORTE SUPPORT

Q: *Is there a Web site where I can type an entire essay without the need of a word processor?*

A: Several Web sites offer online word processors and other programs. They also offer online storage for your documents, which means you can access your work any time from any computer.

My favorite is ThinkFree Office (www.thinkfree.com). It's a Microsoft Office–compatible office suite that you can access anywhere you can get on the Web. It works on any machine that supports Java, including Windows, Macintosh, and Linux. If you're using Windows XP, you'll have to download Java before you can use ThinkFree, but the Web site makes it a painless process.

You can either run the software entirely online or download part or all of it to your hard drive. It runs faster off the hard drive, but it's nice to be able to run it completely online, especially when you're on the road.

Online software is great for people who need to work on the same documents on a variety of different computers. It also makes life simpler for both users and software publishers. Online software installs automatically and is always up-to-date. Many experts believe that this is how all software will work in the next few years.

SATURDAY, AUGUST 24

FOR GEEKS ONLY

Check out the following principles for digital artists according to Vincent Marcone of MyPetSkeleton.com:

- **Always use original media**—Incorporate your own textures and sketches into your digital art. This is the best way to develop your own electrical thumbprint.
- **Get into the habit of writing down your dreams**—Making a connection with your subconscious offers a unique approach to your artistry. If you can incorporate little bits of your subconscious into your image, they leave a long lasting impression.
- **Experiment as much as you can**—Don't be afraid to rearrange your composition between different layers. More often than not, the best effects come by trial and error, not by preplanning.
- **Give your illustration a rest**—After you're finished with a piece, leave it alone for a day or two and then come back to it with a fresh pair of eyes. This new perspective enables you to add just the right touches to your final composition.
- **Listen well to constructive criticism**—Having an opinion of your image through another set of eyes is extremely valuable. However, a constructive critique is just another perspective—it doesn't mean it's the right perspective. If you're genuinely happy with what you've created, you're on the right path.

SUNDAY, AUGUST 25

Back up your data!

PROTECT YOURSELF

My five year old, Henry, once asked me why we always buckle our seat belts before setting out for a drive. "Are you expecting a crash, Daddy?" Of course not, but it's a good idea to be prepared.

That's why I use an Internet security program whenever I'm online. I don't expect hackers to come a knocking, but I want to be ready in case they do. Especially because excellent protection is available for free. I use ZoneAlarm from `www.zonealarm.com`. It works with any Windows PC to prevent intruders from invading your machine.

After you've installed ZoneAlarm, test your Internet security with ShieldsUp at `grc.com`. Its creator, Steve Gibson, does a great job of explaining Internet security issues and how to protect your system.

MONDAY, AUGUST 26

LAPORTE SUPPORT

Q: *I have a WebTV. Do I have to continue to subscribe to its $24.95 per month service? Can't I use another cheaper ISP?*

A: You might be able to use a cheaper ISP, but you still have to pay for the WebTV service, so don't expect to save much money.

WebTV, now MSN TV, offers a mere $10 discount for people who use a different ISP. To save any money you have to find an ISP that costs less than $10 a month. None of the free ISPs currently work with WebTV, nor do AOL or CompuServe. However, most other ISPs do.

To use an alternative ISP with WebTV Classic, select Setup from the home page, click Dialing, and then select Use Your ISP. With WebTV Plus, select Using WebTV from the home page. Then click Dialing and Connecting to get to the Use Your ISP option.

For complete instructions on finding and configuring an alternate ISP visit `www.webtv.com/products/useanisp`.

TUESDAY, AUGUST 27

MAC TIP

If you have Mac OS X, you're probably using the Internet Explorer 5.x that came with it. But there's another browser that's completely Mac OS X-native (written using Cocoa) and even better in many ways than IE. It's called OmniWeb and it's a free download from your iTools disk or from `www.omnigroup.com`.

Not only does OmniWeb do a better job of downloading and unstuffing files (it doesn't mangle them as IE often does), it has a very nice Mac OS X-style bookmark feature, uses the built-in Mac OS X spell checker and keychain facilities for password protected sites, plus support for Java, JavaScript, Flash, secure browsing, and CSS. It also seems to crash much less often.

I have found that some pages don't work quite right with OmniWeb, so I still have to launch IE now and then. But OmniWeb is my workhorse for Mac OS X. It's free to try, $29.95 to buy.

GEEK SPEAK

Multimedia is communication between any combination of two or more media, including the computer, video devices, audio devices, animation, gaming consoles, and so on.

WEDNESDAY, AUGUST 28

WEB TIP

Most people with disabilities can benefit from technology, and this includes the Web. Some of the best places to go are online support groups:

- One of the best sites to address mobility problems is wheelchairjunkie.com, a peer group of enthusiasts with the same fervor as sports car rally drivers, motor-cross enthusiasts, and NASCAR participants.
- Ataxia has its own global online support groups at groups.yahoo.com/groups/internaf and www.internaf.org.
- Another great place that provides useful information to all people with disabilities and their families is HalfthePlanet.com.
- A disabled person can shop online, which extends his or her reach to around the world. You can buy everything from pizza to computers, wheelchair gloves to portable ramps, and personal items to gifts for others.

Web designers would do well to consider the special needs of disabled people when creating Web sites. The Center for Applied Special Technologies, CAST, has a free accessibility tester at www.cast.org/bobby. Does your site pass the test?

THURSDAY, AUGUST 29

WINDOWS TIP

Here's how to choose which program automatically plays your audio CDs when you insert them in your CD-ROM drive:

1. Go to the Start menu, choose Settings, then select Folder Options.
2. Choose the File Type tab and scroll down to Audio CD.
3. Double-click Audio CD. This should open a window called Edit File Type. This is where you change the settings for the default player. You can also use this dialog box to turn CD auto play on or off, and even change the icon.
4. Click Edit. The box with the heading Application Used to Perform Action is your computer's default CD player. You can enter or browse for whichever player you want your computer to run when you pop in a CD (for example, I like to use Winamp, so I would enter C:\PROGRAM FILES\WINAMP\WINAMP.EXE).
5. Close the dialog box, insert a CD, and enjoy.

FRIDAY, AUGUST 30

LAPORTE SUPPORT

Q: In Microsoft Internet Explorer 5, when I delete temporary files (the cache), it also says you can delete all "offline content." What does that mean?

A: Internet Explorer letsyou download the contents of Web pages to your hard drive so that you can browse even when you're not online. This "offline content" can take up considerable space, so when you're done with the data, it makes sense to delete it.

To download Web sites to your hard drive using Internet Explorer for Windows, select Add Favorite from the Favorites menu, then check the Make Available Offline option. With IE5 for the Mac, select Subscribe from the Favorites menu, click the Customize button, select the Offline tab, and then check the Download Site for Offline Browsing option.

One warning here. Offline content also includes any channel data you might have downloaded. If you use Microsoft's Channel Bar, all your channels will disappear after you delete offline content. If you've never heard of Microsoft's Channel Bar, don't worry. It was something Microsoft introduced several years ago that pretty much bombed. It's no longer included with Windows or Internet Explorer.

SATURDAY, AUGUST 31

FOR GEEKS ONLY

If the recent tip on changing your default CD player was too easy, here's another way to do it:

1. Go to the Start menu and select Run. Then type in `regedit` and click OK.
2. Expand the `HKEY_CLASSES_ROOT` key. Scroll down until you get to AudioCD and expand it.
3. Click Shell to expand it. Then click Play to expand it. Click Command.
4. In the right window, right-click Default and select Modify. An Edit String window opens.
5. In the Value Data field, enter the full path to the program you want to use. For example, if I want to use Winamp, I would enter `C:\PROGRAM FILES\WINAMP\WINAMP.EXE`.
6. Exit the Registry. You might need to restart or log out of Windows for the change to take effect.

Why do something the easy way when you can hack the Registry?

TURN YOUR PC INTO A SOUND SYSTEM

By Regina Lynn Preciado and David Spark

Although your Luddite* friends might suggest you hire a live orchestra to entertain you as you pay your bills online, we suggest a less expensive alternative: Use your computer as a sound system.

Volume Control

Before you get started, learn how to adjust your computer's volume.

Many external speakers and audio software programs come with their own volume controls. The speakers often have a regular dial; the software usually includes a slider bar. Still, you should know how to adjust your master system volume.

Windows: Basic Volume Control

1. Look at the row of icons in the lower-right corner of your screen.
2. Click once on the speaker icon to launch a slider volume control.
3. Move your cursor over the slider.
4. Hold the left mouse button down and move it up or down to raise or lower the system volume.

Windows: Fancy Volume Control

1. Look at the row of icons in the lower-right corner of your screen.
2. Double-click the speaker icon.
3. In the new window that appears, move your cursor over the slider under the volume heading.
4. Hold the left mouse button down and move it up or down to raise or lower the system volume.
5. Adjust the other sliders to tweak your wave balance, CD audio balance, and other techie audiophile settings.

Protesters in 19th century England known as Luddites smashed the equipment that was replacing them during the industrial revolution—it has become a generic term for folks who hate technology.

Mac Volume Control

1. Click the Apple icon in the upper-right corner of your screen.

2. Move your cursor down to Control Panels and release the mouse button.

3. Find either the Sound (Mac OS 9) or Monitors & Sound (Mac OS 8.x) control panel and double-click it (move the cursor over the picture or listing and press the mouse button down twice, quickly). (In Mac OS X, open the Sound panel in the System Preferences and adjust the System Volume.)

4. In the Monitors & Sound control panel, click Sound.

5. Adjust the slider to change the volume. Your computer beeps at you every time you adjust the level to demonstrate how loud it is.

Your Computer Is a CD Player

The simplest way to enjoy music through your computer is to pop an audio CD into your CD-ROM drive. Unless you or a friend has changed the default settings of your Windows 98—and if you're a new user, we bet you haven't—that CD automatically starts playing.

If it doesn't play right away, someone might have tweaked your autoplay feature. To check, follow these steps:

1. Move your cursor over the Start button at the lower-left corner of your screen.

2. Press the left mouse button and hold it down.

3. In the menu that appears, move your cursor to Settings.

4. A menu pops up to the side. Slide your cursor to Control Panel and let go of the mouse button.

5. In the new window that appears, double-click the System icon.

6. The System Properties dialog box appears in a new window. See the row of tabs across the top? Click the one called Device Manager.

7. Double-click the CD-ROM drive icon.

8. Double-click the name of your CD-ROM drive (it's probably the only choice there).

9. Now click the Properties button.

10. Click the Settings tab in the new window.

11. Under the Options heading, check or uncheck the box next to Auto Insert Notification to toggle the autoplay feature on or off.

Your Computer Is a Radio

Web radio enables you to listen to all kinds of music and talk from around the world. It's more and more likely that the station you listen to in your car also Webcasts its programming—so the Australians on your instant messenger buddy list can share your commute.

Here's how to find radio on the Web:

- Check out portals such as Broadcast.com (www.broadcast.com), which is like a Yahoo! directory for audio and video, and ComFM (www.comfm.fr/live/radio), which lists thousands of stations in dozens of countries in several languages.
- If your local radio station advertises its Web site, visit it to see if it streams its programming online—that's especially convenient when you're stuck in an office building that jams broadcast signals.
- Use a regular search engine like Google (www.google.com) or Web directory (www.looksmart.com) to find Internet radio stations.
- Browse RealPlayer's station listings using your RealPlayer software.

Most I-radio requires that you have the free RealPlayer software (www.realplayer.com) or Windows Media Player (www.microsoft.com), and you're likely to run across some QuickTime (www.apple.com) audio as well. You can download all of these programs for free from their respective Web sites.

Your Computer Is a Jukebox

If you have an old machine sitting around that has at least a 100MHz processor, 16MB RAM, sound card, and Windows 95/98/NT, you can turn it into your own personal jukebox. (You can do this on your regular machine, too.)

Go through your CDs and pick out the songs you want on your jukebox. Then you have to convert those songs into MP3 format. MP3 songs compress to about 1 megabyte per minute. If you assume that the average song lasts about four minutes, you could conceivably fit about 250 songs on a 1GB hard drive.

The easiest way to create MP3s from audio CDs is to use MusicMatch (www.musicmatch.com). The demo version is limited to converting five songs; the full version costs $29.99, but it's well worth it. With one click, you can convert any audio track into an MP3 file. Typically, this is a two-step process.

You can stop there, but to get the full jukebox experience, go crazy with Winamp and its plug-ins, which you can download at www.winamp.com. After you download each plug-in, copy the files into the Winamp plug-in directory. After they're installed, start Winamp; the program recognizes them. To see all installed plug-ins, right-click the Winamp program, select Options and then Preferences. Tabs for Audio I/O, Visualization, and Misc Plug-Ins appear. All the plug-ins you download can be activated and configured from this area.

Joystick control of Winamp turns your joystick into a remote control for your jukebox. Configure the controller to play, pause, stop, change volume, and skip songs.

Winamp has a feature called Visualization, which creates graphical representations of sound—a must for any video jukebox. There are tons of Visualization plug-ins available, but we chose Prince's 3D OpenGL and Aquamarine 3. Because we couldn't choose between these two, we also installed Visualization Mux—a plug-in that enables you to run multiple visualizations simultaneously. If you're fortunate enough to have a 3D card installed, try Tripex. This 3DFX plug-in dishes up an amazing display. Note: Tripex cannot be used with Visualization Mux.

A lull in the tunes can bring your raging party to a screeching halt. Safeguard yourself with Nullsoft's Crossfading Plug-In. This plug-in starts the next tune as the current one fades out.

Winamp also enables you to add faceplate designs—better known as skins—to Winamp's control panel. Skins are to Winamp what Desktop Themes are to Windows. There are hundreds available, and you can create your own. We chose Cold Fusion 2.02, but you can load tons of them into your skin browser and change them as often as you like.

If your computer speakers aren't up to par, plug the computer into the stereo. Most people need just one magical cable: a stereo 1/8-inch (miniplug) to dual-RCA (phono) cable. Plug the miniplug end into your sound card's line-out port. (You also can plug it into the speaker-out port, but the line out is ideal.) Plug the RCA plugs into your stereo receiver's auxiliary-in ports (or use any other inputs, such as video or tape). Before you turn on the stereo, be sure you have the volume down so the pop sent from your PC won't damage your speakers.

Regina Lynn Preciado and David Sparks both write for TechTV.com.

AH, WILDERNESS

AUGUST

THE "EDUCATIONAL" COMPUTER

It's Back To School time. Time for kids to relearn everything they've spent the last three months forgetting. And parents will, once again, begin to haunt the aisles at Sam's Club looking for computer programs to help Johnny get smarter. But before you pick up the latest version of Merry Marmot's Math Drill and Kill, I'd like to remind you that the lessons kids learn from computers don't all come from educational software titles.

The most important lesson a child can learn is that the PC is fun. Here's why. I divide all computer users into two camps: those who see their digital devices as tools and those who think of them as toys. The tools set uses the computer to get a job done. They see it as a productivity tool and nothing more. They slog away at the keyboard until they've finished their task, and then jump up ready to move on to more entertaining objects, such as the boob tube. The toy folks might use the computer to balance the checkbook, too, but first and foremost they see a computer as a toy, something to have fun with. They enjoy their relationship with the computer.

I believe you end up belonging to one camp or another depending on your first experience with the PC. If you first encountered a computer as a word processor in an office, you're going to be disposed to thinking of it as a tool. On the other hand, if your first experience of the PC was playing a game, listening to music, or surfing the Web, you're more likely to see it as an entertainment device. A toy.

No matter which camp you fall into, I suggest that it's a good idea if your kids think of the computer as a toy, their little plastic pal that's fun to be with, to paraphrase Douglas Adams. Our children are going to be spending a lot of time in front of a computer monitor in their lives. They might as well enjoy it. Plus, to be really proficient with a computer, to really excel as a computer user, you have to like the darn thing. If you see a hammer and saw as tools you'll never be more than a journeyman carpenter. If you see them as pleasurable extensions of your will, you'll be a craftsman, an artist. It's the same with 20th century technologies.

So, before you sit Sally down in front of Mrs. Melmac's Typing Without (much) Pain, let her play a computer game. Let her discover that the computer is fun above all. She'll learn about the drudgery soon enough. And if she really likes the thing, who knows, she might be the next Bill Gates. Now that's a retirement plan!

SUNDAY, SEPTEMBER 1

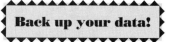

Back up your data!

PROTECT YOURSELF

Most people don't bother to erase their hard drives before selling or recycling their computers. Your hard disk contains a lot of private information, from personal finances to records of what sites you've visited on the Web. It only makes sense to erase it before you pass it on.

In addition, erasing your disk is the ethical thing to do, because most software applications aren't transferable, and giving them to friends or strangers—even when selling those people your computer—can constitute theft.

Dragging these files to the Recycle Bin does not delete them, even if you empty the Recycle Bin later. It merely releases the space the files occupy. All the data is still there. To really erase your private data, format the hard drive. Here's how:

1. Reboot into DOS. You can use your rescue disk to do this.

2. At the command prompt, type FORMAT C:.

3. If you're really ready to delete the disk, acknowledge the warnings and poof, you're data's gone.

Repeat this procedure for all the hard drives in your computer.

Formatting makes the data extremely hard to recover, but if someone is very highly motivated to spy on you, and has the skill and equipment to do so, they can recover data even from a formatted hard drive. The truly paranoid should use an erasing program that uses Department of Defense-approved techniques for overwriting the data. I like the free Eraser for Windows from www.tolvanen.com.

MONDAY, SEPTEMBER 2 (LABOR DAY)

LAPORTE SUPPORT

Q: I downloaded a new version of AOL instant messenger, and now whenever I sign on, it loads this huge window full of ads. How do I turn it off???

A: If you don't want to see AOL's "Today" page—which some people do, because of the local weather forecasts and such—it's easy to turn it off.

1. From your buddy list window, go to the My AIM menu.

2. Select Edit Options.

3. Select Edit Preferences.

4. From the left side of the Preferences screen, click Sign On/Off.

5. Uncheck the box in front of "Show Today window at signon."

6. Click OK.

TUESDAY, SEPTEMBER 3

MAC TIP

How would you like to access your home Mac's hard drive while you're on the road? Sound good? Then follow these instructions to set up remote access in Mac OS 9.

On your home Mac:

1. Open the Remote Access control panel.

2. Choose Answering from the Remote Access menu.

3. In the resulting dialog box, select Answer Calls.

4. Open the File Sharing control panel.

5. Click the Users and Groups tab.

6. Create a user for your own sweet self and click Open.

On your road Mac:

1. Follow the previous instructions.

2. In the pop-up menu, select Remote Access.

3. Click the Allow User to Dial Into This Number option.

VIRUS ALERT

A few viruses to note if you have MS Word 6.x/7.x:

- WM/HELPER.F;G;H
- WM/Eraser.A:Tw

Update your virus definitions and run your antivirus program!

Be sure your computer is secure with an antivirus program. Can't afford one? Visit antivirus.housecall.com for a free online checkup. Or download AVG free from www.grisoft.com. You can't afford *not* to have virus protection.

WEDNESDAY, SEPTEMBER 4

WEB TIP

Many cable TV providers also offer Internet access. Ask your cable company if they offer cable modem access. As with any ISP, the quality of the service depends on the provider, but cable Internet access is, in general, one of the best ways to get online, offering speeds up to 100 times faster than your dial-up modem. On the other hand, there are some negatives you should keep in mind:

- **Limited upload speed**—Most cable connections are limited to 128Kbps upload speed.
- **Expense**—Expect to pay $40 to $60 a month, plus installation.
- **Shared bandwidth**—You and your neighbors share the same cable line. The speed of your connection can go down during peak access times.
- **Potential security problems**—Because you are on a shared network with your neighbors, it's often possible for them to spy on your connection.
- **Read the fine print**—If you run a small business at home, you might not be able to use cable, or you'll pay more. Most providers will not let you run Web sites or other servers on your connection, either.

THURSDAY, SEPTEMBER 5

WINDOWS TIP

For unusual characters, instead of memorizing a long list of Alt number combinations, simply change your language from English-US to United States-International:

1. Open Settings, Control Panel, Keyboard.
2. Choose the Language tab.
3. Press Add.
4. Choose United States-International.
5. Press OK.

You can type in other languages without knowing the Alt codes for a non-English alphabet. For example, type ~ followed by N to get Ñ. An apostrophe followed by any letter will place the appropriate accent on the letter you choose.

FRIDAY, SEPTEMBER 6

LAPORTE SUPPORT

Q: Will we ever run out of available .com domain names? What about .tv, .org, and all that?

A: `allthegoodnamesaretaken.com` (including this one). The Internet is running out of names. Part of the problem is that companies are registering extra names just in case. Proctor and Gamble has registered more than 100 including pimples.com, badbreath.com, and diarrhea.com. I think I'll skip that last site.

That explains some of the strange name choices we're seeing lately. Names like snap-fish.com (free photo processing) and statusfactory.com (Internet bill paying) aren't exactly descriptive.

One solution is to make the names longer. The limit was extended in 2000 from 22 letters to 64. But who wants to type in `www.GrandmaWentToMiamiAndAllIGotIsThisLousy TeeShirt.com`?

Another solution is to add new domains like dot-name, dot-biz, and dot-info. But nothing will have the cachet of the original dot-com.

So we're back to fighting over the few good names left. I checked leo.com, leolaporte.com, and askleo.com—they're all taken. I guess I'll settle for `poorleosalmanac.com`.

SATURDAY, SEPTEMBER 7

FOR GEEKS ONLY

If you want to play old PC games on your hot new Pentium IV, but they run too fast, I recommend a tiny free program called Slowdown (`members.aol.com/bretjohn`). The best way to use slowdown is to create a batch file to run the game. As an example, let's say you want to slow down the computer to 486-33 speed to run `DOSGAME.EXE`. Create a text file named `RUNDOSGAME.BAT` with the following line in it:

```
SLOWDOWN /Q /MHz486:33 DOSGAME
```

Slow it down 50% with this syntax:

```
SLOWDOWN /Q /P:50 DOSGAME
```

If `DOSGAME` has any parameters, you can put them at the end. Make a shortcut to `RUNDOSGAME.BAT` on your desktop and double-click it to run the game from now on. Slowdown turns itself off when you exit the game.

One caution: The batch file `C:WINDOWSDOSSTART.BAT` runs every time you exit to DOS from Windows. If you run Slowdown in it, you'll always slow down when you exit. This may or may not be what you want to do.

Read the Slowdown manual—it's the best source for ways to do this.

SUNDAY, SEPTEMBER 8

Back up your data!

PROTECT YOURSELF

It's a classic scam, the old "bait and switch." You see a fabulous product advertised at an even more fab price. You call, surf, or walk into the store to buy. You're told that the product's out of stock but a more expensive model just happens to be available.

Unless you really think the other product is a bargain, it's best to say, "No thanks." You might be surprised to hear, "What do you know, we just found one of those advertised products in back." In that case, you should still think twice about buying, because the product may be defective. You can also ask for a rain check for the out-of-stock item. No law says a seller must provide one, but some vendors who want your business may make a deal.

Now, here's the modern bait and switch. You see the same tempting offer, and actually buy the product by mail or via the Web. Your credit card may even be charged. Then, a few days later, you get a call back from a company representative who's very sorry, but a mistake has been made. Either the product was mismarked, or the product was out of stock when you bought, or something else seemingly genuine. You're then offered a higher-priced item. Even worse, you could be offered an exchange only (on the item you didn't exactly buy), or charged a restocking fee (on the item you never really sent back), if the vendor doesn't have a money-back plan.

Don't fall for these scams. If you think a merchant is trying to take advantage of you, contact your Better Business Bureau or the consumer protection agency in your state. The Federal Trade Commission consumer protection Web page has valuable advice and a complaint form at www.ftc.gov/ftc/consumer.htm. And for online merchants, contact the Better Business Bureau Online at www.bbbonline.com.

MONDAY, SEPTEMBER 9

TODAY IN COMPUTER HISTORY

Today in 1945, Grace Hopper recorded the first actual computer "bug"—a moth stuck between the relays on the Harvard Mark II.

LAPORTE SUPPORT

Q: I would like to know who created the Internet and who pays for it?

A: The original research was paid for 30 years ago by the U.S. government, but the real credit goes to thousands of volunteer engineers, programmers, and users who have worked on it since then.

The feds stopped funding the Internet in 1995. Since then it's been run entirely as a private enterprise, paid for by people like you and me through our Internet service fees.

If you'd like to learn more about the early days of the Net, visit the Internet Society's home page at www.isoc.org.

TUESDAY, SEPTEMBER 10

MAC TIP

You walk into an office with your iBook. You'd love to open and print a file, but getting on the network is too complicated.

If your computer has a FireWire port, you can connect it to another FireWire-equipped Mac via Target Disk Mode. Your entire computer will show up on the other computer's screen as a hard drive. Then you can open the document on your iBook and print it from the network connected desktop. Here's how:

1. Turn off the target computer (your iBook).

2. Connect the target computer to the host computer (the desktop) with a 6-pin to 6-pin FireWire cable.

3. While holding down the T key, start up the iBook. This puts the system in Target mode.

4. When you see the FireWire icon, let go.

5. Check the host computer for the icon of the target hard drive.

6. You can copy files to the target system's drive, or even boot off of the target's drive.

7. When you're finished, drag the target computer's hard disk icon to the Trash and press the power button on the target computer.

You can purchase the necessary 6-pin to 6-pin FireWire cable at any computer store. Sometimes they're labeled IEEE 1394, which is just another way of saying FireWire. Every Macintosh owner should own one of these handy cables.

GEEK SPEAK

ROM (*read-only memory*)—pronounced rahm—is a computer chip on which data has been prerecorded. Once data has been written onto a ROM chip, it cannot be removed and can only be read.

WEDNESDAY, SEPTEMBER 11

 ## WEB TIP

DSL uses phone lines for a high-speed connection to the Internet. There are several different flavors of DSL, but the most common is asymmetric DSL, known as ADSL. Your phone company will provide the DSL line, but in most areas you have your choice of ISPs. To find out if DSL is available in your neighborhood visit www.dslreports.com.

Pros

- **More flexible options than with cable**—You'll get more options for upload and download speed with DSL if you pay a higher monthly fee.
- **Not a shared line**—The bandwidth to the head end is all yours. This makes your connection to the ISP more secure.

Cons

- **Limited area**—Your home needs to be within 20,000 feet of the phone company's central office. Your phone company might require you to be even closer. The farther you are from the CO, the slower your connect speed. DSL connections are also effected by line quality, older homes and neighborhoods my not receive optimal service.

TODAY IN COMPUTER HISTORY

Last year on this day, the Internet proved a powerful force for good, bringing people together in support and unity when tragedy struck. On this first anniversary of the terrorist attacks on the World Trade Center and the Pentagon, remember those who died with a gift to help the living. Visit www.helping.org for a list of groups that need your help. You can donate money directly from the site or learn about other ways to contribute in your community and beyond.

THURSDAY, SEPTEMBER 12

TODAY IN COMPUTER HISTORY

Today in 1958, Jack Kilby demonstrated the first electronic circuit in which all the components, both active and passive, were fabricated in a single piece of semiconductor material half the size of a paper clip. Kilby is credited, along with Intel founder, Robert Noyce, as the co-inventor of the integrated circuit, the key invention that made the personal computer possible. He won the Nobel Prize in Physics for his discovery in December 2000.

WINDOWS TIP

What if you create a file but can't remember its name or location? For example, you know you created and saved your birthday wish list last Friday, but when you search for file names that contain "birthday" or "list," you can't find the file.

Instead of racking your brain for the filename, try this trick:

1. Open Windows Explorer and press Ctrl+F. (Or select Tools, Find, Files or Folders.)
2. Select the Date tab in the dialog box.
3. Click Find All Files and select either Modified, Created, or Last Accessed.
4. Either select Between for a date range, or specify a number of previous days or months.
5. Select Find Now.

Windows Explorer lists all files or folders created during the time span you specify.

FRIDAY, SEPTEMBER 13

LAPORTE SUPPORT

Q: On AOL, is there any utility for blocking mass mails besides using AOL's mail control?

A: AOL doesn't offer the kind of sophisticated mail filtering you'd need to really stop spam, but you can take some steps.

Most spam comes from the Internet, so use AOL's mail controls to accept mail only from AOL addresses. You can also take it a step further and accept mail only from people you know. That's guaranteed to stop spam, but it also might block some e-mail you'd like to see.

If neither of these solutions is acceptable, you'll have to turn to an outside e-mail service. Most free Web-based e-mail services offer filters that can be used to delete spam before you see it. Some, such as Yahoo! Mail (mail.yahoo.com), automatically send spam to a special folder where you can delete it at your convenience.

SATURDAY, SEPTEMBER 14
FOR GEEKS ONLY

chmod is another innocuous but extremely useful Linux command. What does chmod do? Simply put, chmod allows you to change file permissions. For MS-DOS users, it is many ways similar to the attrib command, except it is much more flexible and powerful.

chmod recognizes four classes of users: user [u], group [g], other [o], and all [a]. These distinctions allow you to tailor permissions without having a blanket effect across the entire system, unless you specify it. With chmod you can either allow [+] or deny [-] the ability to read [r], write [w], or execute [x] a file.

Using chmod

The standard syntax is as follows:

```
chmod [u|g|o|a][+|-][r|w|x] filename
```

- The [u|g|o|a] represent the user specification.
- The [+|-] represents whether you want to allow or deny access.
- The [r|w|x] represent the functions you want to allow or deny.

When you type the command, there is a space between chmod and the commands and a space between the commands and the filename. However, there is *no* space between the commands.

For example, chmod go-rw filename is an example if you what to remove the read and write permissions from the group and other categories.

Absolute Setting

Another way to use chmod is through the absolute setting. The absolute setting replaces the commands [u|g|o|a][+|-][r|w|x] with octal numbers. Octal numbers are a numeric system based on eight (hence the octal). Instead of the [u|g|o|a][+|-][r|w|x] commands, you would use the numbers 0–7 to set permissions.

Here are the absolute settings and their permissions:

Setting	Permission
0	No permission
1	Execute
2	Write only
3	Write and execute
4	Read only
5	Read and execute
6	Read and write
7	Read, write, execute

What about the users, you ask? Instead of number of user types, the absolute setting system uses the octal number placement. For example, the command chmod 012 filename means the following:

- The user has no permissions (0)
- The group has execute permission (1)
- Other has write-only permission (2)

The order is always the same. The first number will always be the user, the second will be the group, and the final number is other. You must list all three numbers when you use absolute setting syntax.

SUNDAY, SEPTEMBER 15

AOL TIP

The Web is a great resource for information. But you might not want your kids to see everything on the Internet. How do you protect them? AOL allows you to set parental controls that limit the access your kids have online.

Here's how to set parental controls in AOL 5.0:

1. Click Parental Controls on the bottom-right side of the Welcome page (or go to Keyword: Parental Controls.)
2. Select Set Parental Controls.
3. At the top of the page, under Edit Controls For, choose the screen name you want to edit. You can set different parental controls for each screen name on your account.

4. At the bottom of the page you can choose a pre-set control based on age: General Access (18+), Mature Teen (16 to 17), Young Teen (13 to 15), or Kid Only (12 and younger).

5. Or you can click on the left side of the page to customize the controls for the following categories: Email, Chat control, IM control, Web control, Additional Master, Download control, Newsgroups, and Premium Services.

With these parental controls, you can do things such as block file attachments (including photos), allow access to kids-only chat rooms, block instant messages, and block explicitly mature Web content.

MONDAY, SEPTEMBER 16

LAPORTE SUPPORT

Q: *Can I connect a second monitor to my iMac to expand my desktop's viewable area? If so, how?*

A: You can connect a second monitor, but it won't increase your desktop real estate.

On most Macs it's possible to use the second monitor as an entirely new desktop. Not so with the iMacs—they can only mirror video. In other words, your external monitor will mirror the contents of the internal screen, no more.

If you still want to do so, it's easy to add a second monitor to the latest iMacs. You'll find a standard video connector on the back of the machine.

The original iMac has an external video port, too, but it's hidden away under the computer. The best way to add a second monitor is to use a $70 attachment called the iPort from Griffin Technology (`www.griffintechnology.com`).

TUESDAY, SEPTEMBER 17

MAC TIP

Did you turn off the "Warn Me If Computer Was Shut Down Improperly" option in your General Controls control panel? If not, the repair window may appear every time you restart your Mac after it crashes. You can get out of this repair window by pressing the Escape key on your Mac's keyboard.

It's hard to tell exactly when to press the Escape key, so try pressing it repeatedly when the repair window first appears. This removes the window as quickly as possible.

Of course, if you have the time, it's best to do the repairs, but banging on the Escape key can be a healthy way to vent frustration with your Mac for crashing in the first place.

GEEK SPEAK

A *byte* is an abbreviation for binary term, a unit of storage capable of holding a single character. On almost all modern computers, a byte is equal to 8 bits. Large amounts of memory are indicated in terms of kilobytes (2^8 or 1,024 bytes), megabytes (1,048,576 bytes), and gigabytes (1,073,741,824 bytes). A floppy disk that can hold 1.44 megabytes, for example, is capable of storing approximately 1.4 million characters, or about 3,000 pages of information.

WEDNESDAY, SEPTEMBER 18

 WEB TIP

Satellite connections used to be expensive and clunky. You needed a modem, as well as the satellite dish for two-way Internet access. But, thanks to clever engineers, two-way satellite service is becoming a viable option.

Pros

- **Competitive Price**—Prices have dropped and the monthly service fees for satellite Internet access are generally competitive with other forms of high-speed access.
- **Availability**—Satellite is a good choice for people who can't get cable modem or DSL access. As long as you've got sky, you can probably use satellite Internet access.

Cons

- Bandwidth is slower than DSL and cable modems. Download speeds top out at 400Kbps. Upload speeds are not much faster than modems. Most services limit the amount of data you can download each month.
- The length of time your data takes to travel to and from the satellite, known as latency, is relatively high. A satellite connection is a bad choice if you like to play high-speed games like Quake III online.

For more information on satellite Internet access, visit www.direcpc.com and www.starband.com.

THURSDAY, SEPTEMBER 19

 WINDOWS TIP

Windows Media Player, which you can download from Microsoft at www.microsoft.com/windows/windowsmedia, offers many integrated features for your listening pleasure.

Not sure what you want to listen to? Click the Media Guide button on the left side of your player. The Media Guide links you to a Web site featuring popular downloads, streaming radio, digital images, and broadband bonuses such as interviews and music videos.

If a CD is inserted into your computer, click the CD Audio button to find a complete listing of every song. Want to know more about the artist? Select Album Profile to find a review of the album and the link to purchase the CD (if you're only borrowing the one in your computer). If you like what you hear, select Artist Search for a complete Internet search on the artist.

If that's not enough, you can choose to copy the CD you own onto your hard drive. Simply select Copy. The song is filed into your player's Media Library.

FRIDAY, SEPTEMBER 20

LAPORTE SUPPORT

Q: Is it possible to compress pictures for an e-mail message? My photos take ages to send.

A: The best way to e-mail photos is to save them in a compressed format called JPEG. (The acronym stands for Joint Photographic Experts Group, a committee of leading computer hardware and software companies.) JPEG files can be squeezed to as little as one-tenth the size of the uncompressed original with very little noticeable loss of quality.

Nearly all graphics programs will save files in the JPEG format. If yours doesn't you can download a file converter to get the job done. For Windows machines I recommend the free PicViewer Lite from Andrew Anoshkin. Get a copy from `www.anixsoft.com`. Mac users can download Thorsten Lemke's Graphics Converter from `www.lemkesoft.com`. The shareware fee is $35 but you can try before you buy.

When you save files in the JPEG format you can choose to trade image quality for file size. Choosing an image quality of 50 to 70 percent should give you a great looking image that's much smaller than the original.

SATURDAY, SEPTEMBER 21

FOR GEEKS ONLY

You've got great looking graphics and stellar content on your Web site. Now you can add sound.

We don't recommend holding your viewers hostage by forcing them to listen to a loop of music while viewing your site, but sound, when tastefully done, can add to the experience.

Many people let users click a link to hear the music. The link looks like this:

```
<a href="http://www.leoville.com/sounds/okbyebye.wav">
```

You also can embed sound into your Web page. It's possible to force visitors to automatically hear a sound as the page loads, but it's better to give them the choice to activate the sound file.

To embed a sound in your Web page, use the `embed` tag:

```
<embed src="nameoffile" type="audio/wav" autostart="false" loop=false></embed>
```

The parts break down as follows:

- **Embed src="nameoffile"**—This is the sound file embedded.
- **Type="filetype"**—This adds the file type. For example, audio/wav.
- **Autostart="false"**—This tells the browser to play the sound file when activated.
- **Loop="false"**—This instructs the browser to play the sound only once. You can tell the sound to keep repeating by adding Loop=true, but unless you want to drive your users crazy, I don't recommend it.

You should always add a console to give your users control to start or pause sounds:

```
<embed src="nameoffile" height="150" width="15" align="bottom" autostart="true"
➥controls="console"></embed>
```

Here's how the console tag breaks down:

- **Embed src="nameoffile"**—This brings the proper sound file up.
- **Height & width**—This determines the size of the console in pixels.
- **Align="bottom"**—The align tag determines the position of the console on the page.
- **Autostart="false"**—Make this true if you're set on forcing people to listen.
- **Controls="console"**—This displays the console.

An even more flexible way to add sound to Web pages is with Beatnik. Beatnik-enabled pages can sound really great, but because most browsers don't support the Beatnik format, users will have to download a plug-in the first time they visit a page using the technology. Read more about it at www.beatnik.com.

SUNDAY, SEPTEMBER 22

 AOL TIP

If you've recently visited a Web site, but can't remember the Web address or URL, AOL can help you access it quickly. The AOL browser stores URLs for Web sites you've visited.

In the center of your toolbar where you enter the Web address, there's a drop-down menu on the right side (look for the down arrow). In AOL 5.0 the drop-down menu is on the left side. Click on that and you'll see all the addresses listed. Click on an address and it will take you to that site.

If your list is getting too cluttered, you might want to clear it and start over. Here's how:

1. Click My AOL in your toolbar.
2. Scroll down to Preferences.
3. Click Toolbar.
4. Click Clear History Now.

MONDAY, SEPTEMBER 23

LAPORTE SUPPORT

Q: When I click Start, Programs, I get one continuous list of programs. I have to scroll down to get to the bottom. How can I get multiple columns so programs are listed across the desktop? I have seen this on other computers.

A: If your Start Menu has too many entries to fit onto the screen, Windows has to find some way to rearrange the items so you can get at them all. In Windows 95 the Start Menu stacked the extra entries into columns. But Microsoft changed the behavior of the Start Menu in Windows 98, giving users a scrolling list with arrows at the top and bottom.

A lot of people hate that scrolling list. So many so that Microsoft now gives Windows ME, 2000, and XP users the chance to turn it off. Go to the Settings entry in the Start Menu, select Taskbar & Start Menu, press the Advanced button and uncheck Scroll the Programs Menu.

For those of us still using Windows 98, help is on the way. Get yourself a copy of Xteq's X-Setup, a truly useful free utility that can change a great many Windows settings, including this one. You'll find it at www.xteq.com.

After you install X-Setup, run it, open the Appearance, Start Menu, Options folder and click Display Options. Check the box reading Show Start->Programs Using Multiple Columns and your old school Start Menu columns will make their triumphant return.

TUESDAY, SEPTEMBER 24

MAC TIP

To start your Mac up from a CD, find the Restore or Install CD that came with your computer. Restart holding down the C key. This tells the system to boot off of the CD.

If this fixes the problem, you might have a corrupt system on your hard drive. You'll need to reinstall the system—luckily, you can run the installer from the Install CD you just booted off.

GEEK SPEAK

An *OS (operating system)* is the most important program that runs on a computer. Every general-purpose computer must have an operating system to run other programs. Operating systems perform basic tasks, such as recognizing input from the keyboard, sending output to the display screen, keeping track of files and directories on the disk, and controlling peripheral devices such as disk drives and printers. Windows, Mac OS, Linux, Unix, and DOS are examples of popular OSes.

WEDNESDAY, SEPTEMBER 25

WEB TIP

Have you ever filled out a form online? Usually, you start by entering your first name in one box. Move your cursor to the second box to enter your last name. This continues through the entire form. If you use your mouse to navigate online forms, try something faster.

Use your Tab key to move from box to box to fill out an online form quickly. If you need to move backwards through the form, use Tab+Shift.

THURSDAY, SEPTEMBER 26

WINDOWS TIP

Most of you know that you can close the active window with the keystrokes Alt+F4. But don't forget the desktop is also a window. Use this quick desktop shutdown:

1. Click anywhere on the desktop to make sure no icons are selected.
2. Press Alt+F4.
3. Release both.
4. When the shutdown dialog box pops up, press Enter.

The option used to close down last time will be selected. If you don't see Shutdown in the drop-down box, press the S key to select it, and *then* press Enter.

FRIDAY, SEPTEMBER 27

LAPORTE SUPPORT

Q: *You recommend ZoneAlarm a lot, but I've heard that it can mess up your computer. Is this true?*

A: I've heard from a few readers who have had problems with my favorite firewall software, ZoneAlarm. Most of these issues can be solved with a visit to ZoneAlarm's support site, `www.zonelabs.com/support.htm`. Some require more serious intervention, like uninstalling ZoneAlarm, and in a few extreme cases, reinstalling Windows.

I've had extensive experience with ZoneAlarm and I'm confident that it's safe and reliable. Millions of people use it without any difficulty at all. Nevertheless, any time you install a new program on your computer you're running a risk. Sometimes a normally well-behaved application can totally muck things up. This is especially true of software that works deep within your operating system.

So before you install ZoneAlarm, or any program, back up your hard drive. Make a note of your network settings. Follow the installation instructions carefully. And if you encounter problems, visit the ZoneLabs Web site for help.

I think the security ZoneAlarm provides is well worth the risk, but that's a decision each user has to make for him or herself.

SATURDAY, SEPTEMBER 28

FOR GEEKS ONLY

You can remove a renegade Add/Remove entry by modifying the System Registry using a program that comes with Windows called REGEDIT:

1. Go to the Start menu.
2. Select Run.
3. Type REGEDIT and click OK.
4. Find the rogue program's name under
   HKEY_LOCAL_MACHINE\SOFTWARE\Microsoft\Windows\CurrentVersion\Uninstall.
5. After you find the obsolete entry, delete it and the reference will be cleared from the Add/Remove Programs control panel.

SUNDAY, SEPTEMBER 29

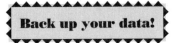

Back up your data!

PROTECT YOURSELF

Don't expect to retrieve an e-mail after you've hit Send. It's just not possible—unless both you and the recipient are on AOL. Then you can unsend, because the e-mail never leaves the AOL server.

Most e-mails are sent between server domains, so most e-mails can't be unsent, any more than you can unsend a letter once you put it in the mail box. Follow this list of rules to help you compose e-mails you won't want to recall.

Top Ten E-mail Rules

1. Don't automatically reply to all.
2. Don't hit Reply instead of Forward.
3. Don't send until you spell-check the entire document.
4. Don't use work e-mail for personal matters.
5. Don't say anything in an e-mail you wouldn't say in person.
6. Don't use all caps.
7. Don't send large attachments.

8. Don't use the CC: field with mass e-mails (use the BCC: field instead).

9. Don't send e-mail if you're angry. Wait. Reread, then send. Or not.

10. Don't pretend that you haven't received an e-mail when you have.

Learn it. Live it. Love it. Why? Because this list might be your only salvation until some genius engineer figures out a way to unsend e-mail.

MONDAY, SEPTEMBER 30

LAPORTE SUPPORT

Q: When recording an LP to a CD I got an error message that reads I/O Error Buffer Underrun. *This canceled the recording. What is a buffer underrun and how can I prevent it from happening again?*

A: When you're burning a disc, the CD recorder must receive a constant flow of data from the source device, typically a hard drive or CD player, but in this case a record player. If the flow of data is interrupted, the disc continues to spin but the drive's writing laser won't have any information to burn onto it. When this happens, the writing process is halted and you end up with a useless CD. This is known as a *buffer underrun*.

Here are the top five ways to prevent buffer underruns.

Close All Apps

During a writing session the only application you should have open is the recording software. Don't do anything else on your computer. The CD writer needs every bit of RAM and CPU power it can get and the hard disk itself should be concentrating exclusively on getting data over to the CD writer.

Don't forget to disable screen savers that could pop up in the middle of a recording session. Background programs such as antivirus and crash-guard software might also activate themselves during a session and wreak havoc.

Defrag Your Hard Drive

When you write data to your hard drive it doesn't land in sequential strips as you might think. Rather, bits and pieces of a whole get written wherever there's space, meaning your song may be fragmented all over the hard drive.

Defragging puts things in logical order and will help the flow of data traveling from the hard disk to the CD move along without interruption. You should defrag about once a week.

Record at a Slower Speed

Recording at high speeds—such as 8X—will empty your buffer faster, increasing the likelihood of a buffer underrun. It's annoying, but recording at 1X or 2X is more reliable.

This is especially true when recording music. (Strangely, few people report greater reliability when recording at higher speeds.)

Take It from the Hard Drive

If buffer underruns get you down, use your hard drive as your sole source device. Only use the record player, the tape deck, or the CD player to transfer data to the hard drive as a virtual image.

Also, be sure your hard drive transfers data quickly. Hard drives that are over 5 or 6 years old use thermal recalibration, meaning they stop mid-task for about a second and a half. That's enough time to cause a buffer underrun to cool down. Today's A/V hard drives take care of this when the hard drive is inactive. Finally, don't write from a hard drive that uses disk compression.

Stay Clean

When recording from a CD player, make sure your source CD, the destination CD, and the recorder itself are clean and dust-free.

Buffer underruns have been virtually eliminated in newer CD recorders using technologies like BURN-Proof and Safe Burn. These techniques allow the laser to stop recording when the flow of data stops, and then resume recording later. If you're buying a new CD recorder be sure it supports one of these technologies. For more information visit www.burnproof.com.

This Month's Feature

TAKE THE SUPERGEEK CHALLENGE: GEEK CULTURE

By Mike Street

"Welcome to Contemporary North American Sociology 104. I'm Professor Natter. If you're not here for Contemporary North American Sociology 104, please leave now. Everyone else, please take a paper handout.

Today's lecture is on geek culture, a fascinating subset of the larger North American upper socioeconomic blah blah blah…"

Do you know the real specs of geek culture? These 10 questions test how well you speak geek chic. Grab a pencil, circle your choice, and play fair—don't look at the answers 'til the end.

The Questions

1. What's geekier than an emoticon?

    A. AOL sound effects

    B. An ad banner

    C. HTML tags

    D. Paper handouts

2. Two bad spellers are chatting about each other's mothers. They repeat their comments over and over, until everyone else in the chatroom sets them to "ignore." This common Internet phenomenon is called a _____.

    A. Heated discussion

    B. Flame war

    C. Chatting primate insurrection

    D. Devolution of the human species

3. What's a general rule for setting up a game server at a LAN party?

    A. Hosts supplies games

    B. Allow 8MHz per player

    C. Leave your Cheetos at home

    D. Don't let Thresh play

4. Which of these is a valid e-mail address?

    A. streetmg@SPAMOFFhotmail.com

    B. streetmg@TIMESLIKETHISIHATESPAMhotmail.com

    C. streetmg@hotmail.com

    D. streetmg@FIRSTWASAPPREHENSIVEBUTLATERWASSPAMFREEhotmail.com

5. Which of these is slang for keywords embedded in a Web page?

    A. Hidey things

    B. Spider food

    C. Tags

    D. Save gems

6. What program helped a Norwegian group write DeCSS?

    A. Visual Basic

    B. Xing DVD

    C. PowerDVD

    D. 3l33t h@X0r tulez

7. Which of these isn't in the Screen Savers Geek Library?

   A. 1984

   B. Wargames

   C. The Curse of Monkey Island

   D. Waiting For Godot

8. Which of these received an honorable mention in Slashdot's Top 10 Hacks of All Time?

   A. Orson Welles' "War of the Worlds" broadcast

   B. Mars Pathfinder

   C. The Great Pyramids in Egypt

   D. SR-71 Blackbird

9. Which bug came first?

   A. A beetle

   B. An industrial defect

   C. A moth in the Mark II Aiken Relay Calculator

   D. Noise on a telephone line

10. Yo, d00d. R U 3l33t?

   A. Pfft... who cares?

   B. I think I'm 3l33t.

   C. I know I'm 3l33t.

   D. I OWN JOO!!!

The Answers

1. What's geekier than an emoticon?

   Answer: (C) HTML tags

<geek history>Long ago, geeks started using emoticons to express emotion. <sarcasm> This was before chat programs automatically changed ASCII emoticons into graphic yellow smiley guys. </sarcasm> </geek history> <bug report> Emoticons aren't standardized, and this can lead to interpersonal misinterpretation. </bug report>

<fix> Today, some geeks set their emoticons aside and replace them with standardized HTML tags. </fix> <example> This is an example. </example> <sensei> An HTML tag is more descriptive than an emoticon, and reflects the true sentiment of your tag-enclosed text. </sensei> <surfer d00d> Like, can you totally imagine what a sensei emoticon looks like? </surfer d00d>

2. Two bad spellers are chatting about each other's mothers. They repeat their comments over and over, until everyone else in the chatroom sets them to "ignore." This common Internet phenomenon is called a _____.

Answer: (B) Flame war

SMITH: "Hello, we'd like to have a flame war, please."

JONES: "Ah yes, a very good choice. It's an excellent year for flame wars."

SMITH: "Can we do it without a computer?"

JONES: "Technically, no, but let's simulate a flame war. First, take a page of insults and sit on opposite sides of the room. Yes, good, now start shouting those capitalized phrases at each other. Oh, don't worry, all of these other people will eventually ignore you."

SMITH: "Okay, here goes nothing... Molly wunker!"

JONES: "Dole bludger! These aren't very nice phrases."

SMITH: "Yes, but you're not very nice people, are you? You barge in here, barking out orders, shouting insults, throwing your Caps-Lock key around like you own the place, drowning out intelligent conversation, drawing nice people into mean chat, proving your predisposition for repetition—it's really a wonder someone doesn't report you to your ISP."

And now for something completely different… (giant foot squishes the flame war sketch)

3. What's a general rule for setting up a game server at a LAN party?

Answer: (B) Allow 8MHz per player

Let's sit up, pay attention, and listen to the prof guy:

"Today we'll discuss the most hallowed geek ritual, a LAN party. Gamers often travel hundreds of miles to attend a LAN party, and pack their PCs, games, food, drinks, and every other geek amenity that fits in a Pinto.

"LAN parties are intense gladiatorial competitions, and rivals fight inside games they play on networked computers. These rivalries can erupt into physical Snaki-cake exchanges, but most participants we surveyed said LAN parties are quite fun. Which is why they're called parties, I suppose."

Wow. Wake me up when he tries to explain a dedicated game server. I'll ask him why a game server is dedicated (it only has to compute game details), why a server is needed (large multiplayer games require more computational power), and the recommended speed of a dedicated server (about 8MHz per connected player). That should keep him busy.

4. Which of these is a valid e-mail address?

   Answer: (C) streetmg@hotmail.com

Geeks don't like spam. Some geeks put phony uppercase text in their e-mail addresses as an extra cushion against spam. The uppercase text confuses spamming programs, but still lets actual people know your true e-mail address.

This is a relatively new phenomenon, and this phony uppercase e-mail text needs a name. I think we should call it "spam jelly."

5. Which of these is slang for keywords embedded in a Web page?

   Answer: (B) Spider food

Some people will do anything to show up in a search engine. They line their pages with spider food (slang for hidden keywords) to attract search engine spiders. Spider food usually is invisible, but you can sometimes see it by highlighting an entire Web page or by looking at the page's source text.

<yoda> Spider food leads to poor spider searches, low productivity from poor searches, much time will you seek and find only spider food sustenance. </yoda>

6. What program helped a Norwegian group write DeCSS?

   Answer: (B) Xing DVD

DVD uses the Content Scrambling System (CSS), which encrypts a DVD's video and audio with a 5-byte (40-bit) key. All hardware and software DVD players need a decryption key to play a DVD. Originally reverse engineered from a Xing DVD player application, DeCSS decrypts DVD video and audio, and allows you to copy a decrypted DVD to your hard drive.

<legal stuff> DVD piracy is bad, so don't use DeCSS to illegally copy a decrypted DVD to your hard drive. </legal stuff> <reality> DeCSS has legitimate applications. If you want to find the outlawed program, do a quick Google search (www.google.com). Don't try too hard. </reality>

7. Which of these isn't in the Screen Savers Geek Library?

   Answer: (D) Waiting For Godot

The Geek Library is your definitive guide to geeky books, movies, and games at www.thescreensavers.com. Every geek should browse the contents of the Geek Library and dip into the storied history of geek. These aren't boring manuals. Geeks refer to these media objects in everyday language, and can help you identify with geek culture. <1984> If you don't understand this reference, please report to room 101. </1984>

8. Which of these received an honorable mention in Slashdot's Top 10 Hacks of All Time?

    Answer: (c) The Great Pyramids in Egypt

Put simply, a hack is a cool piece of engineering that expands the ways something is used. Orson Welles' "War of the Worlds" broadcast expanded the influence of mass media. The SR-71 Blackbird is faster than any other jet plane. Mars Pathfinder was a very cool beach ball. Each of these is a monumental hack and truly deserves a place in Slashdot's Top 10 Hacks of All Time (www.slashdot.org). The Great Pyramids in Egypt only received an honorable mention, probably because the Khufu transmitter hasn't operated properly in thousands of years.

9. Which bug came first?

    Answer: (A) A beetle

Bugs are insects, and are good for swatting, slapping, shooing, and metaphorically describing electrical problems. Hawkin's New Catechism of Electricity (1896) describes a bug as "any fault or trouble in the connections or working of electric apparatus." After telephone lines were laid, people complained about bugs in noisy telephone cables. The first computer bug was a moth in the Mark II Aiken Relay Calculator (1945). Since then, the terms "bug" and "debug" have become part of geek language.

10. Yo, d00d. R U 3l33t?

    Answer: All correct

Internet language and geek culture evolve constantly. An "3l33t d00d" means many different things to different geeks, but most can agree on one point: It means "elite dude" in decrypted English.

HOW DID YOU DO?

1 to 3 correct answers: Good start. Betcha you now know more about geek culture than you ever wanted to. But if you're hooked, tune into TechTV to stay abreast of the latest in all things geek.

4 to 7 correct answers: If you've watched TechTV for a while, you probably fall into this category, and your friends call on you to solve their computer problems.

8 to 10 correct answers: You are the true 3l33t of geek culture! It takes a certain kind of person to ace a Supergeek Challenge like this.

TechTV writer Mike Street grows geek culture in his cool home box.

LEO'S ESSAY

BEWARE GEEKS BEARING GIFTS

These days, we all know one or two true geeks, some guy or gal who lives for computers. A person who would contentedly spend a sunny day huddled in the basement soldering printer cables. It might be the 14-year-old down the street or a member of your Bridge Club. It might even be, heaven help you, a member of your own family. Whatever you do, do not—I repeat do not—let this person anywhere near your computer.

Most geeks know just enough about computers to be dangerous. Ask them a seemingly harmless question like, "How can I rename my Recycle Bin?" and watch out. Two hours later your entire computer will be reformatted, you'll have no idea where your precious documents are hidden, and in all likelihood, your Recycle Bin will have disappeared completely. At that point, the true geek will rise from your computer with a beatific smile, say "Well that just about does it," and return to his basement lair where some cables urgently require soldering, leaving you alone amid the rubble that once was your PC.

Every geek has strong preferences about how a computer should be configured. The problem is that no two geeks can agree on this. And they almost certainly have nothing but disdain for how you've arranged things. The minute they see your desktop they're bound to sniff like an English butler and begin remodeling. In the aftermath of this whirlwind nothing will ever work right again. And the geek will be long gone. I know all this because I am one of them.

Yes, I admit it. I have a drawer full of cables, wires, and assorted computer bits that have no discernable use. My system tray is filled with icons from programs that are supposed to improve performance but do nothing but fight like cats in a sack. I have even soldered a cable or two in my time. And I've messed up more computers than I care to mention. You would be nuts to let me in the same room with your computer.

Your only defense against geeks like me is to learn how to do things for yourself. Become a computer expert. It's easier than you think. And the first step is to start playing with the thing. After you've renamed your Recycle Bin, everything else is a piece of cake. The truth is, it's not hard at all. We geeks just want you to think it's hard so you'll still need us. But with a little work, you can be one of us, and you can start messing up other people's computers. When you're ready, let me know. I have some extra cables and a soldering iron you can buy cheap.

TUESDAY, OCTOBER 1

MAC TIP

Does your iMac or Power Mac G4 slow down when the mouse isn't moving? If so, Apple suggests you turn off the Allow Processor Cycling option in the Energy Saver control panel:

1. Open the Energy Saver control panel.
2. Click the Advanced Settings button.
3. Uncheck Allow Processor Cycling.
4. Close the control panel.

Processor Cycling is designed to save power by slowing down your computer when it's not in use. But on some systems the CPU slowdown can occur at inopportune times. On those systems it's best to disable cycling entirely.

GEEK SPEAK

MP3 is the file extension for MP3 audio files. MP3 is short for the audio compression technology used in the MPEG-1 video specification, sometimes known as MPEG-1 layer 3. (Now you know why everyone just calls it MP3.)

MP3 compression can turn one minute of CD quality music into about a megabyte of data, small enough to store on a computer and transfer over the Internet. And thus are revolutions born.

WEDNESDAY, OCTOBER 2

WEB TIP

Translations of common acronyms used in chat rooms on the Web:

Acronym	Translation
Addy	Address
AFAIK	As far as I know
AFK	Away from keyboard
ATM	At the moment
BRB	Be right back
BTW	By the way
DCC	Direct client-to-client
EG	Evil grin
G	Grin
IMO	In my opinion
IRL	In real life

Acronym	Translation
J/K	Just kidding
L	Laugh
LOL	Laugh out loud
ROTFL	Rolling on the floor laughing
S	Smile
WEG	Wicked evil grin

THURSDAY, OCTOBER 3

WINDOWS TIP

On today's giant monitors it's common to see screen resolutions of 1024×768, 1280×1024, and even 1600×1200. All that extra screen real estate is great, but there is a drawback. Icons and text can shrink to illegible size, especially for older eyes. But you can make your screen more readable at higher resolutions with these tricks:

- Open the Display control panel, click the Appearance tab, and choose one of the Appearance schemes with (large) or (extra large) in the name.
- Open the Display control panel, click the Effects tab, and check Use Large Icons.
- Increase the Zoom factor in your applications. In Microsoft Word, for example, select Zoom from the View menu and choose a higher magnification factor.
- In Internet Explorer, choose a bigger font by clicking the View menu, selecting Text Size, and picking Larger or Largest.

Eye doctors also recommend using reading glasses with a slight magnification, +1 say, if your eyes bug you after a long session in front of the computer. And don't forget to blink frequently and take breaks every few minutes.

FRIDAY, OCTOBER 4

LAPORTE SUPPORT

Q: *In the old days, I paid a lot of attention to* AUTOEXEC.BAT *and* CONFIG.SYS. *Do these files still matter with Windows 9.x?*

A: Probably not. You're seeing the vestigial remains of ancient operating systems, the computing equivalent of fossil bones. AUTOEXEC.BAT and CONFIG.SYS are configuration files used by DOS, the operating system that predates Windows. They're still around to preserve compatibility with older programs.

If all you use is Windows 95/98/Me and all your hardware is supported with drivers for your version of Windows, you don't need those old DOS files at all. If you use hardware that uses real- or DOS-mode drivers, you will need CONFIG.SYS to load them. Both Windows 95 and Windows 98 include a blank CONFIG.SYS file on installation for this purpose. You will also find a blank AUTOEXEC.BAT, unless an installed application expects a command to be present there.

Two other OS bones you might notice lying around are `C:\WINDOWS\WIN.INI` and `C:\WINDOWS\SYSTEM.INI`. These files were used by Windows 3.1 to store settings, but they've been mostly replaced by the Windows Registry. Microsoft keeps them around for compatibility's sake, as well.

SATURDAY, OCTOBER 5

FOR GEEKS ONLY

Have you recently made the switch to Windows 2000, only to find that you can no longer run a favorite application? Many games and applications, such as specialized accounting software, will not run in Windows 2000.

The Windows 2000 registry has stricter registry permission levels than other versions of Windows. Because of this, applications requiring Windows NT or Windows 9.x may not be able to access these restricted levels.

Don't fret. The solution may be an executable file called `apcompat.exe`. `Apcompat.exe` is the Application Compatibility Tool for Windows 2000. Its function is to trick your application into thinking that it is running under an operating system different from Windows 2000. This is especially useful for those programs that give an error message stating that the application is not accessible by Windows 2000. It doesn't work on every application, but it works more often than not.

`Apcompat.exe` can be found on the Windows 2000 CD in the Support folder. (If you don't see it there, check the Tools folder under Support.) Drag this file to your desktop and then double-click the icon. This will bring up the Application Compatibility dialog box.

Once you have the Application Compatibility dialog box open, enter the path of the program you want to test. In the Operating System section, choose the operating system that you would like to trick the program into using. Under the Operating System option are four boxes that can be checked or left unchecked. The following is a description of those options.

Disable Heap Manager on Windows 2000

Compared to earlier Windows versions, Windows 2000 has more varied and complicated ways to manage memory. If you experience memory errors that did not occur in previous Windows operating systems, try disabling the heap manager.

Use Pre-Windows 2000 Temp Path

A few programs limit the number of characters used to store the name and path of the Temp Folder. The location of the Windows 2000 Temp Folder may exceed this limit. If this is the case in your application, check this box.

Correct Disk Space Detection for 2GB+ Drives

If a program uses an unsupported data type to query and read the amount of free disk space in Windows 2000, you may want to check this option. The data types are dependent on the programming language used to code the program. However, the process for detecting available disk space is the same.

Make the Previous Check Box Settings Permanent

If checking the previous options worked for your program, you can check this box to make these settings permanent for this program. It will make the necessary registry entries, and this entire Application Compatibility process will automatically run every time you open this program.

Apcompat.exe only works for a small percentage of incompatible applications, but it's worth a try.

SUNDAY, OCTOBER 6

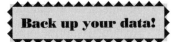

Back up your data!

PROTECT YOURSELF

There's one computer security rule that's more important than all the others. One rule you must never violate. One rule that I want you to etch into your brain. That rule? **Don't open e-mail attachments**. Never. Ever. *Especially* if they come from someone you know. E-mail attachments are the primary way computer viruses spread these days, and they almost always come from friends, family, and co-workers.

When I tell people that attachments are bad medicine, they often ask, but how can I get my job done without them? How am I going to see the latest pictures of my grandchildren? What if Anna Kournikova really does like me?

You can get by pretty well without sending or receiving attachments. Honest. Instead of sending word processing documents, place the text in the body of the message. If you need to preserve formatting use a format that can't spread viruses like Rich Text Format (RTF). All word processors support RTF as a secondary format.

If you want to exchange pictures, put them up on the web instead. Companies like Ofoto (www.ofoto.com) and Yahoo! Photos (photos.yahoo.com) allow you to post pictures and share them with friends for free. If you want to send along the latest joke program, send a link to it on the Web instead.

Your friends will appreciate your concern for their security. And you won't be filling their inboxes or clogging the Internet by e-mailing giant files. When you really must send or receive an attachment, schedule the exchange with your correspondent ahead of time.

You can load up your machine with all the antivirus and firewall software in the world, but they won't do any good if you open your system wide open by opening attachments. So just don't do it. You'll thank me later.

MONDAY, OCTOBER 7

LAPORTE SUPPORT

Q: I am interested in learning how to program. What's the best language for a beginner?

A: Computer programming is a wonderful hobby for all ages. And it can be a very lucrative profession, too. Just ask Bill Gates.

I, like many people, started programming with BASIC. In fact, BASIC was invented for beginners. That's what it stands for: Beginners' All-Purpose Symbolic Instruction Code. Microsoft's Visual Basic for Windows (www.microsoft.com/vbasic) and REALBasic for Macintosh (www.realbasic.com) are powerful, modern languages that are great for learning.

If you plan on pursuing a career as a programmer, you'll need to learn C eventually. C and its big brother C++ are the languages most software is written in today. C is surprisingly easy to learn. I suggest starting by reading *The C Programming Language* by Brian Kernighan and Dennis Ritchie. C compilers on Windows can be expensive, but all versions of Linux come with free C and C++ compilers.

Web programming is almost always done in a language called Perl. It's a really fun language that's designed for ease of use, but it can also be incredibly cryptic. You can get a free copy of Perl for any OS from www.cpan.org.

My new favorite language for learning to program is Python (www.python.org). I like it for several reasons. It's free and available for every kind of computer. It's powerful but easy to learn. There's lots of online documentation available. And Python teaches good programming habits.

If you enjoy using your computer, and you'd like to get deeper into the guts of the system, get programming. It's one of the most satisfying pastimes around.

TUESDAY, OCTOBER 8

MAC TIP

Even if you don't own a video camera, you can still use iMovie, Apple's video editing application (www.apple.com/imovie). You can convert any movie file into a digital video (DV) stream using QuickTime Pro, $30 from Apple (www.apple.com/quicktime, of course) and then edit that stream with iMovie. Here's how.

Launch iMovie and create a new project. Starting a project creates a folder named "media folder" inside the project folder.

Open your video files in QuickTime Pro, and then Save As Digital Video into the media folder. The next time you open your project in iMovie it will ask you if you want to import the new video files. Say yes and you're ready to edit away.

VIRUS ALERT

The WM/KOMPU.A virus, which affects MS Word 6.x, 7.x, and 97, is expected to be active today. Be sure you have updated your virus definitions.

WEDNESDAY, OCTOBER 9

 ## WEB TIP

If you use Internet Explorer or Netscape Navigator and want to save a Web page so you can look at it later, follow these steps:

1. On the File menu, click Save As.
2. Double-click the folder where you want to save the page.
3. In the File Name box, type a name for the page.
4. In the Save As type box, select a file type.

If you're using Netscape Navigator, click Save. If you're using IE, do one of the following before you click Save:

- Click Web Page, Complete to save all the files needed to display this page, including graphics, frames, and style sheets. This option saves each file in its original format.
- Click Web Archive, Single File to save the entire page, graphics and all, as a single archive file. This is usually the most convenient way to store a page, but you'll have to use Internet Explorer to re-open the archive.
- To save just the current HTML page, click Web page, HTML only. This option saves the information on the Web page, but it does not save the graphics, sounds, or other files.
- To save just the text from the current Web page, click Text File. This option saves the information on the Web page in plain text format. No layouts, graphics, or other non-text elements are preserved.

THURSDAY, OCTOBER 10

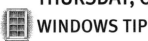

WINDOWS TIP

Web browsers speed up browsing by saving the contents of Web pages locally on your hard drive. If you return to a page that hasn't changed since you last saw it, the browser can load the page from disk, which is much faster than retrieving it from the Internet. This is called *caching* the page. Internet Explorer stores those cached pages in a special folder called Temporary Internet Files, which usually is located in the Windows folder.

This folder can get quite large. It's a good idea to limit how much of your hard drive Internet Explorer can use for its cache.

1. Open Internet Explorer.

2. Mouse over Tools and select Internet Options.

3. In Internet Options select the General tab.

4. In the middle of the General tab is the Temporary Internet Files section. Click the Settings button.

5. On the pop-up window that appears, checkmark the Every Visit to the Page option under Check for Newer Versions of Stored Pages. This will insure updated Web pages always get displayed in your browser.

6. In the Temporary Internet Files Folder field under Amount of Disk Space to Use, set the size to a suitable number based on the amount of hard drive space available. If you have a small hard drive, you'll probably want to make it 10MB or less. It need never exceed 100MB.

7. When you're finished making changes, select OK.

8. Then select OK in the Internet Options dialog box.

FRIDAY, OCTOBER 11

LAPORTE SUPPORT

Q: What's the best digital video camera? I do a lot of presentations.

A: Check for the following before purchasing a digital video camera:

- Look for image stabilization. Optical stabilization is better than digital.
- The power of zoom: If zoom is important to you, go for a camera with a high *optical* zoom. Ignore the inflated digital zoom numbers. Digital zoom looks terrible.
- Lens quality.
- Special effects and editing features you can perform on the camera.

I like Canon and Sony cameras. Canon has a large line of cameras for everyone from the pro (we use Canon cameras in the studio) to the amateur. Some Canon cameras to look at include the Canon ZR-10, and the Canon Optura Pi.

SATURDAY, OCTOBER 12 (COLUMBUS DAY)

FOR GEEKS ONLY

Have you ever considered overclocking? That's running a processor at a faster speed than the manufacturer has rated it for. You can overclock CPUs, video cards, even PDAs.

With processor speeds increasing rapidly and prices dropping nearly as fast, overclocking makes little economic sense, but computer enthusiasts enjoy wringing the last ounce of performance out of their machines.

A word of warning: Manufacturers don't like it when you overclock. It can damage equipment and it will definitely void your warranty. Overclocked systems are often less reliable, and if you push a system too hard it may fail entirely.

Overclocking your Palm PDA is fairly simple. I use a program called FastCPU. It's $10 shareware from www.megasoft2000.com. The program can overclock the 33MHz processor in my Sony Clié up to 55MHz, although I've only been able to get it to 50MHz reliably. Still, that's a 50% increase in speed for just $10.

You can use software to overclock many video cards, too. HardOCP has a how-to guide at www.hardocp.com/articles/video/oc/.

Overclocking your CPU is a little trickier. It usually requires changing some settings in your BIOS setup. Some processors overclock better than others. The 366MHz Celeron, for example, was an overclocker's dream. More recent high-speed processors are already at the limit of what they can do in many cases. Visit www.overclockers.com and check their CPU database for real-world overclocking results. There are good guides there to overclocking most systems.

SUNDAY, OCTOBER 13

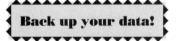

Back up your data!

PROTECT YOURSELF

Optometrist's call it Computer Vision Syndrome (CVS). The tired, gummy feeling your eyes get when you've been at the computer for too long. Several factors contribute to CVS.

When you're staring at a screen you blink less; four times a minute compared to the normal 12 times a minute. That causes your eyes to dry out. Try to blink more often when you're working. And take regular blink breaks to moisten your eyes.

Another CVS prevention technique is to exercise your eyes regularly. While you're taking those breaks, stretch your eye muscles. When you stare at a computer monitor your eyes stay at a fixed focal length, tiring the muscles. To reinvigorate your vision, focus at a distance then close up a few times. I like to look out the window for a while. I also like to rub my hands together briskly until they're warm, then lightly press the heels of my palms into my eyes. The warmth and darkness is very soothing.

Your work environment is very important, too. Glare on your computer screen can really bother your eyes. Computers should never be lit from behind you. Place lighting sources behind the monitor, or use indirect lighting.

I use the Eclipse Computer Light, $30 from `www.thinkgeek.com`. It sits on top of my monitor and directs its light upward at a reflector that spreads the light gently throughout the room.

Never sit too close to your screen, either. Keep it at arms length. Literally. If you can't stretch out your arm in front of you without hitting your screen, you're too close.

For more good advice, and a CVS test for your workstation, visit Dr. Ergo at `www.doctorergo.com`.

MONDAY, OCTOBER 14

LAPORTE SUPPORT

Q: What do I need to know before I upgrade my PC?

A: Important things to keep in mind when upgrading your PC:

* Be sure you know and understand the specifications of your PC before upgrading.
* Know the hardware requirements for the upgrade you want to do.
* Take a parts inventory and make sure you have all the necessary parts with you before you start.
* Research everything before you buy a single thing.

And always allow a day or two to get the upgrade installed and working. Never upgrade your system at a time when you might need it. Wait until the weekend so that you and your machine will have time to recover from the ordeal.

TUESDAY, OCTOBER 15

TODAY IN COMPUTER HISTORY

Today in 1956, IBM published *Fortran 1 Programmer's Reference Manual*. A FORTRAN (short for Formula Translator) was one of the first high-level computing languages. Up until then, computers had to be programmed in the machine's own language—a tough job for humans. High-level languages such as FORTRAN made it possible to write software in a language that was much closer to human languages.

MAC TIP

If, while playing DVD movies on your Mac, you notice large areas of pixelation (where dark areas appear blocky), try the following.

Set the screen resolution to 800×600 and colors to Millions in the Monitors control panel. If you're viewing the movie on an external display, select a resolution of 720×480. Also, select Normal Size rather than Full Screen playback.

GEEK SPEAK

Bitrate denotes the average number of bits that one second of audio data will consume. A typical MP3 is recorded at a bitrate of 128,000 bits per second.

WEDNESDAY, OCTOBER 16

WEB TIP

A Web accelerator is a program designed to speed up Internet access by modifying your TCP/IP settings or elaborate caching algorithms. These programs don't work and often can cause more harm than good.

To check your Internet settings use the free diagnostic tools at `www.dslreports.com/tools`. You can monitor your online speed with AnalogX's free Netstat Live program from `www.analogx.com/contents/download/network/nsl.htm`.

If you're disappointed in the results, I recommend a visit to Speedguide at `www.speedguide.net` or the Navas Cable Modem/DSL Tuning Guide at `cable-dsl.home.att.net`. You'll find many suggestions for fine tuning your system, and they won't cost you a penny.

THURSDAY, OCTOBER 17

WINDOWS TIP

You can find a particular word, number, or symbol in almost any Windows document with a few keystrokes.

Press the Ctrl key and the F key simultaneously. In the dialog box that appears type the word or symbol you are looking for.

Windows will search the document and jump to that word or symbol, if it finds it. This works in Web pages as well as Word Documents, Excel Spreadsheets, and more.

FRIDAY, OCTOBER 18

LAPORTE SUPPORT

Q: How can I split up a very large file so I can put it onto floppies?

A: What you want to do is called *spanning*, dividing a file so that it spans several smaller drives. Most compression programs can span files. Just try creating an archive on the A:

drive and see what happens. If you do this with my favorite file compression program, WinZip, for example, it will prompt you for additional floppies until the entire file has been copied over. Then it will ask you for the first floppy to write some additional data. The resulting disk set can be decompressed by WinZip, restoring the file to its original glory.

The newest WinZip, v8.1, also has a command to expressly divide a file into equal-sized chunks suitable for storing on a variety of media, including floppy, Zip, and Jaz disks.

If you just want to split files without compressing them, try HJ-Split, free from `www.freebyte.com/hjsplit`. There are compatible versions for nearly every operating system.

SATURDAY, OCTOBER 19

FOR GEEKS ONLY

In the 1950s, the first hard drives were up to 20 inches in diameter and only stored a few megabytes of data. Like today's hard drives, these primitive "fixed disks" stored information on a hard platter covered by a magnetic medium. Early geeks sometimes referred to them as "Winchesters," after a codename for a popular IBM fixed disk. No fixed disk ever appeared in a cowboy movie.

Your desktop IDE hard drive probably has three or more platters with two read/write heads for each. Data on each platter is stored in concentric circles called tracks, which are subdivided into arcs called sectors. Sectors are usually grouped together into clusters.

DOS and older versions of Windows use a 16-bit file allocation table (FAT), which creates very large clusters on a large disk partition. Even if a file is smaller than a full cluster, enough room is reserved on your hard disk for the entire cluster. The unused part of the cluster is called *slack space*. Newer versions of Windows support FAT32 and its smaller 4-K cluster sizes, which minimizes wasted slack space.

SUNDAY, OCTOBER 20

AOL TIP

One useful tool in AOL is the AutoComplete feature. When you start typing in a Web address that you've been to before, AutoComplete will automatically fill in the rest of the address for you so that you don't have to type out the whole thing. A pull-down list appears in the browser and you choose the one you're looking for.

To turn on AutoComplete:

1. Click on My AOL in your toolbar.
2. Scroll down to Preferences.
3. Click on WWW.
4. Click on the Content tab.
5. Click on AutoComplete.
6. Check Web Addresses.

MONDAY, OCTOBER 21

LAPORTE SUPPORT

Q: I like to listen to music on my PC at the office. But whenever Windows beeps at me, it's so loud in my headphones my eardrums burst. What can I do?

A: You need to shut off the system sounds so they don't blast you to the ceiling every time you commit an error:

1. Go to the Start menu.
2. Select Settings.
3. Open the Control Panel.
4. Select Sounds & Multimedia.
5. Under Scheme, select No Sounds. All those annoying beeps and boops will disappear. Warning: If you've created an elaborate sound scheme be sure to save it before you change to No Sounds. Click the Save As button to preserve your settings so you can restore them later.

TUESDAY, OCTOBER 22

MAC TIP

If you want to restore an application or two to your iMac, there's no need to run the installer from the iMac's Software Restore CD. Instead, just open the CD's Configurations folder and double-click on the iMac HD.img file. Disk Copy will mount this image file as if it were a separate volume. From there, you can simply drag the applications you want from the disk image to your hard drive.

Remember to copy any support files you might need. For example, if you want to restore AppleWorks 5, you'll need to copy the three different folders. First copy the entire AppleWorks folder. Then go to the image's System Folder and copy the Claris folder. Finally, from within the System Folder, open the Application Support folder and copy the AppleWorks folder.

When you drag these three folders over to your hard drive's System folder, put them in their proper places. The Claris folder goes at the root level of your System Folder. The AppleWorks folder (not the application, but the one you found inside the Application Support folder) goes into its own Application Support folder within the hard drive's System Folder.

Come to think of it, maybe it would be easier just to rerun the installer after all.

GEEK SPEAK

A *scanner* is a device that converts paper documents or photos into a digital format that can be viewed on a computer.

WEDNESDAY, OCTOBER 23

 **WEB TIP**

Internet Explorer has a handy tool to help you find specific information more quickly. (Either that or it will suck you deeper into a Web of info from which you may never escape.)

When you're at a Web page and not finding exactly what you need, but you know you're close, try the Related Links feature. IE will present you with a list of sites similar to the one you're on without taking you away from the current page.

1. In IE, go to the Tools menu.
2. Select Related Links.

The new links appear in a search box along the left side of the browser window.

To close the links section, click the X at the top right of the search box.

THURSDAY, OCTOBER 24

 WINDOWS TIP

The Shift key is far from shiftless. It might be the hardest working key on your keyboard. Just try some of these Shift key combinations:

- Shift+F10 is the equivalent of a right-click.
- Shift+Del deletes immediately without removing to the Recycle Bin.
- Shift+Tab moves to the previous control in the dialog box (Tab alone goes forward, Shift+Tab goes backward).
- Press Shift when inserting a CD-ROM and you can skip auto-run.
- Pressing Shift while holding down Ctrl and dragging to the desktop or to a folder creates an instant shortcut. (Of course, you can do the same thing by clicking and holding the right mouse button, letting go on the desktop, and choosing Create Shortcut.)

FRIDAY, OCTOBER 25

LAPORTE SUPPORT

Q: I'm having problems defragging my computer, even though I don't open anything else while I do it. What gives?

A: Defrag needs to have sole access to your hard drive while it's working. If anything accesses the disk, Defrag must restart; otherwise, the contents of your disk could be scrambled. Be sure to close all programs and background applications, including your screen saver, before you run Defrag.

To turn off your screen saver, right-click on the desktop, select Properties, and then the Screen Saver tab. Choose None to turn off your screen saver.

If you still have problems during the defrag process, try defragging in Safe Mode. While you restart, press F8 continuously until the boot menu loads up. Select Safe Mode and continue booting. Safe Mode loads a minimal set of drivers and applications so there won't be anything to conflict with Defrag. When you're finished defragging, reboot and Windows will load normally.

SATURDAY, OCTOBER 26

FOR GEEKS ONLY

It's not unusual for MP3s to have a few seconds of silence at the beginning or end, but that can be annoying if you're trying to make a music mix with smooth segues between songs. Here are some ways you can eliminate the silence.

If you just want to clobber dead space at the beginning and the end of a file, I recommend mp3trim, free from `www.logiccell.com/~mp3trim`. It can eliminate silence at the beginning and end of a track, fix the levels on quiet recordings, and more.

For fancier editing try Cool Edit 2000, a commercial program from `www.syntrillium.com`. Unlike most other sound editors, Cool Edit 2000 can edit MP3s directly, without first having to convert them to WAV form. You can try Cool Edit 2000 for free or buy it for $69.

SUNDAY, OCTOBER 27

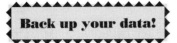

 ## PROTECT YOURSELF

Is your cell phone damaging your health? Information available on this controversial topic is often contradictory and confusing.

No solid evidence exists to prove that cell phones cause brain damage. However, scientists don't fully understand the effects of radio waves beamed right at your skull. That's why some recommend a "better safe than sorry" approach.

So how can you limit your risk if you choose to use a cell phone? While radiation shields are available, we don't know whether they are all that effective. Until further data becomes available, the best strategy is to minimize the use of cell phones—if a land line is available, use that instead.

When looking at the risks, remember good old-fashioned common sense. For instance, you're more likely to be injured by talking on a cell phone while driving than to get a brain tumor from it.

It's important to remember that no amount of research can ever prove conclusively that cell phones don't cause cancer—that's not the way science works. Scientific methods can indicate only whether or not cell phones are a health hazard. That hasn't happened yet.

MONDAY, OCTOBER 28

TODAY IN COMPUTER HISTORY

Bill Gates was born today in Seattle in 1955. Happy Birthday Bill! You might be the richest man in the world, but you'll always be one year older than Poor Leo.

 ## LAPORTE SUPPORT

Q: How do I know whether my iTunes will work with my CD recorder?

A: With the release of version 1.1, iTunes built in compatibility with many third-party CD-RW drives. Apple kindly includes a list of these drives at `www.apple.com/itunes/compatibility`.

However, you might not know what kind of drive mechanism is inside your CD-RW burner. How can you tell?

1. Launch the Apple System Profiler.
2. Click the Devices & Volumes tab.
3. Click the triangle next to the entry for your CD-RW drive.

In the resulting box you will see the model and manufacturer of your drive.

TUESDAY, OCTOBER 29

MAC TIP

PCs won't read Mac disks without special software, but Macs are perfectly content to read PC disks.

To read a Mac Zip disk on the PC, follow these steps:

1. Format the Zip disk as a PC disk using the Mac's Iomega tools.
2. Mount the disk.
3. Copy the files to the Zip disk.
4. Move the Zip disk to the PC.

You might need to add extensions to your file names so the PC will recognize them (for example, .doc for Word files, .mid for MIDIs, and so on). For a list of common PC file extensions (and how to open them on a Mac) visit www.stack.com.

GEEK SPEAK

A *processor* (a.k.a. microprocessor, CPU) is the brains of the entire computer. Macintosh processors are made by Motorola and IBM. PC processor manufacturers include Intel and AMD.

WEDNESDAY, OCTOBER 30

WEB TIP

It's almost Halloween. Is your costume ready? If the lightning bolt of creativity hasn't hit you yet, there's no need to panic. As long as you've got a PC you can make a great mask in minutes.

Before you start, here's what you need:

- A PC or Mac (of course!)
- Scissors
- Stapler
- Rubber band
- Pen
- Heavy stock paper
- Printer (preferably a color printer)
- A desktop publishing or photo-editing program

Here are the basic steps:

1. Pick a piece of clip art or an image from the Web.
2. Paste it into your desktop publishing program.
3. Enlarge the image so it's the size of a single piece of paper.

4. Print it out.

5. Cut the mask out of the paper.

6. Make the strap out of two cut rubber bands tied together.

7. Fasten the rubber bands to the mask with a stapler.

8. Use a ball point pen to poke two eyeholes. (Make sure you're not wearing the mask when you poke out those eyeholes.)

9. Wear and scare!

Have a great Halloween!

THURSDAY, OCTOBER 31 (HALLOWEEN)

WINDOWS TIP

You don't have to purchase a different mouse if you're left handed. Windows recognizes that not everyone favors the right hand.

Follow these steps to turn your mouse into a left-handed device:

1. Click Start, Settings, and select Control Panel.

2. Double-click the Mouse icon.

3. On the button tab under Button configuration select Left-handed.

4. Click Apply.

You just toggled your mouse buttons to reflect a real left-handed mouse.

As a lefty, I'm always looking for mice that don't favor righties. My current favorites: the Microsoft Intellimouse Optical and Apple Pro Mouse. They're good for people of either persuasion.

This Month's Feature

HOW TO MAKE A TV-READY PC

By Leo Laporte

After more than a decade using computers on the air, I've learned a thing or two about how to configure them for the rigors of a live TV show. This is the step-by-step process we go through with all the new machines we install on *The Screen Savers*. You might not want to do everything we do, but there are some things worth trying.

We equip all set computers with dual hard drives to make it easier to back up and restore our data with minimal downtime. It's not unusual that we'll have two or three minutes during a commercial break to get a system back up and running. Having a backup image of a working installation always ready has saved my bacon more than once. We use Norton

Ghost (www.symantec.com/ghost) to create and restore these backups. With Ghost we can rebuild a hard disk in just a few minutes.

Here are the 20 steps to a perfect PC, Screen Savers style:

1. Partition the first hard drive as follows (This is for a 20GB hard drive. Modify the partitions sizes to match your hard drive's capacity): Swap 500MB, Windows 4GB, Programs 6GB, Data 2GB, Media 6GB, Temp 1.5GB. We use PowerQuest Partition Magic (www.powerquest.com) for partitioning but you can use Windows FDISK if you want to save money.

2. Partition the second drive into a single large partition.

3. Format all partitions on both drives.

4. Create a Program Files folder in the Programs partition on drive one. Within that, create a folder called Common Files. Create My Documents, Favorites, and Downloads folders on the Data partition of drive one.

5. Create an Images folder on drive two.

6. Install Windows onto the Windows partition of hard drive one.

7. Install Norton Ghost onto hard drive two.

8. Now use Ghost to back up the Windows install into the Images folder on hard drive two. Name this image WINBASE. Having this makes it easy to re-install Windows in just a few minutes.

9. Configure Windows for Internet access.

10. Connect to the Internet and Run Windows Update and install all patches and upgrades.

11. Open the System control panel, click the Device Manager tab, and confirm that all drivers are correctly installed. Download and install updated drivers from manufacturers' web sites.

12. Configure Internet Explorer as follows:

    • Point to The Screen Savers (www.thescreensavers.com) as home page.
    • Enable small icons only on toolbar, no text.
    • Set 2MB for temporary Internet files.
    • Configure browser to check for updates on every page visit.

13. Configure Outlook Express for mail pickup. Do not pick up mail until after Ghosting (why back up old messages?):

    • Check the Leave Mail on Server option and set it to delete messages after one day. This way, you can get mail on multiple systems if necessary.
    • Set OE to check mail every 10 minutes.
    • Check Empty Deleted Items on Exit.

14. Download WinZip (www.winzip.com) and install it.

15. Download TweakUI (`http://www.microsoft.com/ntworkstation/downloads/PowerToys/Networking/NTTweakUI.asp`) and install it.

16. Open the TweakUI control panel, click the My Computer tab, and configure the Special Folders as follows:

    - Point My Documents to the My Documents folder in the data partition of drive one.
    - Point Favorites to the Favorites folder in the data partition of drive one.
    - Point Program Files to the Program Files folder in the Programs partition of drive one. Point Common Program Files to the folder within Program Files. This will trick programs into using your Data and Programs partitions instead of trying to store everything on the Windows partition. It's a good idea to separate the operating system, programs, and data into separate partitions.

17. Install any applications you'll be using. We typically put Microsoft Office on every system.

18. Delete any extraneous icons from desktop. Only leave My Computer, Network Neighborhood, Recycle Bin, and My Documents.

19. Organize the Start menu. I create subfolders in the Program menu called Accessories, Fun, Graphics, Internet, Multimedia, Office, and System Tools. Then I move the program icons into the appropriate folders. This keeps the Start menu to a reasonable length and makes it much easier to find what I'm looking for.

20. Make a second Ghost image and name it WINFULL. To avoid having to re-install applications, you might want to back up the applications directory as well. These are the backups you'll restore if something really goes wrong. If you make any major changes to your system, don't forget to make a new Ghost backup.

Leo's Dozen Doozies — Must Have Shareware Utilities

Here are my all-time favorite shareware and freeware downloads, in alphabetical order.

- Adobe Acrobat portable document viewer (www.acrobat.com—get the free reader, not the expensive full package)
- AVG Anti-virus (www.grisoft.com)
- Download Accelerator Plus download manager (www.downloadaccelerator.com)
- Free Agent news reader (www.forteinc.com)
- MusicMatch Jukebox MP3 player (www.musicmatch.com)
- NoteTab Lite text editor (www.notetab.com)
- PGP encryption (www.pgpi.com)
- PicViewer Lite image viewer (www.anixsoft.com)
- Sandra system diagnostics (www.sisoftware.demon.co.uk/sandra/index.htm)
- Second Copy 2000 backup utility (www.centeredsystems.com)
- WinZip file compression (www.winzip.com)
- Zonealarm firewall (www.zonealarm.com)

NOVEMBER

Leo's Essay

READ THE FINE PRINT

The holiday shopping season begins this month. Before you head out to the stores to stock up on technology necessities, it's worth remembering this simple motto: There's nothing fine about fine print.

Misleading claims are not the exclusive province of the computer salesman. Every carpenter knows that a 2×4 measures just 1.5 by 3.5. Quarter Pounders weigh only a quarter pound *before* they're cooked. And cereal boxes are never more than two-thirds full. But computer companies have raised these little deceptions to a high art.

You'd be lucky to get more than 45 kilobits per second out of a 56k modem. Fifteen-inch monitors display only 14.5 inches of picture (and even that's measured diagonally). Ten-megabit Ethernet really tops out at six or seven. A 20-gigabyte hard drive contains only 18 gigs useable space. A computer always sounds much quieter in the store.

Is it false advertising? Not if you read the fine print. The problem is that too few of us do. It would be nice if the computer industry made the fine print just a little bit bigger, but they don't seem too inclined to do so. It's up to us, as consumers, to educate ourselves, so we'll know what we're getting. Reading this book is a good start. As is reading the reviews in computer magazines before you buy. And we should all encourage the computer companies to be a little more honest in their advertisements.

Truth in advertising is a good thing, as long as I don't have to start putting my true weight on my driver's license.

FRIDAY, NOVEMBER 1

LAPORTE SUPPORT

Q: I live in an extremely rural area with a very rough power supply. The power occasionally goes out in bad weather and flickers on and off in good weather. I want to buy a UPS, but I'm not sure how much capacity I need or what features are worthwhile.

A: UPS stands for Uninterruptible Power Supply. Essentially, a UPS is a big battery with some control circuitry. It keeps your computer running temporarily during a blackout or power sag. While the power is working, the UPS charges the battery. When the power goes out, the battery takes over. A UPS also acts as a surge suppresser—conditioning the power to protect your computer against spikes.

Most folks buy UPSes that provide about 15 minutes of juice after the power goes out. That's enough to save your work and shut down normally. Businesses tend to invest in massive rack-mount UPS systems that can keep a company's server farm humming until the backup generators take over.

UPS capacity is measured in volt-amps (VA). You can calculate how big a UPS you need by adding up all the power the various pieces your PC requires. If you have a 16–21-inch monitor and Pentium IV system with typical peripherals, you're probably consuming 250–300 watts. To keep that system running for 15 minutes after a blackout you'd need a 400VA UPS. The easiest way to figure out what you need is to use the UPS calculator at `www.apcc.com/template/size/apc/`.

SATURDAY, NOVEMBER 2

FOR GEEKS ONLY

Many systems today come with video services built into the motherboard. But onboard video is usually inadequate for the demands of gaming and other 3D graphics. Here's how to add an after-market video card to a PC with built-in video.

First, open the case and check to see whether you have an available AGP slot. If you do, you should buy an AGP video card. AGP is faster, and you'll have a wider choice of cards. If there's no AGP slot, you're stuck with buying a PCI video card, but there are several good PCI-based video cards on the market. I recommend one based on an nVidia chipset.

On most newer systems you'll just install the new video card and go your merry way. But on older systems you might have to disable the onboard video before the new card will work. You can do this in one of two ways:

1. Move a jumper on the motherboard. Check the manual, or, sometimes, you find instructions inside the case. Use needle-nose pliers to do this, if you don't have truly nimble fingers.

2. Most systems can turn off the onboard video in the BIOS Setup. You enter Setup during booting by pressing a magic key, usually Del, F1, F10, or Esc. Check your manual or watch the screen carefully during boot-up for instructions. When in BIOS Setup look for a command to "disable onboard video." Don't change odd individual AGP settings by accident; just turn the video off.

Now pop in the new card and you're all set!

SUNDAY, NOVEMBER 3

PROTECT YOURSELF

Hauling your computer into a repair shop can give you the same sickly, helpless feeling you get when you take your car to the mechanic. How do you know if the shop is reputable? Will you get charged for things that aren't even broken? Does the repair staff know what it's doing?

Use these guidelines when you take your computer to the repair shop:

- Before you take your sick computer to the doctor, back up all critical data to removable storage. Just because computer experts work at repair shops doesn't mean they won't foul things up. Even the best intentioned repairistas will often accidentally wipe the hard drive. Also, remove all personal and financial information from your hard drive.
- Jot down the serial numbers of all your components. That way, you're able to tell for sure if new parts have, in fact, been added. And ask for parts that have been replaced to be returned to you.
- Be sure you ask what the hourly rate is (expect to pay about $50 per hour) and demand a written estimate. Don't rely on a verbal agreement, and instruct the repair shop to inform you of all changes to the written estimate. Ask to be told what type of replacement parts are used and visit PriceWatch (www.pricewatch.com) to compare the price the shop is charging you to the average street price.
- Ask the repair shop to explain how you might avoid running into the same problem down the road.

MONDAY, NOVEMBER 4

LAPORTE SUPPORT

Q: How do I get my fax/modem and my cable modem to run at the same time? I currently have to pull out the Ethernet card to get the regular phone line modem to work. If I don't, folks get a busy signal when they try to fax me.

A: Some cable modem companies offer only one-way access. The data comes into your house via the cable, but outgoing data travels via modem over the phone lines. If that's your situation, you're out of luck. The telephone will be busy whenever you're online. Ask your cable company when they plan to upgrade to true two-way service.

In most cases, however, the cable modem doesn't use the phone line at all. All Internet traffic travels over your TV cable. If that's how yours works, then there must be a conflict between your modem and your network card.

To resolve this, open the System control panel and select the Device Manager tab. Look for a red x or a yellow exclamation point on either the modem or network card. Either is an indication of a conflict. If both are PCI cards, try moving one to another slot. Many motherboards share resources between card slots, restricting the way you can install cards. You might find a cryptic reference to this in the motherboard manual, but trial and error has always worked best for me. Keep trying slot combinations until all the devices work together.

There's one other voodoo solution that often works. In theory, all device conflicts should be worked out automatically by Plug and Play (PnP). This technology is supposed to arbitrate between devices and arrange it so that they all get along together. In practice, this often doesn't work. But you can kickstart PnP by changing a setting in your BIOS Setup. Enter Setup at boot time, and look for a setting that says something like "Plug and Play OS?" The BIOS is asking whether your primary operating system wants to handle the Plug and Play chores. If not, the BIOS will do it. Sometimes, reassigning PnP responsibilities can resolve conflict. Change the setting, and then reboot. Repeat as needed.

TUESDAY, NOVEMBER 5 (ELECTION DAY)

MAC TIP

Macintosh files aren't like other computer files. They're divided into two parts:

- **A resource fork**—This contains system information, such as menus, fonts, icons, and program code, if any.
- **A data fork**—This contains the data of the file.

This presents a problem when you want to send a Mac file over the Internet. Most Internet operating systems don't understand two-part files and will eliminate one of the parts.

Before sending Mac files over hostile networks, you must process them, turning the dual forks into a single data file. When they're back on home turf, the files can be reconstituted. There are two common ways of doing this.

The oldest is Binhex. Binhex converts the two files into 7-bit text that's guaranteed to make it over even the most inhospitable networks. Binhex files are compatible with every Mac ever made, but they tend to be bigger because text is not the most efficient way to store binary data. Binhex files have the extension .HQX.

The newer MacBinary format uses an 8-bit binary representation of the data that's more compact. Because some really old Internet servers can handle only 7-bit text, MacBinary file transfers can become corrupted when the 8th bit is dropped. This problem is less and less common, but it can still crop up. That's why many Macintosh download sites offer files in both Binhex and MacBinary formats. You should choose MacBinary unless the files you're downloading arrive damaged. MacBinary files have the .BIN extension.

There are standalone Binhex and MacBinary decoders, but Stuffit Expander does the job just fine. It comes with every Macintosh. If you want to create Binhex or MacBinary files, buy Stuffit Deluxe from Aladdin Systems at www.aladdinsys.com.

VIRUS ALERT

Your antivirus program should screen out the following viruses today:

- The Helper Virus
- The Eraser Virus
- The Jackal Virus

Thank goodness for computer protection.

WEDNESDAY, NOVEMBER 6

 ## WEB TIP

Some Web pages these days are beginning to replace text with more add banners and dancing monkeys. If you find this trend extremely distracting, here are two ways to combat online visual pollution.

First, you can turn off graphics altogether. If it's just text you want, open Internet Options in Internet Explorer, click the Advanced tab, scroll to the Multimedia section and turn off animations, sounds, videos, and pictures. Ah, blissful silence.

To turn off graphics in Netscape, select Preferences from the Edit menu, click the Advanced heading, click Images, and select the Do Not Load Any Images option.

If you hate losing the pictures, try "turning up" the text. Follow these steps to increase font sizes within your browser.

Netscape

1. Click View, and you're provided with the options to increase or decrease the font size.

2. Or, hold down Control+] (right bracket) for a larger size or Control+[(left bracket) for smaller type.

Internet Explorer

1. Click View, Text Size, and choose between Largest and Smallest.

2. Or, if you have a wheel mouse, you're able to hold Control and slide the wheel to increase or decrease font size.

THURSDAY, NOVEMBER 7

WINDOWS TIP

Windows comes with several symbolic fonts. Printers call them *dingbats*—typefaces that contain bullets and other graphics instead of letters. But choosing a character from fonts like Symbol, Wingding, and Zapf Dingbats is tough, because there's no particular order to the symbols.

That's when the Windows character map comes in handy. A character map shows you all the characters in any font. You can use this map to find the right symbol for any task:

1. From your Start Menu, open Programs, Accessories, System Tools, Character Map.

2. In the Character Map, select a font (Wingdings is fun).

3. Choose the letter or symbol needed.

4. Press Select.

5. Press Copy.

6. Paste (Ctrl+V) into your document.

You can keep the Character Map window open as you type for easy access. Want more fun symbolic fonts? Try the Dingbat pages at www.dingbatpages.com.

FRIDAY, NOVEMBER 8

LAPORTE SUPPORT

Q: I was wondering how businesses such as AOL and local Internet service providers connect to the Internet. I was also wondering whether a regular home computer is able to cut out the middleman and connect directly to the Internet.

A: Most ISPs get their Internet connections from larger regional companies that buy their bandwidth, in turn, from the telephone companies. These telecoms—Sprint, MCI, AT&T, UUNET and others—own the fiber optic and satellite connections that form the backbone of the Internet worldwide. Larger ISPs, such as AOL and CompuServe, are big enough to have their own cross-country backbones.

You could jump up a step or two on the food chain, but it would cost you. The telcos and regional providers sell connectivity wholesale. In most cases the smallest connection you could get is a T-1 line, which offers 1.44 megabits of throughput in both directions. But it's gonna cost ya.

SprintLink charges a port fee of $2,700 per month (as of 2001), with a 4 percent discount for a year, 6 percent off for two years, and 8 percent off for three years. This does not include the $1,000 installation fee or the POP (point of presence), which can cost as much as $1,300. And all that for only a little more speed than you'd get from a $50/month DSL or cable connection.

Eliminating the middleman when you buy connectivity is like eliminating the butcher. Why buy a side of beef when all you want is a steak?

For an interactive map of Internet backbones worldwide, visit `www.caida.org/tools/visualization/mapnet/Backbones`.

SATURDAY, NOVEMBER 9

FOR GEEKS ONLY

Are you tired of Word crashing? Do Outlook freezes give you the chills? Do you think it's important that Microsoft face *some* competition *somewhere*? You might want to try a non-Microsoft office suite.

It's true. Even though Microsoft Office is dominant with more than 90% market share, there are other office suites to choose from. Some of them are free. Some offer features you won't find anywhere else. Some are easier to use because they're simpler. All offer an alternative to the juggernaut from Redmond.

Here are some of the things to look for when shopping for an office suite:

- If you need to work with other people be sure your suite can read and write Microsoft Office-compatible file formats.
- Feature sets vary widely. Choose a suite that can do the things you need to do.
- Look for a product that's in active development by a company or group that's in it for the long haul. Microsoft is so dominant in this category that many companies have just given up. You need a suite that will be supported for as long as you plan to use it.

The next few Saturdays are dedicated to office suite alternatives.

SUNDAY, NOVEMBER 10

Back up your data!

PROTECT YOURSELF

Even with falling prices, computer equipment is expensive. Protect your investment from light-fingered Louies with the following proven security techniques:

- **Cable anchors**—You've probably seen the rubber-coated security cable anchor constructed of galvanized steel. The cable can be lassoed through an anchor plate that comes attached to most modular wall systems. Most laptops come with a security slot designed for these locks.
- **Computer tracking devices**—LoJack for your laptop. If it's stolen, police can use the built-in transponder to track it down. (Check out www.computrace.com).
- **Laptop alarms**—Loud alarms that go off when your laptop is moved. (For more information, point your browser to www.targus.com.)
- **Barrel locks**—These can be used to keep the PC from being physically opened, thereby protecting CPUs, memory, hard drives, and other components.
- **Locks**—You can purchase drive locks made to restrict access to Zip, CD/DVD, and 3.5-inch disk drives.

For more information on protecting your PC, visit www.computersecurity.com.

MONDAY, NOVEMBER 11 (VETERAN'S DAY)

LAPORTE SUPPORT

Q: What are biometrics and under what circumstances are they used?

A: Thanks to biometrics, we're rapidly approaching the day when a computer can know you better than your own mother does. *Biometrics* is the science of measuring unique physical or behavioral characteristics of the human anatomy. When we talk about biometrics in the computer security field, we're talking about using these characteristics to positively identify an individual.

Often portrayed as futuristic technology in spy novels and science fiction films, biometric technologies are now emerging as practical, effective solutions for guarding high-security environments, conducting fraud-free e-commerce, and preventing time and attendance fraud.

A wide variety of biometric technologies exists today. They mainly break down into two groups: physical characteristic biometrics and behavioral biometrics.

Physical Characteristic Biometrics

- Subcutaneous (below the skin's surface) scanning
- Fingerprinting
- Hand/palm geometry
- Retina and iris scanning
- DNA sampling
- Face recognition
- Ear shape
- Hair sampling
- Body weight and odor

Behavioral Biometrics

- Voice recognition
- Signature
- Keystroke patterns
- Gait (walking or movement)

TUESDAY, NOVEMBER 12

MAC TIP

If you'd like to create disk labels that list the contents of those countless Zip, Jaz, and CD-R discs scattered about your office, turn to Ilja A. Iwas' UnCoverIt, $10 shareware from www.iwascoding.com. This ingenious little application scans your removable media and creates a printout that lists the disc's contents, icons and all. After you've printed the label, just cut it to the correct size and slip it into your Zip or CD-R case.

GEEK SPEAK

Emoticons are pictures of facial expressions made up of certain symbols on the keyboard. These are primarily used in online messages (e-mail, chatrooms, message boards, and so on). For example, :) symbolizes a happy face, :(is a sad face. These are sometimes called *smilies*.

WEDNESDAY, NOVEMBER 13

WEB TIP

Most of us already know that a fast connection makes for a more enjoyable Web experience, but how do you measure the speed of your connection?

Several Web sites offer online tests to determine your available bandwidth.

- DSLReports (www.dslreports.com) has a complete suite of performance analysis tools that can not only tell you how fast your connection is, but can also compare it to results from other users and offer suggestions for improving speed. The tools use Java and so should work on most computers.

- PC Pitstop (www.pcpitstop.com) also evaluates your computer speed for free. It also will analyze the health of your computer in general. Requires Windows and Internet Explorer.
- Toast.net (www.toast.net) offers a simple tool for testing bandwidth, but it's good for a second opinion. And the test runs from several different servers so you can pick one near you to minimize the effect of geographical distance on your connect speed.
- C|net (webservices.cnet.com/bandwidth) is another simple tester.

Generally, these sites work by sending a file of known size and measuring the time it takes to complete the file transfer to your computer. Because the speed of their servers and the Internet at any given time can affect the results, I recommend using all four sites during several different dayparts. The highest number you get is the peak speed your connection is capable of.

THURSDAY, NOVEMBER 14

WINDOWS TIP

Changing the sounds that Windows plays is as easy as opening up the Control Panel and selecting Sounds. You'll see a list of all the events that can have an associated sound effect. The standard system sounds are stored in the C:/windows/media folder, but you can attach sounds from anywhere on your hard drive.

Follow these steps to customize a Windows sound event:

1. Save your favorite WAV files in a convenient place (such as the C:/windows/media folder).

2. Open the Sound Properties window from the Control Panel and select the event for which you would like to add or change a sound.

3. Browse to the WAV file you want played each time the event occurs and click OK.

You can record your own WAV files if you have a microphone attached to your PC. Select the Start menu, Accessories, Entertainment and open the Windows Sound Recorder.

Thousands of Web sites offer free WAV files. Try www.dailywav.com and www.thefreesite.com/free_sounds. Or search for a particular sound effect at www.findsounds.com.

FRIDAY, NOVEMBER 15

LAPORTE SUPPORT

Q: How do I find out whether a certain Internet service provider is going to reliably meet my needs?

A: After you've located a local ISP, the next step is to find out how good it is. The best way to learn the truth about an ISP is to ask its customers. Call a prospective ISP and ask for references, visit the alt.internet newsgroups, or ask around.

Ask the following questions:

- Does it provide good technical support?
- Does its tech support staff understand your operating system?
- Does it have a high modems-to-users ratio so you won't get busy signals? (There should be no more than 10 users per modem; I recommend seven or eight, max.)

You also should try to find out what kind of connectivity to the Internet the ISP has, and how many users share that connection. The bandwidth available to you is equal to the bandwidth of the ISP's connection divided by the number of users connected at any given time. (For example, if seven users simultaneously share a 56Kbps connection, they each get a maximum of 8Kbps bandwidth.)

The final factor is how forward-thinking the company is. Currently, ISPs are like phone companies: They just provide you with a line. But in time, value-added service might become more popular. Multicasting, radio and TV broadcasts, telephony, and faxing are services ISPs will offer in the future. Ask what additional services your prospective ISP plans to offer.

If you want to put up your own Web page, make sure the ISP provides at least 10MB storage for a Web site, without additional charges for downloads, and reasonably priced domain name registration services. It shouldn't cost more than $50 to register a custom domain name through the ISP.

SATURDAY, NOVEMBER 16

FOR GEEKS ONLY

If you're a Linux user, you have several good Microsoft Office alternatives. This is not surprising because Linux is one of the few operating systems Microsoft refuses to develop for.

The granddaddy of office suites for Linux is Sun Microsystem's StarOffice (www.sun.com/products/staroffice). This mature office suite comes with word processor, spreadsheet, e-mail, HTML editing, graphic design, and presentation applications. The only thing it doesn't come with is a price tag. StarOffice 5.2 is freeware and is compatible with Microsoft Office files. There's also a version for Windows. Mac users, visit porting.openoffice.org/mac/ for progress reports on a version for Mac OS X.

If you're running a recent version of Linux, check out Koffice. This free, open-source project is attempting to surpass Microsoft Office in ease of use and functionality. Most Linux distributions come with Koffice, but you can always get the latest version at www.koffice.org. Early versions of Koffice were noticeably incomplete and buggy, but it's been getting better by leaps and bounds.

Also, check out VistaSource's Applixware Office (www.vistasource.com/products/axware). It's native to Linux, so all seven Applixware Office applications are small, stable, and fast. Applixware can import and export Microsoft Office documents, but the free demo version limits document size. The full version of Applixware lists for $99.99.

Just out of the gate is Gobe Productive for Linux (pronounced go-be). This elegant Office Suite was written by the same people who created ClarisWorks for the Mac, and it's very similar to that classic program. There are versions of Gobe Productive for BeOS, Windows, and, soon, Linux. The $125 product is really a works program, combining common office programs into a single all-in-one package. It's singularly easy to use and highly recommended for folks who find the Microsoft Office programs overly complex. There's no Gobe Productive for the Macintosh, but that's probably because Apple's own AppleWorks is really just ClarisWorks updated and renamed.

SUNDAY, NOVEMBER 17

AOL TIP

The Web is a great resource for information, but you might not want your kids to see everything on the Internet. How do you protect them? AOL allows you to set parental controls that limit the access your kids have online.

Here's how to set parental controls in AOL 5.0:

1. Click Parental Controls on the bottom-right side of the Welcome page (or go to Keyword: Parental Controls).

2. Select Set Parental Controls.

3. At the top of the page, under Edit Controls For, choose the screen name you want to edit. You can set different parental controls for each screen name on your account.

4. At the bottom of the page you can choose a preset control based on age: General Access (18+), Mature Teen (16 to 17), Young Teen (13 to 15), or Kid Only (12 and younger).

5. Or you can click on the left side of the page to customize the controls for the following categories: E-mail, Chat Control, IM Control, Web Control, Additional Master, Download Control, Newsgroups, and Premium Services.

With these parental controls, you can do things such as block file attachments (including photos), allow access to kids-only chat rooms, block instant messages, and block explicitly mature Web content.

MONDAY, NOVEMBER 18

LAPORTE SUPPORT

Q: What is the difference between an update and an upgrade? Is it enough just to update when an upgrade is available?

A: If you registered for a program, either purchased in a brick-and-mortar store or down-loaded off the Internet, then you have probably received (or will receive) an offer to update or upgrade that program:

- **Update**—These usually free downloads are pushed by the manufacturer and intended to fix a problem or add new functions.

  I always install updates. If the company is offering a free fix on a program, then I figure why turn it down. And updates often repair critical bugs or security holes, so they're important to keep up with. Updates can break things, though, so I am never the first person to download an update. Wait a week or so. If you haven't heard of any problems with installing the update, then go for it.

- **Upgrade**—This is the next generation of a program and it almost always costs money. Upgrades offer new functions and fixes, but sometimes upgrades go wrong, very wrong. Often, fixes are not made, or added functionality screws up a simple but elegant user interface.

  If you're happy with how a program is working for you, don't feel any pressure to upgrade. Most software companies make the bulk of their profits selling upgrades, so they create new releases for products that don't really need them. Intuit's Quicken and Microsoft Money, for example, upgrade yearly. That doesn't mean you have to.

TUESDAY, NOVEMBER 19

MAC TIP

Many applications, such as Word, Outlook Express, and Photoshop, create scratch files as you work on a document. Often the files are only temporary, and the application intends to delete them when you quit the application.

If your computer crashes, the application might not get the chance to delete these files. Eradicator 1.6 (www.swssoftware.com/products/eradicator.html) is a piece of freeware that enables you to see and delete temporary and invisible files. Using Eradicator 1.6, you might be able to free up hundreds of megabytes of disk space.

GEEK SPEAK

Clock speed is the heart rate of a CPU. Clock speed is measured in megahertz. One MHz (megahertz) equals one million cycles a second. 200MHz equals 200 million cycles a second. 1000MHz is the same as 1GHz (gigahertz). A typical computer instruction takes two or three cycles, but modern CPUs can execute multiple instructions simultaneously, so it's difficult to extrapolate the speed of a processor from its clock speed. When you shop for a computer don't get blinded by megahertz and gigahertz. You can only measure the true speed of a computer by seeing how it handles the real-world applications you use every day.

WEDNESDAY, NOVEMBER 20

WEB TIP

Outlook is much more than an e-mail client—it's a Web browser, too. All your favorite URLs are a click away. Sure, you could get to them through the Favorites menu, but what if you don't want certain URLs in the global list?

Each Outlook folder can have a default homepage if you follow these steps:

1. Right-click an Outlook folder in your Folder Bar and pull up its properties.
2. Click the Home Page tab.
3. Either enter a complete URL (Web address) or browse for a local HTML file.
4. Place a check mark in the Show Home Page by Default For This Folder box.

You can go a step further and add a Web Address Bar to your toolbar. It's easy to do.

1. Right-click your main toolbar.
2. Select the Customize option.
3. Select the Web category.
4. In the right-hand pane, drag and drop the Address field somewhere into your toolbar.

THURSDAY, NOVEMBER 21

WINDOWS TIP

The Windows Product Key is the unique serial number assigned to each copy of Windows. Certainly everyone who has installed Windows can remember having to type out that annoying string of characters before the installation procedure can be completed.

Here is how to find that Product Key number on your Windows installation:

1. Click the Start button and select Run.
2. Type `regedit` and press Enter (be careful not to modify your registry here).
3. Select HKEY_LOCAL_MACHINE.
4. Select Software.
5. Select Microsoft.
6. Select Windows.
7. Select Current Version.
8. Look by the heading ProductKey on the right window pane to see the 25-digit number.

Keep this number handy in case you need to re-install Windows.

FRIDAY, NOVEMBER 22

LAPORTE SUPPORT

Q: *How does RAM work?*

A: When you launch an application, your operating system copies the program from the hard drive into RAM, where the program is run. Your computer uses RAM as its workspace and short-term storage area, because RAM is much faster to work with than the hard drive. That's why adding RAM to your computer often speeds it up.

Most programs are too big to fit in RAM all at once. These programs use various schemes to load parts of the program into RAM as needed, and then unload them when they don't need them. These programs continue to access your hard disk even after they're loaded. Smaller programs load entirely into RAM and don't access the disk again.

RAM also stores data that you are currently working on. That data stays in RAM until it is saved to the hard disk, or until the computer is turned off—in which case the data is wiped out. Your word processing program provides a good example. Changes you make to a Word document are stored in RAM. If you don't save the document to the hard drive before turning off the computer, the changes are lost.

SATURDAY, NOVEMBER 23

FOR GEEKS ONLY

Even though Microsoft Office dominates the shelf space in your local computer store, there are other commercial choices that make a good alternative:

- **Corel WordPerfect Office** (www.wordperfect.com)—This Windows package actually predates Microsoft Word and is still very popular in the workplace. It's a Windows product, although some of the components are available on Linux, too.
- **Lotus SmartSuite** (www.lotus.com/home.nsf/welcome/smartsuite)—IBM now owns SmartSuite and sells it mostly to offices that are already tied to Lotus products. It's a perfectly capable set of applications and compatible with Microsoft Office.

Prices on both these products are competitive with Microsoft Office. In other words, expensive, ranging from $150 to upgrade from a previous version to nearly $500 for the full suite. Both Lotus and Corel offer 30-day free trials if you can handle a 300 megabyte download.

A lesser-known, but technically interesting choice is the ThinkFree Office (www.thinkfree.com). This Web-based office suite is compatible with Microsoft Office documents and runs on any Windows, RedHat Linux 6.1, or Mac OS 9 computer. After you register, you can log in from any Web-connected computer and download the ThinkFree office suite (less than 10MB). You're allowed 20MB of free, secure, online storage for your documents and spreadsheets, but you can also save ThinkFree files to local drives.

ThinkFree is only free for 30 days. After the trial period expires, you have to pay a $49.95 yearly subscription. It runs on a Java virtual machine, which might lock or crash some computers. It also works slowly and isn't much of an alternative for the dial-up user, because you have to be online to use it.

Although you might not need to be a supergeek to use ThinkFree itself, you will be happiest with it if you're computer-savvy. A high-speed Internet connection is a must to use the online version; so is patience with Java.

SUNDAY, NOVEMBER 24

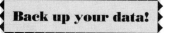

PROTECT YOURSELF

Most of the items for sale on eBay are not being sold by a store but by people like you and me who are trying to purge some junk from their lives and make a buck. But you must be careful, because what might appear to be a great deal on, say, a brand new TV is actually a clever marketing ploy by an electronics store. The high bid for that TV might be a shockingly low $25, but as soon as you bid $30 you're informed that someone has already outbid you. This is because the electronics store has set a reserve bid. A reserve bid is the minimum the electronics store will accept for the TV, which might well be $300. Basically, the low initial bid price is just a false enticement. Despite the sometimes misleading auctions, you can get great deals on new items from Web retailers on eBay.

MONDAY, NOVEMBER 25

LAPORTE SUPPORT

Q: Sometimes when I send an e-mail with a photo in it, the person receives it, but there is no photo in the e-mail. I have tried Outlook Express and Netscape Composer, saving the picture as an HTML file, but there is still no photo. Can you tell me how to do it right?

A: Pasting a photo, or other image, into the e-mail window is not the most compatible way to send it. For this to work, the recipient needs to use an HTML-based e-mail package. E-mail programs use HTML differently, so if you send the photo from Netscape to Outlook, it might look odd.

The best way to send a photo is via an attachment. Just be sure your friends and family know the attachment is not an executable program. Photo attachments, like other pure data files, cannot transmit viruses. Here's how to attach a photo:

1. Create a new message.
2. Click the paper-clip icon (or select Attach from the File menu.)
3. Select the photo file.
4. Send the message.

The photo is not visible in the body of the e-mail message, but the recipient is able to open the attachment to view the photo.

Even better than attaching photos to an e-mail is posting the photos on the Web, where people can download them at their leisure. If you don't have a Web page of your own, there are many free services that will let you upload pictures and share them with friends. My favorite is Kodak's Ofoto, www.ofoto.com. Other online photo albums include Yahoo! Photos (photos.yahoo.com), PhotoPoint (www.photopoint.com) and ClubPhoto (www.clubphoto.com).

Save the originals, though. Many photo album sites have already gone out of business, and I expect the number of sites to shrink down to the top two or three in the next year or so.

TUESDAY, NOVEMBER 26

MAC TIP

Want to change the application that opens when you double-click a document? If so, follow these steps:

1. Get information on a document file by clicking the file's icon or pressing Command+I.
2. Select Application from the Show drop-down menu.
3. Choose an application to open a particular document, or change the default application for all documents of this type.

GEEK SPEAK

GUI (*Graphical User Interface*) is an interactive visual display that uses pictures and words together on the screen. Xerox invented the GUI, but it was popularized by the Apple Macintosh.

WEDNESDAY, NOVEMBER 27

WEB TIP

It happens to everyone. You've been surfing the Web for an hour or so, and all of a sudden, you realize you've created a huge list of bookmarks (or favorites). Unfortunately, it's almost as time-consuming to scan through your list as it is to just type in the site addresses. Here's how you can put your bookmarks in order.

Internet Explorer

1. On the Favorites menu, click Organize Favorites.

2. Click the Create Folder button.

3. Type a name and press Enter.

4. Repeat the steps above as necessary.

5. Drag the shortcuts in the list to the appropriate folders.

Netscape Navigator

1. On the Communicator menu, go to Bookmarks, then Edit Bookmarks.

2. Go to File, then New Folder.

3. Name the folder and click OK.

4. Repeat the steps above as necessary.

5. Drag any bookmark on your list into the folders you've created.

THURSDAY, NOVEMBER 28 (THANKSGIVING)

WINDOWS TIP

When you turn your computer on, do you have enough time for a rousing game of Monopoly before it's ready to use?

Many people leave their computers on because they take too long to boot. Instead of pushing up your electric bill, optimize your computer to boot faster. Here are a few tips you can use:

- Use faster hard drives and RAM
- Remove SCSI cards
- In the bios, use the following settings:
  - PNP OS yes
  - Turn off memory check
  - Boot from C: only
  - Quickstart/Quickboot
  - Turn off floppy seek
- Turn off any programs that do a virus scan at startup
- Turn off ActiveX
- Clean up the registry
- Rebuild your hard drive and do a fresh system installation
- Defragment your hard drive

ALL TURKEY, ALL THE TIME

By far, the best turkey resource on the Web is the National Turkey Foundation (www.turkeyfed.org). There you can find trustworthy advice on how to purchase, store, thaw, roast, carve, and even deep-fry a turkey. There are also scores of great turkey recipes for the main event or your leftovers, as well as interesting turkey trivia.

And for the vegetarians among us, let's not forget the legendary Tofurkey, `www.tofurkey.com`. All soy, all the time.

FRIDAY, NOVEMBER 29

LAPORTE SUPPORT

Q: I have been arguing with a few people over DOS. They insist that Linux, Windows 2000, and other OSes don't use DOS, while I have been insisting that though it is not apparent to the user, some form of a disk operating system has to be in use by the OS. Could you settle this for us?

A: You're both right, sort of.

You can use the technical term "disk operating system" when referring to any OS. However, when people say "DOS," they actually mean the original operating system released by the Microsoft Corporation, which is called *MS-DOS* (*Microsoft Disk Operating System*). Like Kleenex, Band-Aid, or any of the other brand names we've incorporated into daily speech, DOS is commonly accepted to mean MS-DOS.

Every computer uses a disk operating system (not necessarily MS-DOS) at the very heart of its operation. DOS is really just an intermediary between your computer's hardware and your BIOS. Every version of Windows, Linux, BeOS, and OS/2 has some form of disk operating system at the bottom level of communication.

SATURDAY, NOVEMBER 30 (HANUKKAH)

FOR GEEKS ONLY

We conclude our tour of non-Microsoft Office suites with some lesser-known free alternatives.

602Pro PC Suite (for Windows only) (`www.software602.com/products/pcs`) is an amazingly complete package considering the price. Free! It's compatible with Microsoft Office documents. Its three modules, 602Text (word processor), 602Tab (spreadsheet), and 602Photo (graphic editor) are fully functional. I like 602Pro PC Search, an add-on that searches for keywords in the full text of DOC/XLS/HTML/RTF and Outlook e-mail. Plus, doesn't "602Tab" just *sound* geeky?

602Pro PC Suite is missing a few essentials, such as a presentation application, and you have to register it to turn the spell checker on and the pop-up windows off.

Siag Office for Unix and Mac OS X (`siag.nu`) is an office suite with a sense of humor. Their motto: It sucks less. Their word processor is named Pathetic Writer. Yet this is a very capable set of programs that has a dedicated following.

Easy Office for Windows from `www.e-press.com` is designed to be simple not powerful, but the premium version does include a surprising range of programs, including a Web page creator, bookkeeper, contact manager, bar coder, and text-to-speech synthesizer. The free version has all the basics and is Microsoft Office compatible.

Finally, a few tips for folks who choose the road less taken. Unless you work alone, chances are you'll need to share your documents with the Microsoft Office masses. If your suite promises Microsoft compatibility, test it before you rely on it. Microsoft keeps its file formats secret, so creating a fully compatible product is difficult. Often the results are imperfect.

In many cases it's best to save your files in a more standard format, such as RTF for word processing or SYLK for spreadsheets. Most programs, including Microsoft Office, understand these formats.

Some of these products are buggy. Save your work often and back up daily. For some reason few products work as well with Windows as Microsoft's. Hmmm.

Finally, be prepared to be questioned, mocked, even stigmatized. It's not easy going your own way. People don't like renegades, especially in the workplace. But the rewards can be great for the pioneer who strikes out on his or her own to explore new territory in the Office Suite wilderness. Good luck and godspeed.

This Month's Feature

THE ULTIMATE ONLINE SHOPPING GUIDE

By Call for Help and The Screen Savers staff

Shopping online can save you time and money after you get the hang of it. But for many newbies, the e-commerce swamp is frustrating and even overwhelming, making them wish they'd just gone to the mall instead.

The best way to learn how to shop online is to practice. Find a shopping site and click around.

Don't worry about accidentally buying things you don't want—online stores put you through a series of steps when you make your purchase. For example, if you don't click the Click Here to Complete This Order button, your order won't go through.

How To Shop

Most shopping sites give you the choice to search or browse the products. For example, look at Amazon.com (`www.amazon.com`).

Search

Along the left side of your screen is a box that says Search. The section contains a blank box where you can type in your keywords. That area also contains a menu that lets you limit your search to books, music, or other sections of the store. That's optional, but it can speed things up.

To find *The Rest of the Earth* by William Haywood Henderson, we typed "rest of the earth" into the little text box, selected Books from the menu above that box, and clicked the Go button. The site presented us with a choice: hardback or paperback? We clicked on the paperback title.

That brings us to the page where we can learn more about the product. If we decide to buy it, we can click the big Add to Shopping Cart button toward the right of the screen.

We can always remove the item later if we change our mind. (In fact, we don't even have to do that—we can wander away to eat dinner, or surf to another site, or check e-mail, and if we don't return to my shopping site within a certain amount of time, the order simply goes away.)

Browse

If you're not looking for a specific title, you can choose to browse instead of search the site. Just under the Search box is the Browse list.

We want a book, so we click Books. The books page highlights certain books. You can click Mystery & Thrillers from the list of subjects in the Browse box (still at the left side of the screen), and so on. You can click through Amazon's products pretty much the same way you click through Web sites at LookSmart (www.looksmart.com) or Yahoo! (www.yahoo.com).

Most shopping sites have a similar setup. Take some time to look around when you first arrive, and you'll soon figure out how to get to the products you want.

Types of Online Stores

Online stores come in many forms. Of course, so do offline stores, but at least online you won't have to drive all over town to visit all of them. Most of us are already familiar with basic shopping sites—it's not much different from the classic Sears catalog experience. But with the Net have come do-it-yourself auctions and even "backward" commerce models that give you more power over your purchasing.

Regular Store

The most prevalent type of virtual store mimics its offline counterpart. The seller offers products at a price; the buyer wanders through, finds what she wants, and buys it. These stores range from huge department-style emporiums that carry products from all kinds of manufacturers, to one-person shops that sell their own in-house merchandise. These stores also cluster in online malls.

You can often find bargains online as vendors compete for your business.

Auctions

Online auctions have become so popular that some established regular stores have added auction sections. The most famous auction-only site is eBay (`www.ebay.com`), which sports a new users section (see the big blue graphic at the top right) that explains how to buy and sell on the site.

Tips for shopping on eBay are offered later in this article.

Something in Between

Priceline (`www.priceline.com`) and its ilk turn the commerce model upside down. They offer products from regular vendors, just like regular stores, but invite the customer to set the price, more akin to an auction.

In other words, you tell the seller what you're willing to pay, and if the seller agrees, blam! You've made the transaction. Unfortunately, at that point there's no going back, so be careful where you click unless you're serious about the purchase.

Is Online Shopping Safe?

For some folks, it feels strange at first to send a credit card number out into cyberspace. What if someone hacks in and steals the number? Havoc would ensue!

Don't Worry About Your Visa

E-commerce proponents point out that it's easier for an unscrupulous store clerk or waitress to jot down your number than it is for a hacker to steal it. Regardless, as long as you report any fraudulent charges within a reasonable amount of time (check your bank for the limit), you aren't held responsible for the amounts. Which means that in the extremely unlikely event that the waitress absconds with your Visa and runs away to Maui, or if a thirteen-year-old boy charges a new computer system online, you don't have to pay for it.

We do recommend that you use a credit card rather than your ATM/debit card when shopping online. You don't want any checks to bounce in the time it takes to clear up any fraud with your account.

Protect Your Privacy

Most reputable online stores post their privacy policies in a fairly obvious manner. A privacy policy outlines exactly what the company will and won't do with the information you provide when you place your order. This includes your e-mail and street addresses, phone numbers, and so on. You should at least skim through the privacy policy to be sure you know what you're getting into.

For example, some sites snag your e-mail address so they can send you sales and promotions. Others might share those addresses with other companies. If you don't want that, you can usually opt out. If you can't, you might want to shop elsewhere.

Put a Shopbot to Work for You

A shopbot most definitely helps you narrow down your search for the perfect Christmas gift. *Shopbots* (short for "shopping robots") are basically programs and applications that search through lots of data and bring back results. You tell them what you're looking for, and they track down the lowest price online. A shopbot scours the Web looking for the items you want at the price you designate while you do other things. When it finds what you're looking for, the program alerts you and gives you the chance to buy.

For your general shopping needs, try MySimon (www.mysimon.com) and DealTime (www.dealtime.com).

The more specific the bot is, the better your results will be. In other words, a bot that only searches for the products you're looking for, as opposed to the entire World Wide Web, produces a more comprehensive and detailed list of results.

When you go through a specialty bot, the results often include the total cost of the item, including shipping and tax. Often they tell you whether or not the item's in stock. Such is the case with Computers.com (www.computers.com). Here, you get information about shipping, store location, tax, and merchant ratings for computer-related products. Don't expect to find this amount of detail in a bot that searches for more general products, such as MySimon.

Botspot.com (www.botspot.com) lists all the shopbots online and lets you test a variety of bots, or browse for one that meets your specific shopping needs.

Just remember, when you're choosing a bot, look for one that searches more than just a handful of merchants. Look for unbiased search results and examine for the features the bot offers: merchant ratings, the ability to sort, shipping charges, where the store is, if the item's in stock, and so on.

How To Shop eBay

You can search through millions of items for sale on eBay at any given moment, and the breadth of what's on the auction block boggles the mind. For example, we decided we wanted some Genesee Beer memorabilia (the Rochester, New York brewery). A search on Genesee Beer yielded more than 70 items. Astonishing.

If you know what you're looking for (like Genesee Beer), the best way to find it is to type the item name in the search box on eBay's front page. If you don't know specifically what you want to buy, but you know the general category, use the category listings. For example, if you're interested in buying an old map, click the Antiques and Art category and then on Maps and Atlases, where you can browse through more than 1,300 offerings.

Before you can bid on anything, you need to register with eBay. It's a simple process that requires you to give up a little personal information, but there's nothing that says you can't lie about yourself if you want to (you need to provide your real e-mail address to respond to the confirmation letter eBay sends you after you have completed the registration form).

When you win an auction, the seller e-mails you to arrange a payment and delivery method.

You should always be sure you know exactly what you're bidding on. Before you bid, e-mail the seller if the information he or she has posted isn't entirely clear. Some sellers even include their home phone numbers.

Also, check the reputation of the seller. After each seller's name is a seller rating in parentheses. Click it to see the seller's scorecard, including links to comments about the seller. Of course, it wouldn't be too hard to re-register with eBay under an assumed name if you acquired a very poor seller rating.

If you're not the type of bidder who plans on repeatedly returning to an auction to ensure that no one has outbid you, you can place a proxy bid. Let's say an item is on the block for $10, but you're willing to pay $25. With a proxy bid, you bid $11 but also state the maximum you're willing to pay ($25) for a particular item. Then, if anybody outbids you ($12), eBay automatically makes a bid on your behalf ($13) until your maximum bid amount has been reached ($25). To place a proxy bid, just state the highest price you're willing to pay for an item in the "maximum bid" box and eBay sneakily takes care of the rest.

SHARE THE WEALTH

It's been a wonderful year. And now that it's drawing to a close and the season of giving draws nigh, perhaps it's time to consider what you've achieved over the past 12 months. Assuming you're not reading this in the bookstore in March (so buy the book already!), you've worked your way through the year, picking up information day by day, and gaining in mastery. By now, you might even begin to consider yourself something of a computer expert. Bravo! You have tamed the beige beast. Word processors cower when you pass by. Now would be a good time to consider giving a little back.

Computer expertise is a precious thing, but you must not hoard it. The days when the computer priesthood kept its secrets closely guarded are long gone. No one gains when geeks hold on to their knowledge, so spread the wealth. Help your neighbor become an expert too. Don't do it *for* her (see October's essay). Show her how to do it for herself.

You might say, "I'm not enough of an expert yet. There are still too many things I don't know." Don't let that stop you. The best way to learn more is to take on new challenges. I'm not suggesting you fake it. If you don't know something, admit it, and say "Let's find out together." But don't turn your back on ignorance. Tackle it. Vanquish it.

There's a school nearby that needs your help. A senior center, too. Computers are such valuable tools that everybody needs to know how to use them. Take what you've learned in this book and share it with the people around you. Keep learning, keep experimenting, keep sharing what you know. And we'll be back next year with a whole new almanac, full of new things to learn and try. See you then!

SUNDAY, DECEMBER 1

Back up your data!

PROTECT YOURSELF

Some Web pages are evil. You visit the evil page—either purposely or accidentally—and it makes itself your home page, overwriting the home page that you set yourself. And as if that weren't bad enough, the new home page prevents you from restoring your original home page.

Fortunately, in the end, good always triumphs over evil. If you've been the victim of an evil Web page, you can get control again by using this Registry hack. This hack works for Internet Explorer. As usual, before you mess with the Windows Registry, read the warnings in the January 26 entry.

To change your home page settings when you can't do it the standard way

1. Open the Registry by clicking Start, selecting Run, typing `regedit`, and clicking OK.
2. Click Current HKEY_Current_User.
3. Click Software.
4. Click Microsoft.
5. Click Internet Explorer.
6. Click Main.
7. Find the key with the value "Start Page."
8. Double-click the key and change the value to the address of the page you want to display as your home page—for example, `http://www.techtv.com/screensavers/`.

MONDAY, DECEMBER 2

LAPORTE SUPPORT

Q: A close friend of mine is a computer enthusiast (read: geek). Being the holiday season, what can I buy him as a gift?

A: Finding the right geeky gift can be challenging. Here are some tips:

- **Newbie and non-techie shoppers**—Rely on the "sure things." Affordable peripherals such as scanners, cameras, printers, speakers, or joysticks are great gifts. Look at software that enables you to do creative things or be productive at home. Books that teach new skills are very helpful.
- **Shoppers with technical savvy**—Remember, you're shopping for someone else. You need to know the specifications of the gift recipient's computer if you want to give a hard drive, CD-ROM, or DVD drive. Graphics cards and CPUs especially need to fit

specifications. Use the Belarc advisor (www.belarc.com) to list the specifications of a computer. For Mac users, try the AnyMac database (www.anymac.com) .
Always research the product first. Read the product reviews on TechTV. Look into computer magazines, and check user review sites such as www.epinions.com. Don't forget to check the manufacturer's Web site for specifications.

If you still end up getting the wrong gift, you'll be glad you saved the receipt. If you buy software, make sure it still has the shrink-wrap or seal to show that it has never been opened. Some stores won't accept software returns that look as though they've been opened.

TUESDAY, DECEMBER 3

MAC TIP

If you want to get serious about Mac programming (you know you want to), Metrowerks' CodeWarrior (www.codewarrior.com) is the way to go. There's a $49 learning edition that's great if you're just starting out. The full version is $600 for the standard edition, $200 for students. CodeWarrior is also available for Windows, Linux, PalmOS, and Solaris.

The program includes C, C++, and Java compilers and many useful development tools. Metrowerks also sponsors free courses, including an introduction to Macintosh programming and developing.

If you're on a budget, Apple offers the Macintosh Programmer's Workshop free to developers. It's an excellent assembler that includes a C and C++ compiler. The command-line interface is not as elegant as CodeWarrior's Integrated Development Environment (IDE), but it's very powerful. Read all about it at developer.apple.com/tools/mpw-tools.

For the Mac hobbyist who wants to dabble in programming, I highly recommend REALbasic (www.realbasic.com) , an award-winning, visual, object-oriented BASIC development environment for both Macintosh and Windows platforms.

GEEK SPEAK

A *word processor* is a computer program used to create a text document.

A *spreadsheet* is a computer program that enables the user to create a table with rows and columns. Most spreadsheet programs can perform calculations on the contents of the rows and columns.

WEDNESDAY, DECEMBER 4

WEB TIP

Children use computers to have fun and learn. Computers are especially useful for teaching specific concepts or providing information to children who like to work at their own pace, need repeated practice, or have difficulty absorbing verbal presentations.

But each child's internal wiring system is unique. It's easy for children to become over stimulated by a computer's multisensory format (visual, auditory, and kinesthetic). A computer can be especially engaging for a child with a short attention span, providing a tremendous amount of simultaneous stimulation.

Warning Signs of Overuse

One of the greatest dilemmas parents face is balancing a child's computer use with real-world activities. If you notice the following, a child might be using the computer too much:

- Has no desire to do anything but be on the computer
- Has tremendous difficulty disengaging or is overly irritable when asked to stop
- Chooses computer time over friendships and social interaction
- Won't let anyone else have a turn

Regulate Computer Use

Parents need to help kids learn to self-regulate the amount of time they spend using the computer. Provide a set amount of computer time tickets daily. Kids can use these tickets all at once, bank them for another day, or share time on the computer with a friend. If your child values the computer more than social interaction, provide computer tickets in relationship to how much time the child spends with family and friends.

THURSDAY, DECEMBER 5

WINDOWS TIP

Fed up with your system and ready to reinstall Windows? Be sure you back up all your stuff before you hit format. Here are five things to save before you reinstall:

- Files, files, files. Back up any of your data that you don't have a copy of. Start with the My Documents folder, but remember not all programs use it. Saved games are often in the game's folder. Checkbook programs can store their data in the program folder, as well.
- Favorites/bookmarks and cookies.
- System configuration information (network settings, e-mail settings, display info, TCP/IP settings, and so on).
- Passwords and software keys.
- Drivers.

The basic backup rule of thumb is make a copy of everything you don't already have a copy of.

GEEK SPEAK

Codec is short for *compressor/decompressor*. It describes a program that compresses real-world data such as images, audio, or video for transmission and storage, and then decompresses it for playback. Common codecs for video include MPEG 1 and 2, DivX, Sorenson, Indeo, and Cinepak. Popular audio codecs include MP3, WMA, and RealAudio.

Don't confuse the codec with the player or the file format. Windows Media Player plays back AVI video files using a variety of different codecs. You can add additional codecs to the player by installing them into your system.

FRIDAY, DECEMBER 6
LAPORTE SUPPORT

Q: What is compression?

A: Compression uses mathematical equations to scan a file for repeating patterns in the data. Then it replaces the data with smaller representations that take up less room. For example, compression software replaces repeating text characters such as XXXXXXXX with 8X, reducing the size of the text in this case by 75%. In an image, it might replace a swath of red pixels with information about the shade and the number of pixels. The more redundant information there is in a file, the more it can be compressed.

Different compression algorithms are used for different forms of media, such as audio (MP3), image (JPEG), and video (MPEG).

Lossy Versus Lossless

When compressing images, audio, and video you'll get the best results using a *lossy compression* technology. Lossy compression removes some of the data from the original for extra compression. Because the human eye and ear can fill in the gaps, the losses are barely noticeable. Common lossy formats include JPEG, MPEG, and MP3.

Lossless compression can't reduce file size by nearly as much as lossy compression. Use it in situations when you can't afford to lose a single bit, such as compressing programs and documents. The most common lossless compression formats are ZIP and SIT.

How Far Can Compression Go?

We found an excellent place for arguments on theoretical compression limits and pretty much anything else compression-related on the comp.compression newsgroup. They also have an excellent FAQ section (`www.faqs.org/faqs/compression-faq`).

SATURDAY, DECEMBER 7

FOR GEEKS ONLY

Ever installed a new device and find it just didn't work? You might be suffering from duplicate device drivers. Leftover drivers from previous installations can conflict with the newer drivers. Ridding your machine of duplicate device drivers might make later hardware installs easier. However, don't do this unless you're very comfortable with playing with your device drivers and safe mode. You can really mess up your computer doing this:

1. First, boot up in safe mode. (Geek filter: If you don't know how, you probably shouldn't mess with this tip).
2. Right-click My Computer.
3. Select Properties.
4. When the Properties dialog box launches, choose the Device Manager tab.
5. Investigate each device by clicking the + sign.
6. If you find duplicate device listings, delete both of them. (Another annoying warning: Don't delete it if you're not sure you still have the driver.)
7. Restart your computer. Windows re-finds most of the devices. You need the drivers for the others.

You get no immediate gratification other than the peace of mind that future hardware installs have a greater chance of going smoothly.

SUNDAY, DECEMBER 8

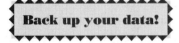

PROTECT YOURSELF

If you're like most e-mail users, you receive "virus alert" chain letters on a regular basis. They describe some horrible new threat to computing, they claim no antivirus software can detect it, and they urge you to notify all your friends.

Sadly, many of these alerts are hoaxes, perpetuated by duped computer users.

Here are three ways to tell whether a virus alert is probably real or probably just a hoax:

- **Did a genuine computer security expert send you the e-mail?**—If you received the alert from your mother-in-law, who received it from her dentist, who received it from her secretary's daughter, who received it from… Well, you get the hint.
- **Does the e-mail urge you to forward it to everyone you know?**—Genuine computer security alerts don't ask you to participate in a chaotic e-mail distribution scheme.
- **Does the e-mail point to an authoritative details page?**—True virus alerts don't describe a virus in detail. Instead, they should summarize the threat and provide links to Web pages where you can go to learn more.

To dispel the hysteria created by hoax virus alerts, many antivirus firms debunk hoaxes on their Web sites. Visit the Symantec Anti-virus Research Center (www.sarc.com) or Trend Micro's Virus Advisory site (www.antivirus.com/vinfo) for reliable virus warnings. You also might check out Vmyths (www.vmyths.com), which not only debunks virus hoaxes, but throws in urban legends for good measure.

MONDAY, DECEMBER 9

LAPORTE SUPPORT

Q: What language do programmers use to code operating systems?

A: Operating systems are not all coded in the same language. However, most are written in the C programming language with an assist from assembly language in performance critical sections.

Microsoft Windows is written in C and C++. The Linux kernel is coded in C. The original Macintosh operating system was written in Pascal, but all current development is in C and C++. Mac OS X supports a form of C called Objective C. Some Mac OS tools are in Objective C, but the guts of Mac OS X are in plain old C.

Ultimately, every piece of software ends up running in the microprocessor's own language, machine code. But because humans have a hard time grasping machine code, they generally work in higher-level languages like C and C++, reserving machine code for those time-critical parts of the program where every byte and cycle counts.

TUESDAY, DECEMBER 10

MAC TIP

If you're looking for older, unusual hardware for your Macintosh, visit MacTreasures (www.mactreasures.com). It specializes in hardware and software no longer available through retail. If MacTreasures doesn't have it, it'll go searching for you.

GEEK SPEAK

Peer-to-peer, or *P2P networking*, has been around for a while. It just means networking without a central controlling computer. If you connect two computers to share files, you're creating a peer-to-peer network. However, P2P became all the rage in 2000 thanks to a program called Napster. Napster let people share music files over the Internet. Because there was no centralized file server, the system was called peer-to-peer.

Many companies, such as Intel, IBM, and Hewlett-Packard, are researching P2P in business. Advanced P2P applications bring computers together to share not only files, but processor power, memory, and other resources as well.

WEDNESDAY, DECEMBER 11

 ## WEB TIP

Tired of launching your browser to type in a URL? Avoid the hassle with this tip to quickly launch an Internet site:

1. Click Start.

2. Click Run.

3. Enter the Web address. For example, type www.yahoo.com. No "http://" is needed.

Try this tip without using your mouse at all. Access your Start Menu by pressing the Windows key+R, then type in your favorite Web site. If your keyboard doesn't have a Windows key, press Ctrl+Esc, and then use the arrow keys to navigate to Run.

GEEK SPEAK

Sometimes referred to simply as the processor or central processor, the *CPU* (*Central Processing Unit*) is where most calculations take place. The CPU is to a computer as a brain is to a human.

THURSDAY, DECEMBER 12

 ## WINDOWS TIP

You can make your mouse work overtime by increasing the sample rate that updates your pointing device's location on the screen.

This tip is beneficial to people with really large monitors, avid gamers who use fast frame rates, and curious folk who want smoother cursor movement.

To overclock your mouse in Windows 2000:

1. Click Start, Settings, Control Panel.

2. Double-click the Mouse option.

3. Click the Hardware tab.

4. Click Properties.

5. Choose Advanced Settings.

6. Change the Sample Rate. I recommend setting the Sample Rate to 100Hz (maximum setting—it's still inferior to PS/2 rate, but it's better than nothing).

7. Up the Input Buffer Length to about 400 to avoid a buffer overrun from the higher sampling speed.

Note that this feature is not supported if you are operating with a USB mouse.

FRIDAY, DECEMBER 13

LAPORTE SUPPORT

Q: How do I view pictures as thumbnails in windows?

A: In Windows 98, ME, 2000, and XP, you can preview a photo by having its icon appear as a thumbnail.

To use this feature in Windows 98, follow these steps:

1. Launch Windows Explorer, then find the folder that contains your images.

2. Right-click the folder and select Properties.

3. With the General tab open, check the Enable thumbnail view box.

4. Click OK to close the dialog box.

5. Now open the folder with the images.

6. Click the View menu, and select Thumbnails.

To activate this feature in Windows Me, 2000, and XP, follow these steps:

1. Open the folder in which you store your photos.

2. Click the View menu, and select Thumbnails.

SATURDAY, DECEMBER 14

FOR GEEKS ONLY

Thinking about digging that old 386 out of your basement and putting it to use running Linux? Most geeks will tell you that Linux (or BSD, for that matter) runs just fine on an old 386 or 486 PC with as little as 4MB of memory and a 200MB hard drive.

There are some limitations to what you can do with such an old system, however.

Forget about running X Window with its easy graphical user interface (GUI). Those older systems don't have the horsepower to paint pretty windows on the screen. This means you'll be living in the world of the Linux command line. And turn off all unnecessary services to save processor cycles. Your 486 is plenty to run a Web server or proxy server, but it might not have enough oomph to do both.

You'll have to install a distribution that works with that older processor. Many distros are optimized for P5 or P6 processors. They won't run on a 386 or 486. Visit `www.linux.org` for a complete list of distributions, and then check the distribution's specs to see how the kernel is configured. Of course, you can always roll your own by recompiling the kernel yourself.

For more information on making Linux do with less, visit the Four MB Laptop HOWTO (`www.linuxdoc.org/HOWTO/4mb-Laptops.html`). It works for desktops, too.

SUNDAY, DECEMBER 15

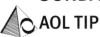

AOL TIP

An instant message, or IM, is just what it sounds like. It's a message that you send through the Internet, lightning fast, to the recipient. Once you connect to the IM service, your typed conversation with one or more people moves at the speed of your fingers. In other words, it's almost instantaneous.

According to America Online spokespeople, AOL Instant Messenger (AIM) has more than 35 million users. Those users send more than 403 million instant messages each day.

But wait, AOL only has 13 million subscribers (as of 2001)—where do the other 22 million users come from? You don't have to subscribe to AOL to use AIM. In fact, AIM is built right into the toolbar of the latest versions of Netscape Navigator. It's an independent program, though, and you don't need Netscape to use it. You can download your own AIM or use the Web-based version from AOL's Web site (`www.aol.com`).

MONDAY, DECEMBER 16

LAPORTE SUPPORT

Q: *I know I'm supposed to delete my temp files sometimes, but where do I find them and how do I do it?*

A: Thanks for reminding me. I just deleted 128MB worth of files from my system. All of these were temp files—files that my applications used at one point but then forgot, leaving them to litter my hard drive.

In theory, temporary files are automatically deleted when a program is finished with them. In practice, programs often leave them behind. To delete these files in Windows 98 and later, close all open applications, and then

1. Open My Computer.
2. Right-click a hard drive—any hard drive—and select Properties from the pop-up menu.
3. Press the Disk Cleanup button.
4. Check any and all boxes, including Temporary Files.
5. Click OK.

You also can delete these files by hand. Search for the TEMP folder (it's usually in the Windows directory) and delete the contents.

TUESDAY, DECEMBER 17

MAC TIP

As Macintosh users, we've always felt immune to Internet attacks, but changes in Mac technologies have finally made us vulnerable. The built-in file sharing in Mac OS 9 now works over TCP/IP, and wireless Airport signals can be intercepted. Mac users need to think about security just like everybody else.

Even if the work you do on your computer isn't classified, you might still be in danger. Spying eyes can check for your credit card number when you order products online. Nasty people can even use your computer as a gateway when they attack other computers, making the criminals invisible, and making you look guilty.

Firewalls protect your data from the Internet. Most hardware routers have simple, built-in firewalls. They're relatively inexpensive, and crash less often than desktop firewalls. If you intend to share your Internet connection with multiple computers, a broadband router offers a quick way to share a single IP address and put a firewall between you and the wild Web world.

The next two Mac Tips describe the different types of firewalls for the Macintosh.

VIRUS ALERT

The Acid virus is supposed to affect Microsoft Word version 97 on the Windows platform today. If your antivirus is relatively up-to-date this should not pose any problem, so why not update it right now?

WEDNESDAY, DECEMBER 18

WEB TIP

The following Web sites can assist you in troubleshooting computer problems should they arise:

- **The PC Guide** (www.pcguide.com)—Charles Kozierok created this labor of love that is one of the best sources of information about how PCs work and how to fix them. When I need to understand something, I turn here first.

- **Annoyances.org** (www.annoyances.org/)—Originally a Web site, it's now a series of books that focuses on customizing and taming Windows. It has some of the best tips on the planet. If Annoyances doesn't know how to do it, it can't be done.
- **MacFixIt** (www.macfixit.com/)—If you have a Mac and it needs some fixin', turn to MacFixit for some solid troubleshooting tips and the latest updates for solutions to your Macintosh computing woes.
- **ZDNet's updates.com** (updates.cnet.com/)—Keep abreast with the latest tech news and advisories at ZDNet's updates page.
- **Google Groups** (groups.google.com)—Newsgroups can be your best source for tech help. Google Groups (formerly Deja News) has a dedicated list of forums just for computing. Surf the variety of newsgroups for answers to your problems, search all groups for your issue, or post a message in hope of an answer.

And don't forget to check vendors' Web sites, too. As more and more companies put their documentation online, the Internet is becoming the best place to get help. For help with Microsoft's products, visit the searchable Knowledge Base at search.support.Microsoft.com. Apple's Knowledge Base is online at kbase.info.apple.com. You must sign up for a free account before you can use it, however.

THURSDAY, DECEMBER 19

WINDOWS TIP

Having options is a very good thing. Why open a file with a single program each and every time, when you can choose PhotoShop or Adobe Elements or Word or Notepad? Follow these steps to keep your options open:

1. Open Windows Explorer.
2. Select View, Folder Options, and File Types.
3. Find the file type you desire (GIF Image for example) and double-click it.
4. Open Edit File Type, and select Actions.
5. "Open" displays in the Action Box. This opens the file into your default.
6. To add an entry, press New.
7. In the New Action box, type the name of the action. For example, type Open (Adobe Elements) or Open with the name of the application in parentheses.
8. Browse to locate the application you want to perform the action.
9. Click OK.
10. Highlight the action you want to open as a default and press Set Default.

The application you selected above becomes the default when you double-click a certain file, such as .gif. If you right-click a .gif file, all the entries you selected in the Action box appear, so you can easily choose another application to use to open the file.

FRIDAY, DECEMBER 20

LAPORTE SUPPORT

Q: *What features should I consider when buying a notebook computer? What do you recommend?*

A: The biggest differencebetween desktops and notebooks are that notebooks aren't as easy to upgrade. Try to get as many features as you can afford up front. This notebook must meet your needs for years, not months.

Before you buy, determine your priorities. They help narrow your choices. You might want to consider the following:

- Processor performance
- Graphics performance
- Display size
- Keyboard size and layout
- Portability
- Price

Be realistic about your expectations. Everyone wants gaming performance from a three-pound notebook. Unfortunately, you usually need to compromise between size and performance. Here's how to determine what you need:

- If you value performance above all else, a desktop replacement is for you.
- If you want portability, stick with an ultraportable.
- Do performance and portability rate equally on your list? The thin-and-light class might fit your needs.
- Price is most important for most of us. Unless it falls comfortably within your price range, forget about the gigahertz processor and 15-inch display.

SATURDAY, DECEMBER 21

FOR GEEKS ONLY

If you have piles of videotapes crowding your home entertainment center, it's probably time to consolidate the tapes and upgrade your system. You can transfer the videos to CD and watch them in a DVD player.

Moving videos from tape to CD requires two steps:

1. Digitize the video.
2. Record that data onto a CD (as described next Saturday, December 28th).

Digitizing is a way to convert analog video into data you can store on your hard drive. To do this, you need a video capture card or, if you have a digital video camera, a 1394 or FireWire port. The ATI All-In-Wonder is a good video card with capture capabilities. If you don't want to replace your video card, pick up a standalone capture card such as Pinnacle Systems Studio DC10 Plus. The Studio DV is a good choice for digital video cameras.

Capture your video to hard drive using the best quality possible with a color depth of at least 24 bits per pixel. The chief limitations here are the speed of your system and size of your drives.

Depending on how many videotapes you have, this should keep the kids busy for the first half of winter break.

SUNDAY, DECEMBER 22

Back up your data!

PROTECT YOURSELF

Many virus utilities offer real-time scanning for viruses. The scanner loads at startup, and can really kill performance because it must scan every program file as it is being loaded into memory. Some antivirus programs can slow your computer by as much as 10%.

If you're willing to get by with a bit less virus protection, you can speed up boot times by turning off real-time scanning. Instead, schedule a task to run a standard virus scan at least once a week. Not only does this shorten boot times, but it makes your system faster for any disk access.

Always use the antivirus's own program options to disable automatic scanning. Antivirus programs protect themselves against viruses that attempt to use any other technique to disable protection.

MONDAY, DECEMBER 23

LAPORTE SUPPORT

Q: *How do I alphabetize my Start menu?*

A: These steps vary slightly depending upon which version of Windows you use, but it's fairly intuitive after you get started:

1. Click Start.
2. Select Settings.
3. Choose Taskbar and Start Menu.
4. Select the Start Menu (or Advanced) tab.
5. Click Advanced.

6. A list of the Start menu programs appears. Go into the Programs folder.

7. Click the bar called Name above the list of programs. That alphabetizes the list.

In Windows 2000, instead of steps 6 and 7, click the Re-sort button in the Advanced tab.

In most versions of Windows you can also right-click on any folder in Start's Programs menu and select Sort by Name to re-sort that folder.

TUESDAY, DECEMBER 24

MAC TIP

If you have only one computer, or you have a spare Mac available to set up as a dedicated router/firewall, a software firewall will work for you. In addition to potentially saving you money, software firewalls have better functionality, giving you more options on what and how you filter. They're also more likely to enable you to track when an intruder tries to attack.

Intego NetBarrier ($59 from `www.intego.com`) is a powerful and reasonably priced firewall for the Mac. For Mac OS X users I recommend Brian Hill's Brick House ($25 shareware from `personalpages.tds.net/~brian_hill/brickhouse.html`). It turns on and configures the built-in Mac OS X firewall.

GEEK SPEAK

CAD (*Computer Aided Design*) refers to computer programs that use graphics to assist in engineering and architecture project designs.

WEDNESDAY, DECEMBER 25 (CHRISTMAS DAY)

WEB TIP

How many times have you clicked a link someone e-mailed you and the Web site opened up in a browser that you don't like? If you prefer Internet Explorer, you can set it as your default Web browser:

1. Open Internet Explorer.

2. Open the Tools menu (in IE 5.x) or View menu (in IE 4) and select Internet Options.

3. Click the Programs tab.

4. At the bottom of the window is a check box that says Internet Explorer Should Check to See Whether It Is the Default Web Browser. Check this box.

5. Restart IE.

If Netscape (4.x and under) is what you want to use, follow these steps:

1. Search for a file on your computer called `prefs.js`. It should be in the Netscape Users folder. When you find it, don't double-click it. Right-click it and select Edit.

2. Find the line that says `user_pref("browser.wfe.ignore_def_check",true);`. Change the `true` to `false`.

3. Save the file as `prefs.js` and replace the old file.

4. Restart Netscape.

In Netscape 6 and later, follow these steps:

1. Select Preferences from the Edit menu.

2. Click Desktop Integration in the Advanced menu.

3. Check all the boxes that apply, and then click OK.

CHRISTMAS FUN

Check out the following Christmas sites for kids and parents:

- **Northpole.com** (`www.northpole.com`)—Has illustrated stories, how to e-mail Santa, and crafts.
- **Claus.com** (`www.claus.com`)—Contains interactive games and activities for kids.
- **Santa Claus.com** (`www.santa-claus.com`)—Send Christmas cards or ask Santa to phone a child anywhere in the world.

THURSDAY, DECEMBER 26

WINDOWS TIP

Sending a file to the Recycle Bin is easy. Just single-click the file and hit the delete button. You're greeted by the Delete confirmation dialog box, which asks you whether you really want to delete the file. This fail-safe feature isn't necessary, because you can rescue the file from the Recycle Bin if you need it at a later date.

Put an end to the Delete confirmation dialog box by following these steps:

1. Go to your Desktop.

2. Right-click the Recycle Bin and choose Properties.

3. In the Global tab feature of the Recycle Bin properties, uncheck the Display Delete Confirmation Dialog Box option.

FRIDAY, DECEMBER 27

LAPORTE SUPPORT

Q: Internet Explorer keeps asking about my proxy server. Why does this happen, and can I stop it from asking?

A: Some ISPs steer your browser through their proxy server to speed up your connection. In my experience at home, it actually does the opposite.

To disable the proxy search:

1. Open the Internet Options control panel.
2. Click the Connections tab.
3. Press the LAN Settings button.
4. Uncheck the Proxy Server box.

You might try it with the Automatically Detect Settings option checked and unchecked, then pick the setting that works best for you. I leave all three boxes unchecked for the best response time.

SATURDAY, DECEMBER 28
FOR GEEKS ONLY

Now that you have digitized your videos (which we all did last week, right?), it is time to record them onto a CD.

After you have the movies on your hard drive, the simplest thing to do is to burn a CD with the captured video files. You'll need a computer to view those videos, and there's no central user interface.

It's a little slicker and friendlier to your viewers to record the CD as a video CD or VCD. This is a standard for creating CD-based movie discs that predates DVD. VCDs can play on most modern DVD players as well as on most computers. The only drawbacks to VCDs are that each disc can hold only about an hour of video and the quality is poor, slightly worse than a VHS tape.

Some capture software can save the resulting video in VCD-compatible MPEG-1 format. If not, save it as an AVI and use a free program called AVI2VCD (www.mnsi.net/~jschlic1) to convert it. The AVI2VCD page has useful information on what kind of files a VCD needs.

Then use a VCD authoring program to record your VCD. One common solution is Roxio's Easy CD Creator Deluxe (www.roxio.com/en/products/cdrpc.jhtml). It costs less than $100 for the package.

Easy CD Creator arranges your video files onto a CD and can create simple menus so you can navigate your files.

SUNDAY, DECEMBER 29

PROTECT YOURSELF

Many people who play 3D games from the first-person perspective might find themselves experiencing the effects of motion sickness (nausea).

When you play a first-person game, two parts of your body detect motion. First, your eyes read the virtual movement of your character. Second, your inner ear contains a balance mechanism that enables you to judge your center of gravity and not fall over when walking. When you play a 3D game, this mechanism senses that you're sitting still.

When these two sensory readings conflict, the central nervous system decides to react to this confusion by unsettling your stomach.

I don't recommend Dramamine because it's sure to affect your game performance, but here's what you can do:

- From my experience, the quality of the image on your computer screen can make a difference. Some game effects such as textures and dynamic lighting can bog down the speed of the game and give it a choppy, jumpy pace that can make one feel ill. Experiment in the video options menu by turning down the effects to produce a smoother speed.
- You can also play the game without it filling up your entire monitor. This can give your eyes some perspective, although you aren't as likely to get as immersed in the game.
- Some games allow you to disable "head-bob." Do it. For many people it's the bobbing motion that really causes problems.

The irony is that the very appeal of these games—the illusion that you are directly part of the action—is the cause of your condition. The upside is that you're not the only one who has this problem, and hopefully this will cause the industry to come up with a solution.

MONDAY, DECEMBER 30

LAPORTE SUPPORT

Q: I just switched from a Mac to a Windows 2000 machine. Is there a Microsoft drawing program similar to ClarisWorks?

A: Yes, there is a drawing program in Microsoft Word:

1. Open Word and right-click somewhere in the toolbar.
2. Click Drawing to expose a toolbar with shapes.

3. Go to AutoShapes at the bottom of your screen to make arrows or other geometric shapes.

4. Just click and drag within Word to resize it.

You can also import GIFs and JPEGs from any graphics program into Word. Use the Microsoft equation editor that comes with Microsoft Office to manipulate words and shapes.

TUESDAY, DECEMBER 31 (NEW YEAR'S EVE)

MAC TIP

Let's conclude this month's focus on Mac security using firewalls. If you plan to share an IP address with routing software, you might want to use Vicom SoftRouter Plus (www.vicomsoft.com) ($245 for 10 users) or Sustainable Software's IPNetRouter (hwww.sustworks.com) ($90), which include protection tools. IPNetRouter in particular includes powerful, but basic filtering tools and rules. Although Sustainable Software has a useful tutorial on its Web site, its software is more difficult to configure than a dedicated firewall application.

You might occasionally find your firewall to be a burden. It might block you from doing certain Internet tasks. For instance, you might have a problem setting up chat, or Web conferencing. When this happens, you need to reconfigure your firewall. Much as with virus software, you need to download updates to your firewall as new protocols become popular and as the firewall vendors find new ways to protect your vulnerabilities.

TODAY IN COMPUTER HISTORY

December 31, 1999, many people feared that the passage into the year 2000 (commonly referred to as *Y2K* in the computer field) could have catastrophic repercussions. The fears were diverse and some quite complex, but a common fear was the possible disarray that could result from computers and programs unable to comply with the date change. Happily, the year change came and went with few hitches.

This Month's Feature

TOP FIVE WORD TRICKS

By Martin Sargent

I'll go head-to-head with anyone in a Microsoft Word tricks competition. Sure, the German champ Dieter Hadan is a legend. The Canadian rookie "Alt+Tab" Reynolds can attack a keyboard with a quickness never seen before. But look out. My personal Word trainer and I have developed some tricks that are sure to catch them both off guard at the World Championships this year.

Insert Horizontal Lines

If you want to separate portions of a document with fancy horizontal lines, use one of these methods:

- To create a thin continuous line, type three hyphens and press Enter (---).
- To create a thicker, bolder line, use underscores (___).
- To create a dotted line, use asterisks (***).
- To create a double line, use equal signs (===).
- To create a wavy line, use tildes (~ ~ ~).
- To create a triple fat line, use pound signs (###).

Insert Today's Date and Time

You can insert the current date into a Word document by pressing Alt+Shift+D. You can insert the current time by pressing Alt+Shift+T.

Every time you open or print the document, the date and time are updated, so don't use this method if, for example, you're adding a date that must remain the same, as in a journal entry.

Use Placeholder Text

When you want to enter nonsense text into a document to experiment with formatting, line spacing, and so on, type =rand(4,5) and press Enter.

Here's what you get:

The quick brown fox jumps over the lazy dog. The quick brown fox jumps over the lazy dog. The quick brown fox jumps over the lazy dog...

Use a Precision Ruler

By default, the Word ruler bar is demarcated by tenths of an inch. If you need precision down to hundredths of inches, hold down the Alt key while working the ruler.

Save All Docs at Once

Let's say you're working on four Word documents and the phone rings. You want to save all your documents, but if you try to save each individually, the answering machine might beat you to your caller.

To save all of your documents at once, hold down the Shift key and open the File menu. The File menu gives you two new options, Save All and Close All.

Martin Sargent, a true geek, writes for TechTV.com and often appears on The Screen Savers.

A P P E N D I X **A**

TECHTV QUICK FACTS

Boasting the cable market's most interactive audience, TechTV is the only cable television channel covering technology information, news, and entertainment from a consumer, industry, and market perspective 24 hours a day. Offering everything from industry news to product reviews, updates on tech stocks to tech support, TechTV's original programming keeps the wired world informed and entertained. TechTV is one of the fastest growing cable networks, available around the country and worldwide.

Offering more than a cable television channel, TechTV delivers a fully integrated, interactive Web site. Techtv.com is a community destination that encourages viewer interaction through e-mail, live chat, and video mail.

TechTV, formerly ZDTV, is owned by Vulcan, Inc.

AUDIENCE

TechTV appeals to anyone with an active interest in following and understanding technology trends and how they impact their lives in today's world—from the tech investor and industry insider, to the Internet surfer, cell phone owner, and Palm Pilot organizer.

WEB SITE

Techtv.com allows viewers to participate in programming, provide feedback, interact with hosts, send video e-mails, and further explore the latest tech content featured on the television cable network. In addition, techtv.com has one of the Web's most extensive technology-specific video-on-demand features (VOD), offering users immediate access to more than 5,000 videos as well as expanded tech content of more than 2,000 in-depth articles.

INTERNATIONAL

TechTV is the world's largest producer and distributor of television programming about technology. In Asia, TechTV delivers a 24-hour international version via satellite. TechTV Canada is a "must-carry" digital channel that will launch in September 2001. A Pan-European version of TechTV is planned for 2002.

TECH LIVE QUICK FACTS

Tech Live is TechTV's unique concept in live technology news programming. Tech Live provides extensive coverage, in-depth analysis, and original features on breaking technology developments as they relate to news, market trends, entertainment, and consumer products. Tech Live is presented from market, industry, and consumer perspectives.

Mission

Tech Live is the leading on-air resource and ultimate destination for consumers and industry insiders to find the most comprehensive coverage of technology and how it affects and relates to their lives, from market, industry, and consumer perspectives.

Format

Tech Live offers nine hours of live programming a day.

Tech Live is built around hourly blocks of news programming arranged into content zones: technology news, finance, product reviews, help, and consumer advice.

Tech Live news bureaus in New York City, Washington D.C., Silicon Valley, and Seattle are currently breaking technology-related news stories on the financial markets, the political arena, and major industry players.

The TechTV "Superticker" positioned along the side of the screen gives viewers up-to-the-minute status on the leading tech stocks, as well as additional data and interactive content.

Tech Live runs Monday through Friday, 9:00 a.m.–6:00 p.m. EST.

NETWORK PROGRAM GUIDE

The following is a list of the programs that currently air on TechTV. We are constantly striving to improve our on-air offerings, so please visit www.techtv.com for a constantly updated list, as well as specific air times.

AudioFile

In this weekly half-hour show, Liam Mayclem and Kris Kosach host the premiere music program of its kind that dares to explore music in the digital age. From interviews with artists and producers, to insight into the online tools to help create your own music, *AudioFile* discovers how the Internet is changing the music industry.

Big Thinkers

This weekly half-hour talk show takes viewers into the future of technological innovation through insightful and down-to-earth interviews with the industry's most influential thinkers and innovators of our time.

Call for Help

This daily, hour-long, fully interactive call-in show hosted by Becky Worley and Chris Pirillo takes the stress out of computing and the Internet for both beginners and pros. Each day, *Call for Help* tackles viewers' technical difficulties, offers tips and tricks, provides product advice, and offers viewers suggestions for getting the most out of their computers.

CyberCrime

This weekly half-hour news magazine provides a fast-paced inside look at the dangers facing technology users in the digital age. Hosts Alex Wellen and Jennifer London take a hard look at fraud, hacking, viruses, and invasions of privacy to keep Web surfers aware and secure on the Web.

Extended Play

In this weekly half-hour show, video game expert hosts Kate Botello and Adam Sessler provide comprehensive reviews of the hottest new games on the market, previews of games in development, and tips on how to score the biggest thrills and avoid the worst spills in gaming. This show is a must-see for game lovers, whether they're seasoned pros or gaming novices.

Fresh Gear

A gadget-lover's utopia, host Sumi Das supplies viewers with the scoop on the best and brightest technology available on the market. In this weekly half-hour show, detailed product reviews reveal what's new, what works, what's hot, and what's not and offers advice on which products to buy—and which to bypass.

Silicon Spin

Noted technology columnist John C. Dvorak anchors this live, daily, half-hour in-depth look at the stories behind today's tech headlines. CEOs, experts, and entrepreneurs cast a critical eye at industry hype and separate the facts from the spin.

The Screen Savers

Whether you are cracking code, are struggling with Windows, or just want to stay up to speed on what's happening in the world of computers, *The Screen Savers* is here to help. Leo Laporte and Patrick Norton unleash the power of technology with wit and flair in this live, daily, hour-long interactive show geared toward the tech enthusiast.

Titans of Tech

Titans of Tech is a weekly hour-long series of biographies profiling high tech's most important movers and shakers—the CEOs, entrepreneurs, and visionaries driving today's tech economy. Through insightful interviews and in-depth profiles, these specials offer viewers a rare look at where the new economy is headed.

INDEX

C

COMPARING INDEX

E

START MENU

INDEX

TYPES

INDEX

U

V

WINDOWS

INDEX

shortcuts, 259
- *horizontal lines, 259*
- *inserting dates and time, 259*
- *placeholder text, 259*
- *ruler bar, 259*
- *saving documents simulatneously, 259*
- viruses, 73

Word Macro viruses, 73

word processing, 242

World Language Resources Web site, 53

writing. *See also* **burning; programming; recording**
- 3D games, 35
- data, 183
  - *defragmented, 183*

X

X Window System, 50

X-Setup, 180

Xteg X-Setup, 180

Y

Yahoo! Mail Web site, 174

Yahoo! Messenger, 74

Yahoo! Photos Web site, 196

Yahoo! search engines, 60

Yahoo! TV Coverage Web site, 103

Yahoo! Web site, 76, 97, 138, 234

Z

ZDNet's updates.com Web site, 251

ZoneAlarm, 181

ZoneAlarm Web site, 35, 87, 95, 157, 181, 211

ZoneLabs Web site, 181

zooming, digital cameras, 129

ZOOMING

INDEX

Everything you always wanted to know about technology*

*But didn't know who to ask

TechTV's expertise in the technology lifestyle, along with the network's well-recognized on-air hosts and Que Publishing's 20 years as the leader in computer publishing, create a new standard for educational books and videos aimed at the technology consumer. The TechTV and Que Publishing partnership expands on TechTV's daily on-air and on-line "help and how to" segments.

Check your local television listings for TechTV.

BOOKS

BOOKS

VIDEOS

TechTV's Starting an Online Business
Frank Fiore
August 2001
ISBN: 0789725649/$24.99

TechTV's Technology Survival Guide
TechTV with Lorna Gentry
November 2001
ISBN: 0789726017

TechTV's Cutting the Cord
TechTV with Joyce Schwarz
December 2001
ISBN: 0789726483

TechTV's Microsoft Windows XP for Home Users
Jim Louderback/Nov. 2001
ISBN: 0789726513

TechTV's Upgrading Your PC
Mark Edward Soper and Patrick Norton/Sept. 2001
ISBN: 0789725991/$24.99

TechTV's Digital Camera and Imaging Guide
Les Freed and Sumi Das
December 2001
ISBN: 0789726394

Poor Leo's 2002 Computer Almanac: Presented by TechTV
Leo Laporte
November 2001
ISBN: 0789726912

TechTV's How to Build a Website
Sumi Das and Tom Merritt
October 2001
ISBN: 0789726661

TechTV Solves Your Computer Problems
as seen on
The Screen Savers

TechTV's Digital Video for the Desktop

TechTV's How to Build Your Own PC

TechTV's Digital Audio for the Desktop

Visit www.techtv.com or your favorite retailer for more information